D1795652

Parliamentary Opposition in
Old and New Democracies

Issues of political opposition, and of parliamentary opposition in particular, are at the very heart of the study of democratic processes in different parts of the world. This volume offers a broad comparative assessment of the many faces of parliamentary opposition in different political, legal and cultural settings. It looks both at the core features of the parliamentary opposition itself and its role in the legislative and wider political process. This includes an inquiry into the manifold challenges that the parliamentary opposition in many countries has come face in the more recent past. The countries covered in this volume include the old democracies of the Anglo-Saxon world, continental Europe and Japan, and the new democracies and democratising regimes in Central and Eastern Europe, Latin America and South Africa. Another chapter looks at the manifestations of parliamentary opposition within the multi-level system of the European Union. All chapters have been written by leading scholars in the field.

This book was previously published as a special issue of the *Journal of Legislative Studies*.

Ludger Helms is Professor of Political Science at the University of Innsbruck.

Library of Legislative Studies
Edited by Lord Philip Norton of Louth, University of Hull, UK.

Parliamentary Opposition in Old and New Democracies

Edited by Ludger Helms

Routledge
Taylor & Francis Group

LONDON AND NEW YORK

First published 2009 by Routledge
2 Park Square, Milton Park, Abingdon, Oxfordshire OX14 4RN

Simultaneously published in the USA and Canada
by Routledge
711 Third Avenue, New York, NY 10017, USA

First issued in paperback 2016

Routledge is an imprint of the Taylor & Francis Group, an Informa business

© 2009 Edited by Ludger Helms

Typeset in Times by Techset Composition Ltd., Salisbury, UK

British Library Cataloguing in Publication Data
A catalogue record for this book is available from the British Library

ISBN 13: 978-1-138-97795-2 (pbk)
ISBN 13: 978-0-415-39070-5 (hbk)

Contents

List of Contributors

Rudy B. Andeweg is Professor of Political Science at Leiden University and a Member of the Royal Netherlands Academy of Arts and Sciences. His research interests include political representation, executive–legislative relations, and coalition government. He co-directed the Dutch Parliamentary Studies of 2001 and 2006, based on interviews with MPs. On the basis of these studies he published articles in journals such as *The Journal of Legislative Studies*, and *Legislative Studies Quarterly*. He co-authored *Governance and Politics of The Netherlands* (Palgrave Macmillan, 2nd edn., 2005).

Flemming Juul Christiansen is a Ph.D. Student in the Department of Political Science, University of Aarhus. He is primarily interested in political parties, parliaments, interest organisations and Scandinavian politics. His latest publication (with Elin H. Allern and Nicholas Aylott) is: 'Social Democrats and Trade Unions in Scandinavia', *European Journal of Political Research*, 46/5 (2007), pp.607–35.

Erik Damgaard is Professor of Government in the Department of Political Science, University of Aarhus. His professional interests include legislative studies, parliamentary government, coalition studies and democratic theory. He has published widely in books and journals on Danish and Nordic parliaments and politics over the past several decades. His latest publications (with H. Jensen) include 'Europeanisation of Executive–Legislative Relations: Nordic Perspectives, in K. Auel and A. Benz (eds.), *The Europeanisation of Parliamentary Democracy* (New York: Routledge, 2006), pp.92–109, and 'Assessing Strength and Weakness in Legislatures: The Case of Denmark', *The Journal of Legislative Studies*, 12/3–4 (2006), pp.426–42.

Lieven De Winter obtained his Ph.D. on 'The Belgian Legislator' from the European University Institute. He is the director of the Centre de Politique Comparée and co-director of the PIOP (Point d'appui Interuniversitaire de l'Opinion Publique). His research interests include electoral behaviour and electoral systems, parties (especially ethnoregionalists) and party systems, government formation, cabinets, parliaments, clientelism and patronage, and ethnic conflict, in Belgium as well as in comparative perspective.

Ludger Helms is Professor of Political Science at the University of Innsbruck. He has held previous appointments, inter alia, at Harvard University, the University of California at Berkeley, the London School of Economics, the

University of Heidelberg, Humboldt University, Central European University, and the University of Tokyo. He is the author of five single-authored books and more than 70 journal articles and book chapters on political institutions, governance and leadership in old and new democracies. His work has appeared in such journals as *Government and Opposition, Political Quarterly, Parliamentary Affairs, Electoral Studies* and *West European Politics*. Among his recent book publications are *Presidents, Prime Ministers and Chancellors: Executive Leadership in Western Democracies* (Palgrave Macmillan, 2005), and *Die Institutionalisie-rung der liberalen Demokratie* (Campus, 2007).

Takashi Inoguchi is Professor Emeritus, University of Tokyo and Professor of Political Science, Chuo University, Tokyo. His research interests focus on Japanese politics and international relations. His latest publications include: *Citizens and the State* (Routledge, 2007, co-authored with Jean Blondel) and *Japanese Politics* (Trans Pacific Press, 2005).

André Kaiser is Full Professor and Chair in Comparative Politics at the University of Cologne and in the International Max Planck Research School 'The Social and Political Constitution of the Economy'. His recent publications include *Mehrheitsdemokratie und Institutionenreform* (2002), *Demo-kratietheorie und Demokratieentwicklung* (2004), *New Labour und die Modernisierung Großbritanniens* (2006) and articles, among others, in *European Journal of Political Theory, European Union Politics, Journal of Theoretical Politics, Party Politics, Political Studies, Politische Vierteljahresschrift, Regional and Federal Studies, West European Politics*, and *Zeitschrift für Politikwissenschaft*. His research focuses on new institutionalist approaches to comparative politics and empirical democratic theory.

Petr Kopecký is a Research Fellow of the Netherlands Organization for Scientific Research (NWO) based at Leiden University. He was senior lecturer at the University of Sheffield, and Visiting Fellow at the European University Institute in Florence, the South African Institute of International Affairs in Johannesburg, and the Ghana Centre for Democratic Development in Accra. His current research focuses on party patronage in contemporary democracies. He is the author of *Parliaments in the Czech and Slovak Republics: Party Competition and Parliamentary Institutionalization* (Ashgate, 2001), co-editor of *Uncivil Society? Contentious Politics in Eastern Europe* (Routledge, 2003), and editor of *Political Parties and the State in Post-Communist Europe* (Routledge, 2007).

Scott Morgenstern is currently an Associate Professor at the University of Pittsburgh, having also taught at Duke University, the University of

Salamanca, and CIDE (Mexico). He earned his Ph.D. from the University of California, San Diego in 1994. He is author of *Patterns of Legislative Politics* (Cambridge University Press, 2004) and author and contributor to *Legislative Politics in Latin America* (Cambridge University Press, 2002) as well as *Pathways to Power* (Penn State University Press, 2008). His research has also appeared in various collected books and journals including *Comparative Politics*, *Comparative Political Studies*, *Journal of Politics*, *British Journal of Political Science*, *Party Politics* and *Electoral Studies*.

Wolfgang C. Müller is a Professor in Comparative Government and former Director of the Mannheim Centre for European Social Research (MZES). Previously he taught at the Universities of Vienna, Humboldt University Berlin, University of California, San Diego, Institute d'Études Politiques de Lille and was Academic Visitor, Nuffield College, Research Fellow University of Bergen, and Joseph A. Schumpeter Fellow at Harvard University. His book publications include *Policy, Office, or Votes? How Political Parties in Western Europe Make Hard Decisions* (co-ed. with Kaare Strøm, Cambridge University Press, 1999), *Coalition Governments in Western Europe* (co-ed. with Kaare Strøm, Oxford University Press, 2000), *Delegation and Accountability in Parliamentary Democracies* (co-ed. with Kaare Strøm and Torbjörn Bergman, Oxford University Press, 2003). His articles have appeared in journals such as *Electoral Studies*, *European Journal of Political Research*, *Journal of European Public Policy*, *Journal of Theoretical Politics*, *Legislative Studies Quarterly*, *Party Politics*, *Political Studies* and *West European Politics*. His research interests include political representation, delegation relationships, government coalitions, political parties, and political institutions.

Juan Javier Negri is a doctoral student in the Department of Political Science at the University of Pittsburgh. His research interests are Latin American and European political institutions; in particular legislatures and legislative behaviour, political parties and electoral systems. He holds a MA in political science from Pittsburgh (2007) and a BA in political science from the Torcuato Di Tella University in Buenos Aires, Argentina (2002). He was awarded a Fulbright Scholarship (2005–7).

Philip Norton (Lord Norton of Louth) is Professor of Government and Director of the Centre for Legislative Studies at the University of Hull. His recent publications include *Parliaments in Western Europe* (3 vols., 1998–2002), *Parliament in British Politics* (2005) and (with others) *Politics UK* (6th edn., 2006). He was elevated to the peerage, as Lord Norton of Louth, in 1998 and was founder Chairman of the House of Lords Select Committee on the Constitution. He also chaired the Conservative Party's Commission to Strengthen Parliament. He has served as President of the Politics Association in the UK and of the British Politics Group in the USA and as co-chair of the Research Committee of Legislative Specialists of the International Political Science Association.

Aníbal Pérez-Liñán is Associate Professor of Political Science at the University of Pittsburgh. He works on issues of democratisation and institutional design in Latin America. Among his recent publications are *Presidential Impeachment and the New Political Instability in Latin America* (Cambridge University Press, 2007) and 'The Effects of U.S. Foreign Assistance on Democracy Building, 1990–2003' (with Steven Finkel and Mitchell Seligson, *World Politics*, 59/3 (2007), pp.404–39).

Robert A. Schrire is Professor and Head of the Political Studies Department at the University of Cape Town where he also directs the Institute for the Study of Public Policy. He has held faculty appointments at several universities abroad including Sciences Po in Paris, Johns Hopkins, Princeton and the University of Western Australia in Perth. He has done research in opposition politics and strategy at both the theoretical and empirical levels. In addition to his research, which has been published in leading journals and books, he has been a consultant to several major opposition parties in South Africa and has assisted them in the development of public policies and electoral strategies. He was an adviser to the South African parliament on the relationship between democratic politics and floor crossing in a proportional representation system. In addition to his work on South African politics, he has conducted research into political economy and international relations and was an editor for the UNESCO Living Encyclopaedia research project.

Maria Spirova is a Lecturer in the Department of Political Science at Leiden University, the Netherlands. Her research and publications focus on political parties, electoral politics, and minority policy in the post-communist world. She is the author of *Political Parties in Post-Communist Societies: Formation, Persistence and Change* (Palgrave Macmillan, 2007).

Studying Parliamentary Opposition in Old and New Democracies: Issues and Perspectives

LUDGER HELMS

Historically, establishing liberal democracy was very much an extended exercise in limiting the power of the government or, more precisely, the power of the executive. While this included in particular the gradual introduction of constitutional constraints specifically designed to check the executive, these institutional constraints were gradually complemented by rights that allowed political and social actors to criticise and oppose the actions and policies of the government publicly. Unsurprisingly, therefore, democratic theory has highlighted (legitimate) opposition, alongside participation, as one of the two basic defining features of 'polyarchies',[1] setting the latter apart from the many different forms of 'illiberal' and/or non-democratic regimes. Robert Dahl's seminal effort to move political oppositions to the centre-stage in the study of democratic politics[2] has been echoed in the more recent literature on the nature of liberal democracy. As Ian Shapiro has emphasised, 'democracy is an ideology of opposition as much as it is one of government'.[3]

Given the widespread scholarly acknowledgment of the importance of 'opposition issues' for democracy and democratic theory, it is remarkable how comparatively patchy our knowledge and understanding of the different aspects of political opposition has remained. Needless to say, this assessment does not apply to all sub-fields of opposition research in equal measure. Political minorities, including ethnic and religious minorities, have clearly attracted growing scholarly attention, as the recent launch of specialised year-books and journals, such as the *European Yearbook of Minority Issues* or the *International Journal of Minority and Groups Rights*, suggests. Also, inter-national research on the phenomena of protest and contention, which have always had a place in the study of democracy, has intensified and extended in scope, as is demonstrated impressively by the broad range of topics covered by the prestigious *Cambridge Studies in Contentious Politics*. There exists now a theoretically and empirically rich literature on old and new social movements as well as on more specific non-state actors, such as non-governmental organisations (NGOs), which have been analysed in differ-ent settings and from comparative perspectives.[4]

Regrettably, there is no equivalent research regarding the sub-field of parliamentary opposition. While issues of parliamentary opposition have never been completely off the agenda of international political research, there are few truly major works, and hardly any genuinely comparative studies. Indeed, a large proportion of contributions to the field could be described as 'occasional papers' by authors specialising on other areas and aspects of legislative research.

Several different factors can help explain the scarcity of political research on parliamentary oppositions. Among the more immediate causes, the shortage of established theoretical frameworks which would allow the integration of empirical findings from different studies and the systematic accumulation of knowledge, merits first mention. Most international volumes on opposition have been considerably more substantial in their empirical analysis than in their theoretical parts,[5] whereas there is (to the best knowledge of this author) not a single recent book-length study focusing primarily on the theoretical dimensions of parliamentary opposition. Many theoretical propositions concerning parliamentary opposition or the relation-ship between governments and oppositions have been formulated by authors from different sub-disciplines of political research who would hardly define themselves as opposition scholars.[6] To a large extent the strikingly a-theoretical character of many works on parliamentary opposition is just a reflection of the marked 'theory-resistance' of its objects of study, a fate that political research on parliamentary oppositions shares with several other sub-disciplines of comparative politics, such as the field of leadership studies in particular.

Perhaps even more importantly, the 'governance turn'[7] in comparative politics has done much to push issues relating to the parliamentary opposition even further towards the margins of the mainstream debate about politics in old and new democracies. The key feature linking the numerous and competing concepts of 'governance' is the notion of a changing relationship between state and society which includes important new roles for private sector actors, and the gradual replacement of hierarchical forms of decision-making by more cooperative modes.[8] There is generally little sympathy among authors working within the governance paradigm for parliaments and parliamentary actors, which are widely perceived as the institutions of a different age; more positive ideas of evaluations of parliaments are largely reserved for transnational parliamentary assemblies in international organisations.[9]

The widespread disregard for parliamentary actors and institutions in contemporary political research is largely unjustified, especially (though not only) in normative terms as even most advocates of the normative variants of the governance paradigm would seem ready to admit. Indeed, few if any of the various concepts of accountability that have been put forward in different contexts would appear to work in practice without including parliaments and genuine parliamentary devices.[10]

In empirical terms, the performance of parliaments has been found to be a key factor in the complex process of democratic consolidation in young democracies.[11] Yet the particular democratic potential of parliaments is obviously not confined to young and emerging democracies. In particular the popular contention that parliaments are rather powerless actors anyway and that they essentially represent the state rather than society cannot be sustained.

Firstly, parliaments in parliamentary regimes may appear rather powerless when being judged by the amount of independent 'policy-making power' they hold, but many of the most critical assessments simply fail to understand the working logics of parliamentary government. Unlike legislatures in presidential regimes, parliaments in parliamentary democracies cannot reasonably be expected to be the chief agenda setters or the principal decision-makers.[12] Their activities focus more on holding governments accountable, and the fact that they generally perform this task without threatening the persistence of the regime in which they operate is a powerful reminder of the great capacity of parliamentary democracy in balancing competing public demands for political stability and change. Secondly, and even more importantly in our context, compared to most other actors participating in public–private decision-making networks, parliaments can hardly be classified as institutions or actors representing the state only. Even though most countries now fund parliamentary party groups through public money and in some cases even pay a public salary to the leader of the largest opposition party, parliaments clearly represent citizens and society, certainly to a greater extent than the host of non-elected office-holders in 'non-majoritarian institutions' or many of the most powerful non-state actors of the 'governance age', such as the truly major companies.

As in parliamentary democracies the governing parliamentary party groups and the executive form a functional 'unit' which somewhat limits the functional independence of the majority parties and their visibility as independent players in the political process, the functions of the parliamentary opposition for the political system as a whole are often more, rather than less, tangible than that of the majority parliamentary party groups. Most authors consider the functional profile of the parliamentary opposition in parliamentary democracies to include the three tasks of criticising the government, scrutinising and checking governmental actions and policies, and representing a credible 'alternative government'.

Alongside the considerably lower degree of party discipline in legislative voting, the notable lack of the 'alternative government' function in presidential (and other non-parliamentary) systems provides the strongest argument against the existence of a genuine parliamentary opposition outside parliamentary democracies. However, conceptually-oriented debates regarding the prerequisites and characteristics of 'parliamentary opposition' in the narrower sense have not been confined to the field of comparing parliamentary and non-parliamentary regimes. For some authors, even those parties in parliamentary democracies that hold seats in the parliament but either do not aspire to become a governing party or fail to be considered as a possible coalition partner by the other parties fail to quality as genuine representatives of the parliamentary opposition.[13]

As in any other field of study, overly strict terminology and conceptual narrowness may prove as much an effective hindrance to knowledge accumulation as the more widely acknowledged pitfalls of 'concept stretching'.[14] Research on the nature of politics in the legislative assemblies of non-parliamentary democracies (such as the United States or Switzerland) or transnational regimes (such as the European Union), suggests that decision-making in these settings is not that fundamentally different from legislative politics in parliamentary regimes to preclude any meaningful comparisons.[15] In fact, contrasting the different manifestations of majority-building and voicing dissent, and comparing their functional relevance in different political-institutional settings, may not only teach us a lot about the working logics of non-parliamentary systems, it can also deepen our understanding of the more 'natural' environments of parliamentary oppositions, that is, parliamentary democracies.

Even when the study of parliamentary opposition is confined to parliamentary democracies, the search for functional equivalents may prove exceptionally instructive. In particular, it may help unravel how central or powerful a player the parliamentary opposition actually is in a given system. The de facto transfer of 'opposition functions' from the parliamentary opposition to other actors, such as interest groups or mass media, normally indicates a structural weakness of the former. Not surprisingly, the potential character of structurally transformed mass media as '*ersatz* opposition' was first identified in political settings marked by a functionally impaired parliamentary opposition, such as Japan.[16] The hyper-stability of governments (in terms of the party complexion of the cabinet) or the existence of 'grand coalitions' and other 'surplus-majority coalitions' may have other functional repercussions as well, such as and in particular the development of 'sectoral opposition' from within the government.[17] Even these cursory observations leave no doubt that only an inquiry reaching well beyond the parliamentary arena may produce a realistic picture of the parliamentary opposition in a given system.

STRUCTURAL PARAMETERS SHAPING THE CHARACTER OF PARLIAMENTARY OPPOSITIONS IN OLD AND NEW DEMOCRACIES

Whereas only a skilful synthesis of different factors and dynamics can do justice to the complex phenomenon of parliamentary opposition, any serious analytical assessment has to start with distinguishing and disentangling the different structural parameters that shape the parliamentary opposition and its room for manoeuvre in the democratic process.

Institutional Factors

As to the structural features of the parliamentary opposition (which have to be distinguished from the actual patterns of behaviour), the specific design of political institutions and institutionalised social settings both external to and within parliament are widely acknowledged to mark a crucial set of variables to be analysed. Most authors consider the party system the single most important variable determining the shape of the parliamentary opposition in a given system. In fact, as parliamentary opposition in parliamentary democracies (though not only there) is virtually always party-based, the structure of the party system can be expected to have an exceptionally powerful impact on the structural features of the parliamentary opposition. Yet party systems do not emerge from nowhere and, at least to some extent, they are shaped by institutional factors (if they are not treated as institutional features of political regimes in their own right).

While there is a notable trend in recent research on electoral and party systems to shift attention away from studying electoral systems as independent variables,[18] and a growing scepticism towards deterministic assumptions about the effect of electoral systems on the structure of party systems, there can be little doubt that electoral systems usually do have a major effect on the structure of the party system. Those effects may only rarely, if ever, correspond neatly to 'Duverger's law', an overly ambitious set of propositions concerning the causal relationship between electoral systems and party systems,[19] but more often than not there are notable correlations between the basic character of the electoral system and the structural features of the party system. Other things being equal, PR systems are more likely than plurality systems to produce multi-party systems which then tend to leave their mark on governmental institutions by giving rise to coalition governments and multi-party parliamentary opposi-tions. The fact that 'other things' tend to be rather unequal in politics is respon-sible for the recurrent disappointments of our theoretical expectations. In much of Eastern Europe, 'Duverger's law' has not only failed to work but has been wholly disproved. In fact, many of those countries that adopted majoritarian electoral systems experienced exceptionally high levels of party system frag-mentation, higher even than in many countries operating PR systems.[20]

Especially for opposition parties, rules and regulations concerning the financial resources of parties mark important components of the institutional parameters of party competition. Public subsidies for political parties have become a widespread phenomenon in both old and new democracies. At least in Europe public funding regimes seem to have led to neither a freezing of party competition nor an institutionalised bias in favour of the governing parties.[21] It has even been argued that in many countries public subsidies helped new parties stabilise themselves and that changes in the party complex-ion of governments increased rather than decreased after the introduction of state subsidies for political parties.[22] From a global perspective on the insti-tutional parameters of party competition, many African countries – most of which do not provide any state subsidies to political parties – stand out as regimes that strongly favour the parties in power, while keeping the opposition at bay from both public money and political office.[23]

Institutions are important also and in particular within the parliamentary arena itself, where they shape the structural room for manoeuvre of the parlia-mentary opposition and the structure of government–opposition relations more generally. It has long become common practice in opposition research to examine the institutional opportunity structure of political actors, an approach originally developed by scholars of social movements.[24]

Rights to address oral and written questions to members of the government can be found in any parliamentary democracy, but even some of the most sophisticated procedures of parliamentary questioning have been considered a pointless exercise, especially as only a fraction of (written) questions sub-mitted is ever answered.[25] Among the many different formats of parliamentary questioning, only 'Prime Minister's Question Time', an institution that has found few genuine equivalents outside the family of Westminster democra-cies, marks a real event for both government and opposition.

Unlike parliamentary questions, the vote of censure or no-confidence vote – which marks the ultimate weapon of parliaments in any genuine parliamentary democracy – can only to a limited extent be considered to form part of the parliamentary opposition's opportunity structure. This is all the more true for systems operating a specific variant of the no-confidence vote, which requires the support of an absolute majority of MPs for an alternative candidate to make the no-confidence vote effective against the incumbent head of government (the so-called 'constructive' vote of no-confidence, to be found in Germany, Spain and Belgium as well as a range of East European countries). But even less restrictive variants of that instrument will have their ultimate effect, i.e. causing the government to step down, only if wielded by an absolute majority of MPs, which – save the exception of minority governments – is normally out of reach for opposition parties. That said, even launching a vote of no-confidence that is (most likely) destined to fail may prove an important opportunity for the parliamentary opposition to voice their dissent.

There are several institutional devices that have had a greater and more direct impact on the parliamentary opposition's room for manoeuvre. The extent to which the parliamentary opposition is involved in parliamentary agenda-setting, the ability of ordinary members or minority parliamentary groups to initiate parliamentary bills, the structural features of the committee system (including the formal and informal rules for the selection of committee chairs), the right of minorities to establish investigation committees, and the rules for passing constitutional amendments (that is, the requirement of qualified majorities) are all highly relevant components of the institutional opportunity structure of the parliamentary opposition in the parliamentary arena. In some countries, such as Germany and Australia in particular, second chambers have traditionally been considered the single most important institutional resource of the parliamentary opposition, even though the veto powers of the second chamber are obviously available to the parliamentary opposition only during periods of 'divided government'.[26]

Several other components of the institutional opportunity structure of the parliamentary opposition – such as the existence of a constitutional court that has the right to annul government bills or laws and may be invoked by a parliamentary minority, or of referendums – are located outside the parliamentary arena and formally come into play only after the completion of the parliamentary stages of the wider decision-making process. Nonetheless, they may, and actually tend to, develop strong anticipatory effects that may considerably strengthen the opposition even in the parliamentary arena.[27] Switzerland remains the prototype of a country whose legislative and executive politics, in fact most of its more recent political history, have been shaped by the existence and frequent use of referendums,[28] whereas countries such as Germany or France (since 1974) provide generous evidence for the significant effect of strong constitutional courts on parliamentary opposition.[29]

Cleavages, Strategies, and Culture

Needless to say, purely institutional approaches do not even get close to a proper understanding of government–opposition relations in contemporary democracies. This holds true even for the most basic elements, such as the key characteristics of party systems and the structure of party competition. There is considerable evidence that party systems are, first and foremost, manifestations of major cleavages emerging from social divisions.[30] As Bartolini and Mair have emphasised, social divisions turn into cleavages that give rise to political parties only if and when they are organised as such,[31] which could help explain why the cleavage-related foundations of party systems in young democracies can remain underdeveloped and shaky for a considerable period of time. But this does not change the fact that cleavages form the social basis of party systems, which to great extent holds true even for the post-communist democracies of Central Eastern Europe.[32]

However, whilst cleavages constitute the societal foundations of party systems, more specific patterns of party competition are clearly not determined by social cleavages. At the electoral level, 'issue-voting' has significantly increased in many established democracies at the expense of more traditional voting patterns.[33] This has manifested itself in rising levels of volatility in the majority of older democracies, while many younger democracies (especially in Eastern Europe) have been highly volatile from the outset.[34]

Important components of party competition and also of government–opposition relations emerge from the dynamic relations between individual parties, which is particularly true at the governmental level. In general, smaller opposition parties tend to profit from an open structure of competition within a given party system, which has been analytically distinguished from a closed structure of competition.[35] In the former, both wholesale alternations and partial alternations in office are possible (which acknowledges the possibility of coalition governments). Also, the system is open for innovative governing formulae, that is for different and new party complexions of governments. Finally, access to government in systems belonging to this category is open to most or even all parties, which indicates that there is a broad range of different, politically viable governing coalitions (or in somewhat more technical terms, a limited amount of 'segmentation').

Party systems are marked by different combinations of these aspects but even a single element associated with a closed structure of competition can give the opposition a hard time when it comes to winning office. For example, the Italian party system before 1992 did allow partial alternations and the formation of differently composed governments, some of which could be described as 'unfamiliar' governing formulae (such as the recurrent Christian Democratic minority governments, and the Spadolini governments of the early 1980s that were led by a prime minister from a party that controlled a mere three per cent share of parliamentary seats). This notwithstanding, the Communists (PCI), who temporarily controlled more than 30 per cent of all seats in the *Camera dei Deputati*, remained one of the system's eternal opposition parties, excluded from office for decades.[36] Chiefly responsible for this was the infamous *conventio ad excludendum*, a strictly adhered to agreement between most of the other relevant parties of the system not to accept the PCI as a coalition partner. In most multi-party parliamentary systems there are certain coalition formulae that are considered possible in theory but not in practice, though few, if any, 'non-options' have been as deeply institutionalised as the famous Italian one.

Conventions and more general cultural parameters do not only have a major impact on the government question; they also shape government–opposition relations in constitutional practice. Normally, the cultural parameters in a given system correspond more or less closely with the existing institutional parameters. This should not come as too much of a surprise, as institutions reflect the basic political and cultural preferences and values that prevail within a given polity.[37] More strictly speaking, they reflect the political and cultural settings of a previous period of time during which institutions were designed and established. However, there is significant evidence to suggest that the basic institutional decisions once made have powerful and enduring effects. Specifically, they have a strong impact on later decision-making processes, as they effectively constrain alternative choices and major alterations of the status quo.[38] There is even evidence that a specific set of institutions established may shape the political culture of a given polity.[39]

In most systems, there is considerably more consensus-seeking and cooperation than purely institutionalist perspectives would lead us to expect. Normally, neither the institutional freedom to manoeuvre nor the available veto resources are exploited to the full. Rather, government initiatives, veto threats by oppositions and reactions (including anticipatory actions) from governments tend to create extremely complex decision-making situations from which decisions emerge that are to a large extent compromises between competing interests, preferences and strategic considerations. More recent research on parliamentary governance in Western Europe has identified a set of different factors that are all suspected to increase the chances for cooperative government–opposition relations across different types of parliamentary democracies. Amongst them are the growing similarities in the social backgrounds of governing and opposition elites and the creation of public funding systems for political parties that provide both government and opposition parties with a structural incentive to develop cooperative working relationships with each other. The latter aspect is part of a larger scenario famously described by Richard Katz and Peter Mair as the emergence of the 'cartel party'.[40] Another key component of the changing set of parameters shaping government–opposition relations in many parliamentary democracies is the significantly increased complexity and 'longevity' of some policy decisions, on issues as different as nuclear power, genetic research or pension reform, which are widely considered to benefit from a broad pooling of political expertise and authority.

Some systems have become famous for their high levels of cooperation and compromise that cannot be explained by actors' constitutional or institutional opportunities and constraints. In Western Europe, Italy, again, would appear to mark a classic case.[41] Austria, too, has seen considerably more inter-party cooperation than the institutional opportunity structure of the parliamentary opposition would seem to suggest.[42] To many, the notable degree of consensus or, more precisely, the widespread absence of outright conflict in the British Westminster system may be even more remarkable. As Denis Van Mechelen and Richard Rose have revealed, the unanimity score in parliamentary voting on legislation in the House of Commons has been quite significant.[43] That said, 'constructive' contributions of the parliamentary opposition in Britain have remained considerably less numerous and more limited in scope than in most other European countries, which reflects institutional choices as well as deeper cultural underpinnings of British politics. Possible exceptions apart, the basic conviction among oppositions prevails, 'that it is better to give the government enough rope to hang itself with'[44] than demonstrating its fitness for office and trying to win the voters' trust by helping the government to govern.

THIS VOLUME

The papers gathered in this volume seek to shed new light on the parliamentary opposition in different political, institutional and cultural settings. Most contributions develop a comparative focus that includes systems that share at least one key variable, such as the basic institutional framework, the prevalence of a certain type of government or a set of similar cultural legacies. In some cases the systematic variable is combined with a specific regional focus, such as in the chapter by Scott Morgenstern, Juan Javier Negri and Aníbal Pérez-Liñán on parliamentary opposition in the non-parliamentary regimes of Latin America.

The terms 'old' and 'new democracies' are being used rather loosely. This is particularly true for the latter category of systems, which includes not only the post-communist regimes of Central and Eastern Europe and Latin America, but also post-Apartheid South Africa, a country that could in fact be described as both an old and new democracy.[45] The term 'new democracy' is stretched even further in the case of the European Union, a transnational regime whose democratic credentials continue to be contested, though more recent developments have strengthened the position of those willing to consider the European Union as some new kind of a democratic order. The category of 'old' democracies, being represented in Part I of this volume, is not fully homogeneous either. Japan, in particular, may be considered a young democracy when compared with some of the other countries represented in this section, such as the United Kingdom, Belgium or the Netherlands. However, in comparison with the countries studied in Part II Japan, Japan clearly deserves to be classified as a fully consolidated 'older' liberal democracy.

Key aspects to be addressed in each of the chapters that follow include the make-up of the parliamentary opposition (especially in terms of parties representing the opposition), the political and institutional opportunity structure of the parliamentary opposition, their role in the legislative and wider political process, relations between the parliamentary opposition and non-parliamentary oppositions, such as the mass media or interest groups, as well as the political clout of the parliamentary opposition in relation to these extra-parliamentary political players.

As to the periodical focus, most chapters concentrate on developments in the past two or three decades, but wherever deemed appropriate and necessary for a deeper understanding of the more recent features of the parliamentary opposition in a given context, historical aspects were duly considered. In other regards, too, authors were given a free hand to include aspects from beyond the 'core set' of issues to be tackled.

Overall, this compilation of analyses of the parliamentary opposition in old and new democracies suggests that oppositions in parliament and beyond remain extremely difficult to theorise, and sometimes even difficult to understand in empirical terms. From a scholarly perspective, this may seem rather daunting. In political terms, by contrast, the unpredictability of the democratic process and its outcomes may secure a milder judgement. Indeed, as Klaus von Beyme has suggested,[46] a greater consistency of behavioural patterns in the relationship between governments and oppositions might easily clash with the very spirit of liberal democracy among whose structural properties contingency has always held a special place.

NOTES

1. R.A. Dahl, *Polyarchy: Participation and Opposition* (New Haven, CT and London: Yale University Press, 1971).
2. R.A. Dahl, *Political Oppositions in Western Democracies* (New Haven, CT and London: Yale University Press, 1966).

3. I. Shapiro, 'The Fallacies Concerning Minorities, Majorities, and Democratic Politics', in I. Shapiro, *Democracy's Place* (Ithaca, NY and London: Cornell University Press, 1996), p.51.

4. H. Kriesi, R. Koopmans, J.W. Cuyvendak and M.G. Giugni, *New Social Movements in Western Europe. A Comparative Analysis* (Minneapolis, MN: University of Minnesota Press, 1995); M.G. Guigni, *Social Protest and Policy Change: Ecology, Antinuclear, and Peace Movements in Comparative Perspective* (Lanham, MD: Rowman & Littlefield, 2004).

5. This is true for the volume by E. Kolinsky (ed.), *Political Opposition in Western Europe* (London: Croom Helm, 1987) as much as for the special issue of *Government and Opposition*, 32/4 (1997) on political opposition.

6. A systematic overview of several theoretical propositions on the political behaviour of parliamentary oppositions can be found in L. Helms, 'Ansätze einer Handlungstheorie der politischen Opposition', *Österreichische Zeitschrift für Politikwissenschaft*, 26 (1997), pp.423–35.

7. B. Kohler-Koch and B. Rittberger, 'The Governance Turn in EU-Studies', *Journal of Common Market Studies*, 44 (2006), pp.27–44.

8. The governance paradigm would deserve a more expansive critique in its own right, especially for its sometimes 'caricature-like' notions of more traditional approaches to studying politics, which cannot be offered here. See however, for example, M. Marinetto, 'Governing Beyond the Centre: A Critique of the Anglo-Governance School', *Political Studies*, 51 (2003), pp.592–608.

9. See, for example, B. Rittberger, *Building Europe's Parliament: Democratic Representation Beyond the Nation State* (Oxford: Oxford University Press, 2005), pp.204–8.

10. R.D. Behn, *Rethinking Democratic Accountability* (Washington, DC: Brookings Institutions Press, 2001); M. Flinders, *The Politics of Accountability in the Modern State* (Aldershot: Ashgate, 2001); R. Mulgan, *Holding Power to Account: Accountability in Modern Democracies* (Basingstoke: Palgrave Macmillan, 2003); M. Bovens, 'New Forms of Accountability and EU-Governance', *Comparative European Politics*, 5 (2007), pp.104–20.

11. S.A. Fish, 'Stronger Legislatures, Stronger Democracies', *Journal of Democracy*, 17/1 (2006), pp.5–20.

12. There have been notable shifts regarding the criteria for assessing and comparing legislatures even within the discipline of legislative research. The 'standard framework' for comparing legislatures that has dominated the international debate for many years has been devised by M. Mezey, *Comparative Legislatures* (Durham, NC: Duke University Press, 1979), pp.24–6. More recent conceptual contributions challenging the 'Mezey categories' include P. Norton, 'Parliaments: A Framework for Analysis', *West European Politics*, 13/3 (1990), pp.1–10, and D. Arter, 'Conclusion. Questioning the "Mezey Question": An Interrogatory Framework for the Comparative Study of Legislatures', in a special issue of the *Journal of Legislative Studies*, 12/3–4 (2006), pp.462–82 entitled *Comparing and Classifying Legislatures*, Guest Editor D. Arter.

13. K. Niclauß, *Das Parteiensystem der Bundesrepublik Deutschland* (Paderborn: Schöningh, 1995), p.50.

14. G. Sartori, 'Comparing and Miscomparing', *Journal of Theoretical Politics*, 3 (1991), p.249.

15. On the United States see, for example, D.R. Mayhew, *America's Congress. Actions in the Public Sphere, James Madison Through Newt Gingrich* (New Haven, CT and London: Yale University Press, 2000), pp.106–22; on Switzerland, P. Sciarini, 'The Decision-Making Process', in Ulrich Klöthi *et al.* (eds.), *Handbook of Swiss Politics* (Zurich: Verlag Neue Zürcher Zeitung, 2007), pp.465–99; on the European Union, N. Ringe, 'Government–Opposition Dynamics in the European Union: The Santer Commission Resignation Crisis', *European Journal of Political Research*, 44 (2005), pp.671–96.

16. See E.S. Krauss, 'The Mass Media and Japanese Politics: Effects and Consequences', in S.J. Pharr and E.S. Krauss (eds.), *Media and Politics in Japan* (Honolulu: University of Hawaii Press, 1996), p.360. The rise of the mass media as genuinely political players with a considerable veto power obviously marks a much more widespread phenomenon. Most observers consider the broad international trend towards commercialisation of the mass media as the single

most important factor for the media's significantly increased political independence and power. See D.C. Hallin and P. Mancini, *Comparing Media Systems: Three Models of Media and Politics* (Cambridge: Cambridge University Press, 2004), Chapter 8.

17. Austria and Switzerland in particular were long considered to mark paradigmatic cases of different forms of 'intra-government opposition'. See F.C. Engelmann, 'Austria: The Pooling of Opposition', in R.A. Dahl, *Political Oppositions in Western Democracies* (New Haven, CT and London: Yale University Press, 1966), pp.260–83; H.H. Kerr, 'The Structure of the Opposition in the Swiss Parliament', *Legislative Studies Quarterly*, 3 (1978), pp.51–62.

18. See, for example, J.M. Colomer, 'It's Parties That Choose Electoral Systems (or, Duverger's Laws Upside Down)', *Political Studies*, 53 (2005), pp.1–21; M. Gallagher and P. Mitchell (eds.), *The Politics of Electoral Systems* (Oxford: Oxford University Press, 2005).

19. In essence, Duverger argued that simple majority single-ballot electoral systems will produce bipolar two-party systems; M. Duverger, *Les parties politiques* (Paris: Seuil, 1951). For a recent assessment of the various theoretical and empirical aspects of 'Duverger's Law' see K. Benoit, 'Duverger's Law and the Study of Electoral Systems', *French Politics*, 4 (2006), pp.69–83. Italy in the 1990s has been widely considered to provide one of the few cases of party system change that matched Duverger's propositions: see S.R. Reed: 'Duverger's Law is Working in Italy', *Comparative Political Studies*, 34 (2001), pp.312–27.

20. G. Tiemann, *Wahlsysteme, Parteiensysteme und politische Repräsentation in Osteuropa* (Wiesbaden: Verlag für Sozialwissenschaften, 2006), p.338.

21. S.E. Scarrow, 'Party Subsidies and the Freezing of Party Competition: Do Cartel Mechanisms Work?', *West European Politics*, 29 (2006), pp.619–39.

22. H. Naßmacher, 'Parteiensysteme und Parteienfinanzierung in Westeuropa', in O. Niedermayer, R. Stöss and M. Haas (eds.), *Die Parteiensysteme Westeuropas* (Wiesbaden: Verlag für Sozialwissenschaften, 2006), pp.507–19.

23. I. van Biezen and P. Kopecký, 'The State and the Parties: Public Funding, Public Regulation and Rent-Seeking in Contemporary Democracies', *Party Politics*, 13 (2007), pp.235–54.

24. H.P. Kitschelt, 'Political Opportunity Structures and Political Protest: Anti-Nuclear Movements in Four Democracies', *British Journal of Political Science*, 16 (1986), pp.57–85; H. Kriesi, 'New Social Movements and Political Opportunities in Western Europe', *European Journal of Political Research*, 22 (1992), pp.219–44.

25. K. von Beyme, *Parliamentary Democracy: Democratization, Destabilization, Reconsolidation* (London: Palgrave, 2000), p.82.

26. Indeed, the great power of the German Bundesrat and the Australian Senate is largely owed to the fact that there has been split party government in the German and Australian bicameral systems for about two-thirds of the time post-1945.

27. On the effects of judicial review on the political process see A. Stone Sweet, 'Constitutional Courts and Parliamentary Democracy', in M. Thatcher and A. Stone (eds.), *The Politics of Delegation: Non-Majoritarian Institutions in Europe* (London: Cass, 2002), pp.77–100. The systemic effects of referendums have been tackled on an abstract theoretical level by S. Hug and G. Tsebelis, 'Veto Players and Referendums around the World', *Journal of Theoretical Politics*, 14 (2002), pp.465–516.

28. See K.W. Korbach, *The Referendum: Direct Democracy in Switzerland* (Aldershot: Dartmouth, 1993); Y. Papadopoulos, 'How Does Direct Democracy Matter? The Impact of Referendum Votes on Politics and Policy-Making', in J.-E. Lane (ed.), *The Swiss Labyrinth. Institutions, Outcomes and Redesign* (London: Cass, 2001), pp.35–57.

29. A. Stone Sweet, *Governing with Judges. Constitutional Politics in Europe* (Oxford: Oxford University Press, 2000).

30. S.M. Lipset and S. Rokkan, 'Cleavage Structures, Party Systems, and Voter Alignments: An Introduction', in S.M. Lipset and S. Rokkan (eds.), *Party Systems and Voter Alignments: Cross-National Perspectives* (New York: Free Press, 1967), pp.1–64; A. Ware, *Political Parties and Party Systems* (Oxford: Oxford University Press, 1996), Chapter 6.

31. S. Bartolini and P. Mair, *Identity, Competition, and Electoral Availability: The Stabilisation of European Electorates 1885–1985* (Cambridge: Cambridge University Press, 1990), p.216.

32. I. McAllister and S. White, 'Political Parties and Democratic Consolidation in Post-Communist Societies', *Party Politics*, 13 (2007), pp.197–216.
33. R. Dalton, 'Political Cleavages, Issues, and Electoral Change', in L. LeDuc, R.G. Niemi and P. Norris (eds.), *Comparing Democracies 2. New Challenges in the Study of Elections and Voting* (London: Sage, 2002), pp.189–209.
34. J.-E. Lane and S. Ersson, 'Party System Instability in Europe: Persistent Differences in Volatility between West and East?', *Democratization*, 14 (2007), pp.92–110.
35. P. Mair, *Party System Change: Approaches and Interpretations* (Oxford: Clarendon Press, 1997), p.212.
36. The other major player excluded from office was the fascist *Movimento Sociale Italiano*. The classic study on the party system of the 'first republic' is G. Galli, *Il bipartitismo imperfetto. Comunisti e democristiani in Italia* (Bologna: Il Mulino, 1966); see also L. Lotti, *I partiti della Repubblica: la politica in Italia dal 1946 al 1997* (Florence: LeMonnier, 1997), and S. Colarizi, *Storia dei partiti nell'Italia repubblicana* (Rome: Laterza, 1994).
37. The largest discrepancies between institutions and culture can be expected to be found where specific institutions have been imported from different cultural settings. On the problems of international and intercultural transfers of political institutions, see A. Przeworski, 'Institutions Matter?', *Government and Opposition*, 39 (2004), pp.527–40.
38. P. Pierson, *Politics in Time. History, Institutions, and Social Analysis* (Princeton, NJ: Princeton University Press, 2004).
39. The Federal Republic of Germany would appear to be a classic case in point. R.M. Lepsius, 'Die Prägung der politischen Kultur der Bundesrepublik durch institutionelle Ordnungen', in R.M. Lepsius (ed.), *Interessen, Ideen und Institutionen* (Opladen: Westdeutscher Verlag, 1990), pp.63–84.
40. R. Katz and P. Mair, 'Changing Models of Party Organization and Party Democracy: The Emergence of the Cartel Party', *Party Politics* 1 (1995), pp.5–28.
41. M. Cotta, 'The Rise and Fall of the "Centrality" of the Italian Parliament: Transformations of the Executive–Legislative Subsystem after the Second World War', in G.W. Copeland and S.C. Patterson (eds.), *Parliaments in the Modern World: Changing Institutions* (New York: Michigan University Press, 1994), pp.59–84.
42. W.C. Müller, 'Executive–Legislative Relations in Austria: 1945–1992', *Legislative Studies Quarterly*, 18 (1993), pp.467–94.
43. During the first four post-war decades no less than three-quarters of bills were passed unanimously. See D. Van Mechelen and R. Rose, *Patterns of Parliamentary Legislation* (Aldershot: Gower, 1986), pp.59–60.
44. A. Birch, The British System of Government (London: HarperCollins, 8th edn., 1991), p.131.
45. See the chapter by Robert Schrire in this volume.
46. K. von Beyme, *Die politische Klasse im Parteienstaat* (Frankfurt: Suhrkamp, 1993), p.183.

Parliamentary Opposition in Westminster Democracies: Britain, Canada, Australia and New Zealand

ANDRÉ KAISER

Despite a promising start with Robert Dahl's 'Patterns of Opposition',[1] comparative research on parliamentary opposition is still in its infancy. This article seeks to develop our knowledge further in two ways. Theoretically, it suggests including policy preferences in a field that has up until now largely focused on institutional arrangements. In order to conceptualise parliamentary oppositions as collective actors we need first to identify two elements: their policy preferences and the institutional constraints under which they act. Empirically, the article compares parliamentary oppositions in four Westminster democracies – Britain, Canada, Australia, and New Zealand. These countries are similar in terms of their cultural and institutional as well as socioeconomic contexts. One major difference is with regard to the territorial organisation of the political system. Australia and Canada are federal political systems, where parties compete for votes and seats on the national as well as the sub-national level. Britain has, since the late 1990s, established regional parliaments in Scotland and in Wales, but not in England. Finally, New Zealand is a unitary political system throughout. This mix of institutional similarities and differences is underlined by Arend Lijphart's two-dimensional analysis of democracies between 1945 and 1996.[2] Regarding the first dimension, which basically measures to what extent decision-making power is concentrated or dispersed in executive–legislative relations at the national level, all four countries are strongly majoritarian. Regarding the second dimension, which takes into account institutions such as federalism, bicameralism, or constitutional courts that may serve as institutional veto points for parliamentary minorities, Australia and Canada clearly diverge from Britain and New Zealand (see Table 1).

In an ideal majoritarian democracy, only two parties are represented in parliament, one which commands a majority of seats and therefore can govern with no institutional restrictions, and the other which is in a minority and functions as 'Her Majesty's Opposition'. The only task of the latter is publicly to criticise the government in order to give voters on election day the possibility of making informed decisions between the two different political teams and policy packages. This is the model on which accounts of parliamentary oppositions in Westminster systems are usually based. It is grounded on two implicit assumptions. Firstly, it assumes that there are only two parties in parliament. Secondly, it ignores any institutional arrangements alongside the linkages between the government and the parliament – or, to be more precise, the first chamber in the cases of Britain, Canada, and Australia – which may be used by political actors to further their aims. Together, these assumptions

TABLE 1
THE WESTMINSTER DEMOCRACIES IN LIJPHART'S TWO-DIMENSIONAL MAP

	Dispersion of power in executive–legislative relations	Other institutional veto points
Minimum	−1.64 (Jamaica)	−1.78 (New Zealand)
Australia	−0.78	1.71
Britain	−1.21	−1.12
Canada	−1.12	1.78
New Zealand	−1.00	−1.78
Maximum	1.77 (Switzerland)	2.52 (Germany)

Source: A. Lijphart, *Patterns of Democracy. Government Forms and Performance in Thirty-Six Countries* (New Haven, CT and London: Yale University Press, 1999), p.312.

lead to a static concept, unable to account for the way parliamentary opposition within these countries actually functions.

There are three reasons for this gap between the model and reality. Firstly, party system fragmentation has increased (see Figure 1). In Britain and Canada there have always been more than two parties in the first chamber. In the British case, the absolute number of parties (ANP) in the House of Commons has increased from nine in 1992 to eleven in 2005.[3] In Canada, the ANP ranged between three and five parties. The introduction of a mixed-member proportional system in the mid-1990s in New Zealand has led to an explosion of the number of parties in the House of Representatives. The ANP increased from three and four in the last first-past-the-post general elections in the early 1990s to eight in 2005. Only in the Australian case do

FIGURE 1
THE NUMBER OF PARTIES IN PARLIAMENT 1990–2006
(A) ABSOLUTE NUMBER OF PARTIES 1990–2006
(B) EFFECTIVE NUMBER OF PARTIES 1990–2006

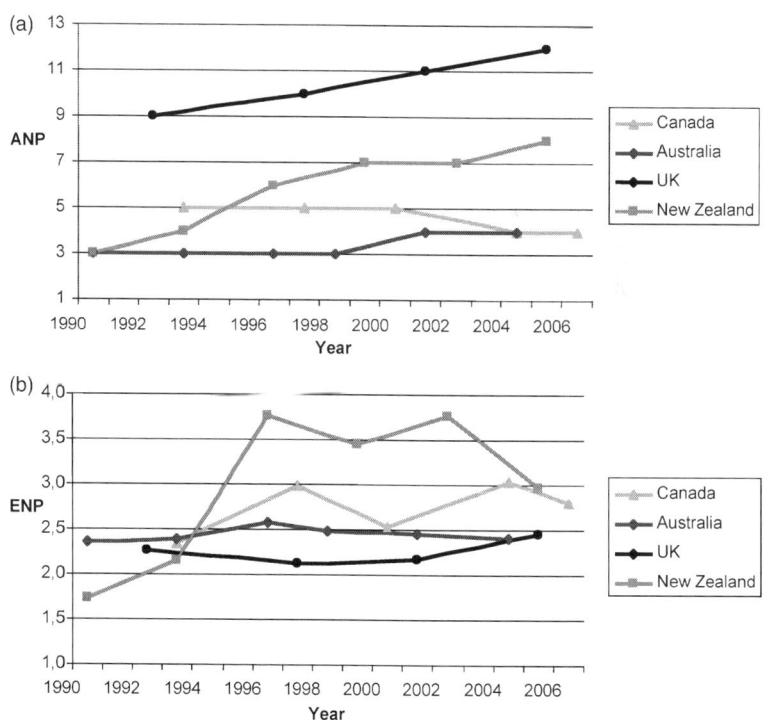

Source: Computations by author.

we still find a quasi two-party situation with the Australian Labor Party on the one side, and the long-term coalition of the Liberal Party and the National Party on the other. Depending on whether we count the coalition as constituting one or two parties, the ANP is, nonetheless, consistently at two or three.[4]

Following common practice within party system research and using the Laakso–Taagepera index of effective number of parties (ENP) instead of the ANP,[5] we see that only the Australian and British party systems with ENPs below 2.5 can be classified as two-party systems, whereas in Canada the ENP has increased to 3.0 and in New Zealand to more than 3.5 effective parties in parliament.

Secondly, and as a consequence of party system fragmentation, a majority government may not be achieved under all circumstances. Canada has a long tradition of oscillating between majority governments and minority ones, which are dependent on the cooperation of opposition parties. More recently, with the advent of proportional representation, New Zealand has seemingly developed a system of persistent Scandinavian-style minority government constellations.[6]

Finally, at least regarding the Australian case, the bicameral parliament exhibits two different patterns of parliamentary opposition. Whereas executive–legislative relations in the House of Representatives, Australia's first chamber, are based on a dominant government and an institutionally rather powerless opposition, minor parties and even single independent MPs in the Senate, the second chamber, have been able to exert influence on government policies way beyond their numerical strength.

This article proceeds as follows. The next section distinguishes between different concepts of parliamentary opposition in Westminster democracies. It is argued that the standard version – opposition with a capital 'O' – as a purely institutional approach is inferior to an actor-centred concept that takes parties' policy positions into regard and understands opposition politics as a problem of coordination.[7] The third section compares the institutional opportunity structures for opposition parties in Westminster democracies. Section four focuses on parties' policy positions within a fundamental left–right dimension. On this basis, we can infer what level of influence non-governmental parties have when attempting to solve coordination problems in their confrontation with the government of the day. Specific attention is concentrated on minority government constellations in Canada and New Zealand. In section five, institutional veto points external to executive–legislative relations in the first chamber are included in the analysis. Australian bicameralism serves as a particularly instructive example of how veto points, such as a powerful second chamber or federalism, may have repercussions on opposition politics. The final section recapitulates the findings.

AN ACTOR-CENTRED APPROACH TO PARLIAMENTARY OPPOSITION

Who constitutes the parliamentary opposition? The classical approach adopts institutional criteria to answer this question.[8] Following the binary logic of parliamentary democracy, the opposition is formed by those parties that are not in government. In the ideal Westminster world, only two major parties exist, so assigning the role of the opposition is simple. However, with real-world multiparty constellations the situation is far more complex. 'In the English-speaking world, all thought about opposition has been dominated by simple two-party models – to which multiparty systems are a kind of unsatisfactory and probably temporary exception.'[9] Based on constitutional conventions, the Speaker of the House makes the decision regarding which party leader becomes the Leader of the Official Opposition. With this title – first introduced in Canada in 1905, then in the United Kingdom in 1937 – considerable resources are spent: an official salary at a ministerial level as well as a privileged position in the allocation of parliamentary speaking time. Complications arise when non-government parties are similar in strength or when a regional party becomes the strongest non-government party, that is, when the simple criterion that the non-government party with the most seats should become the Official Opposition does not suffice. Especially in Canada –both on the national and the provincial levels – there have been a number of disputes in the run-up or following on from the Speaker's decision.[10]

What is more significant is that the constitutional recognition of a party as the Official Opposition does not offer us valuable information about how the opposition works. Do the non-government parties act together? Or do opposition parties oppose each other? Does one of them, in effect, function as a legislative support party of the government? To put it in Laver and Schofield's terms,[11] the interplay between government and opposition, as well as the coordination of behaviour between those parties that do not form the government, are varied in bipolar and multipolar competition, in particular when the overall institutional framework of democracy is highly majoritarian, as in Westminster systems. In order to analyse opposition politics, it is necessary to gather information on how 'cohesive' non-governmental parties act, as Dahl has already noted.[12] I suggest adopting the policy positions of parties as a proxy for potentially cohesive parliamentary behaviour. This rests on the assumption that the opposition's quality as a collective actor depends on its closeness in policy terms. The following sections cannot present a fully-fledged spatial analysis on the situations in the four Westminster democracies. However, as an approximation we will start with the parties' ideal points regarding a fundamental left–right dimension. To clarify the argument, imagine three scenarios, all based on the same alignment of policy positions (see Figure 2).

FIGURE 2
GOVERNMENT AND OPPOSITION PARTIES' IDEAL POINTS ON A LEFT–RIGHT
DIMENSION

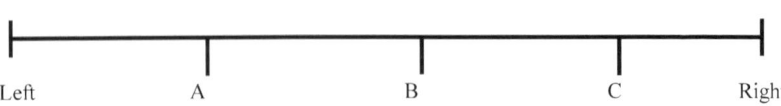

Left   A   B   C   Right

In the first scenario, party B is in government, while parties A and C are not. This is a situation of a bilateral opposition in which the government is in a privileged situation in the expectation that parties A and C have little chance to act together. Party B, in addition, covers the centre ground. Even if it forms a minority government, it can expect to be relatively safe from votes of no confidence. This is a situation often found in Scandinavian democracies.[13] In scenario 2, party A is in government and holds a majority of seats. However, B and C have adjacent policy preferences on the left–right dimension and may act together to make difficulties for the government. In this case, the opposition is more inclusive than the Opposition Leader's party. When no single-party majority government can be formed the situation becomes significantly more complicated. There is still considerable reluctance to form coalition governments in the English-speaking world.[14] In the third scenario, party A forms a single-party minority government. It is probable but not certain that party B will support the government on essential policy decisions. In this case, parties B and C, although with adjacent policy positions, will not cooperate.

In the following we will utilise the concept of parliamentary opposition in an actor-centred sense.[15] We will have to take into regard the parties' policy preferences and potential for coordinated parliamentary behaviour. However, as a first step, institutional opportunities and restrictions for the parliamentary opposition have to be clarified.

INSTITUTIONAL OPPORTUNITY STRUCTURES OF PARLIAMENTARY
OPPOSITION

Scholarship on executive–legislative relations in majoritarian democracies begins with the hypothesis that opposition parties can exert less influence on policy content than in consensus democracies. As long as governments have a majority status and parties behave cohesively, opposition parties will normally not be able to affect legislation directly. The parliamentary opposition depends on indirect opportunities to affect parliamentary decisions in two arenas. The first one is in parliamentary committees. Here, so the argument goes, policy expertise might be more relevant than party political affiliations of MPs, resulting in a cross-party mode of executive–legislative relations.[16] The second arena consists of the opposition using plenary debates to affect the public agenda.[17] Parallel to these ideas, Herbert Döring has put forward an argument in recent years stating that opposition parties in parliamentary democracies differ regarding the extent to which they can make use of procedures for setting the parliamentary agenda.[18] The core idea is that the power of the opposition with regard to the timing of different parliamentary stages and the sequence in which amendments to a bill are voted upon are inversely related. To illustrate, in the British House of Commons, the government can make use of the guillotine motion to drastically reduce the amount of time spent on a bill but it does not have the so-called last amendment power.[19] The power to decide which amendments will be debated and voted on rests with the Speaker. This presupposes, of course, that the Speaker is fully independent in his or her rulings from the government of the day. Whereas in Britain, Canada, and New Zealand this is usually the case, the convention that the Speaker acts in a party-politically neutral way has never been accepted in Australia.

From these hypotheses, a number of indicators can be derived, which help us to measure the indirect influence of the parliamentary opposition. However, there are astonishingly few attempts actually to employ them in comparative research. The following analysis is mainly based on three accounts. Firstly, Kaiser's analysis of institutional reforms in Westminster democracies contains an index of institutional opportunities for the parliamentary opposition based on data provided by the Inter-Parliamentary Union in 1976 and 1986 and a written survey of the Clerks of the New Zealand House of Representatives and the first chambers of Australia, Britain, and Canada.[20] The choice of indicators in this study is mainly determined by the research focus on institutional change over time. Therefore, those instruments had to be taken into account which were included by the Inter-Parliamentary Union in its 1976 and 1986 handbooks.[21] Secondly, Schnapp and Harfst's detailed analysis of parliamentary information and control resources in 22 established democracies is used to classify the four Westminster democracies in a more encompassing group.[22] Thirdly, Schnapp and Harfst's findings are contrasted with the results querying the role of the opposition in an expert survey from the late 1980s.[23]

How much do the four countries differ with regard to institutional opportunities for the opposition to influence parliamentary decisions? Based on three indicators (see Table A1) continuously available from the 1970s to the 1990s – whether the number of committees is large enough to have a differentiated grip on different policy areas; whether committee domains actually mirror the portfolios of ministries; and whether committees' information rights are comprehensive or not – we see that the situation remains more or less stable over time in the cases of Australia and Canada. In New Zealand, a committee reform in 1985 increased institutional resources for the opposition and a comprehensive parliamentary reform in 1995 prepared for the advent of proportional representation by introducing, inter alia, a consensus-oriented business committee to decide upon the parliamentary agenda. The introduction of a system of select committees alongside the standing committees in 1979 in Britain created new opportunities for the parliamentary minority. In terms of a rank ordering, the United Kingdom arrived at a level more or less similar to Canada and New Zealand, whereas Australia adopted a lower position. If we allow for all indicators available at the different time points – and accordingly ask whether committee chairs are distributed on a proportional basis; whether there is a business committee that seeks to make decisions upon the parliamentary agenda by consensus; whether a committee minority has the right to publish a minority report; whether the opposition parties have the right to control the parliamentary agenda (the so-called 'Opposition days') on at least ten days per session; and, finally, whether the committee stage takes place before the major principles of a bill are decided upon in the plenary – we get a similar picture. Australia is at the bottom whereas New Zealand and the United Kingdom are at the top. Only Canada falls behind its rank based on only three indicators and is placed in the middle. We can infer two facts from this analysis of the four Westminster democracies. Firstly, the institutional resources of the parliamentary opposition are not static. There is change over time. Secondly, there is variation between countries – in fact, more variation than a textbook version of Westminster parliaments would have us believe.

Schnapp and Harfst base their choice of indicators for measuring the strength of parliamentary oppositions in OECD democracies on three different prerequisites for an effective parliamentary monitoring of government activities[24]. Firstly, the control structures: the number of committees, the average committee membership and the mirroring of portfolios. Secondly, control resources: the number of staff per MP and committee, the number of research staff in the parliament and in its library, the number of volumes in the library. Thirdly, control rights: the summoning and information rights of committees, the timetable for budget laws, support by audit offices and ombudsmen. In this way, they are able to paint a highly differentiated picture. Britain, Australia, and Canada rank very low with regard to control structures, whereas New Zealand is not far from middle-ranked countries such as Norway and the Netherlands. In terms of control resources, Canada fits well at the top end of the countries, Australia and Britain rank in the middle, whereas New Zealand is at the lower end. Finally, with regard to the rights of control, Britain achieves a rank near the top, whereas the other three countries belong to the middle-ranked group of countries. The Schnapp and Harfst study shows that as soon as we consider a larger number of indicators for oppositional influence in parliament, the findings are more differentiated than summary indices would have us believe. These findings are in stark contrast to an index from a late 1980s expert survey by Laver and Hunt that is still often used in empirical democracy research.[25] Here Britain is at the bottom end, New Zealand ranks 14th, Canada 11th and Australia 7th in a sample of 19 countries. The astonishingly high ranking of Australia has mainly to do with the fact that experts did not distinguish between the influence of the opposition in the House of Representatives and the Senate. However, as we will see below, opposition politics in these two chambers follows very different patterns.

In addition to instruments which aim at influencing policy during the parliamentary term, there are procedures targeted at improving the performance in the polls. A good example of this is question time. Commonly believed to be mere window dressing, recent research by Rob Salmond and others demonstrates that its effects can be considerable.[26] Question time is a central feature of plenary activities. Due to the fact that it is televised in Westminster democracies, it is the most visible part of parliamentary activity. It is mainly an opportunity for the opposition to criticise the government and to respond to the public agenda. No-notice questions and follow-up questions are allowed.[27] Given that questions and answers have to be short, question time is highly interactive, combative and spontaneous. In a sample of 22 countries, Britain, Canada and New Zealand significantly lead the table with regard to how many questions are asked within one hour.[28] This Westminster-type question period is not only found to be associated with higher levels of political engagement of the citizens (knowledge, partisanship and turnout) but it can also help the opposition to improve its stance in opinion polls. Salmond's case study of New Zealand demonstrates that a well-performing opposition leader during question time can have a notable effect on voting intentions.[29]

However, all these findings should not distract us from the fact that these are only indirect instruments to either affect legislation or improve prospects at the next general election. As long as the government commands a majority in parliament and its MPs follow party lines, it has a firm hand on legislative output in Westminster democracies. This is underlined by the immense time pressure under which bills have to be dealt with. Nevertheless, even in this regard, there is more variance in the group of Westminster parliaments than hitherto acknowledged. Whereas in Britain and Canada, during the first half of the 1990s, between 0.3 and 0.5 parliamentary bills were adopted per sitting day, the equivalent number in New Zealand was at 1.7 and in Australia a startling 2.8.[30] The major reason for these differences is that the first two countries have a tradition of holding a very high number of sitting days, which is not the case in Australia and in New Zealand. However, even with half a bill adopted per sitting day, it is clear that opposition parties have to concentrate on a few policy issues if they want to use their indirect influence in the parliamentary process effectively.

POLICY POSITIONS AND POTENTIAL FOR COORDINATED OPPOSITION
BEHAVIOUR

Having reviewed the astonishingly diverse institutional opportunity structures
for the parliamentary opposition, parties' policy positions on the left–right
dimension will now be added to the analysis. Policy preferences are assessed
on the basis of a quantitative textual analysis of election manifestos[31] and
measured according to the Franzmann–Kaiser modification of the original
Comparative Manifesto Group's procedure.[32] On this basis, we can infer to
what extent non-governmental parties have to solve coordination problems
when confronting the government of the day. Specific attention is given to
minority government constellations in Canada and New Zealand. If a government has a minority status, it looks for support from one or more of the opposition parties – either in the longer term or on an issue-by-issue basis. This
inevitably leads to a division in the opposition camp between parties that
simply oppose the government and those that choose a legislative support
status without joining the government; a status elegantly described by Tim
Bale and Torbjörn Bergman as the 'grey area between opposition and office
– in governance but not in government'.[33]

In the period from 1990 to 2006, there have only been majority governments
in Australia (see Figure 3a) and Britain (see Table A2). The situation was the
least complex in Australia. With the exception of a few independents without
any bargaining power, the government was confronted by a single opposition
party (or, in the case of the Liberal–National coalition, by a perennial party
bloc). Accordingly, the coordination costs for the opposition were very low.
Given its minimal institutional opportunities to influence government decisions,
the only option to criticise the government publicly and to prepare for an alternation after the next election remained open. In the Australian case, therefore,
we do not need to consider policy positions.

In the British case, we find that the opposition is split between many groups,
dramatically differing in strength. Most of them are small, such as the Northern
Irish parties, nationalist parties from Scotland and Wales, one-MP groups and,
on occasion, independents. More importantly, the major opposition party –
Labour until 1997 and the Conservatives from 1997 onwards – had to cope
with an increasingly strong third party, the Liberal Democrats. Was there any
potential for cooperation between the two largest opposition parties? If we
take into account the policy positions on an encompassing left–right dimension,
we see that the Liberal Democrats held very similar positions to the Labour
Party throughout the period observed here (see Figure 3b).

In the first half of the 1990s, this created an opportunity for a coordinated
opposition of Labour and Liberal Democrats against the Conservative government. Hence, it came as no surprise when the Liberal Democrats heralded a

'constructive' opposition to the Blair government after the Labour victory in 1997 and even participated in a joint consultative committee with the government up until 2001.[34] Adjacent policy positions can be a double-edged sword for an opposition party, however. The Liberal Democrats may have been more influential than the Conservative Party with regard to policy decisions in recent years, but they had to balance this advantage carefully by ensuring voters understood them to be a party with an independent profile. Hence, the internal discussion about the equidistance maintained between the Labour government and the Conservatives as the major opposition party never stopped within the realm of the Liberal Democratic leadership. Britain illustrates a situation where two opposition parties had similar institutional opportunities – although the much stronger Conservative Party held the position of 'official' opposition – but with differing options to affect the policy decisions of the government majority.

In the cases of Canada and New Zealand, the situation is more complex (see Table A2 and Figures 3c and 3d). After an unusually long period of majority governments in the 1990s and early 2000s, since the general election of 2004 Canadian governments have had to find support from opposition parties at least with regard to confidence and supply votes in order to stay in office. Upholding a traditional pattern from the 1960s and the 1970s, the Liberal government under Paul Martin (2004–6) was supported by the social democratic New Democratic Party on the basis of a number of policy compromises. Again, this is a situation whereby an opposition party gained influence on government policy way beyond its parliamentary strength.

Finally, amidst a corruption scandal, the New Democrats requested from the government a list of policy compromises which Martin was unwilling to fulfil. Consequently, all opposition parties united in a vote of no confidence at the end of 2005. In policy terms, this episode is interesting because the policy distances between opposition parties were significant. Nevertheless, they hoped for extra votes in a general election due to the fact that Liberal support in the polls had dropped dramatically. The situation of the current Conservative government of Prime Minister Stephen Harper (since 2006), although also in a minority position, is different. There is no longer-term agreement with any one of the opposition parties whatsoever. Instead, the government has had to find support on an issue-by-issue basis from at least one other party. Given the fact that the opposition parties are at odds with one another on a number of central policy issues,[35] they have great difficulty coordinating their activities. So far, Harper has succeeded in winning all essential votes.

The most interesting case is New Zealand (see Figure 3d). After the general elections of 1990 and 1993, both held under the traditional first-past-the-post system, the National Party under Jim Bolger was able to form a majority government. However, the introduction of a proportional

FIGURE 3
(A) LEFT–RIGHT PARTY POSITIONS IN AUSTRALIA
(B) LEFT–RIGHT PARTY POSITIONS IN BRITAIN
(C) LEFT–RIGHT PARTY POSITIONS IN CANADA
(D) LEFT–RIGHT PARTY POSITIONS IN NEW ZEALAND

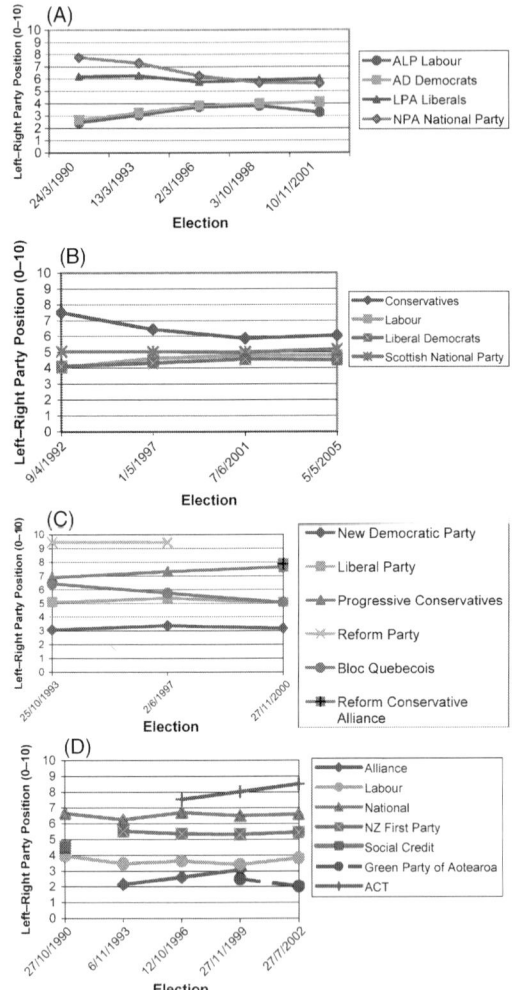

Source: I. Budge, H-D. Klingemann, A. Volkens, J. Bara and E. Tanenbaum, *Mapping Policy Preferences.*
Estimates for Parties, Electors, and Governments 1945–1998 (Oxford: Oxford University Press,
2001); H.-D. Klingemann, A. Volkens, J. Bara, I. Budge and M. Macdonald, *Mapping Policy Prefer-*
ence II: Estimates for Parties, Electors and Governments in Eastern Europe, the European Union and
the OECD, 1990–2003 (Oxford: Oxford University Press, 2006); S. Franzmann and A. Kaiser, 'Locating Political Parties in Policy Space. A Reanalysis of Party Manifesto Data', *Party Politics*, 12 (2006).

representation system based on the German model – combining a constituency with a list vote with an overall proportional distribution of seats to parties, known as 'mixed member proportional system' – led to party system fragmentation well before the first general election under the new system in 1996.[36] The National government soon lost its majority due to the fact that party cohesion eroded and a number of MPs left to establish their own parties in order to exploit the new opportunities. Nevertheless, the government succeeded in staying in power by negotiating support on essential votes and they finally signed a formal coalition agreement a few months prior to the next general election in 1996. The 1996 election, the first one held under the new rules, resulted after protracted negotiations in a rather unstable majority coalition government of National and New Zealand First. From 1999 onwards, all governments, now led by Helen Clark of the Labour Party, have been minority governments. Formally, all three governments since then were of the minority coalition type (Labour plus a left-leaning group that rearranged itself consistently and stood under different names in the general elections). In addition, in all three cases there were formal agreements with further parties, agreeing to support the government on confidence and supply motions – in 1999 with the Greens; in 2002 with the Greens plus United Future; and in 2005 with New Zealand First and United Future. This, however, did not inhibit the legislative support parties from voting against the government on other policy issues. To complicate the situation further, the 2005 government formation introduced two other innovations. Firstly, the Greens, formally no longer a legislative support party, still agreed not to vote against the government on supply and confidence. This means that, in practice, they abstain in such votes. Secondly, and most astonishingly, the two legislative support parties, New Zealand First and United Future, do not formally belong to the government, but each has one minister outside cabinet. This arrangement allows these parties still to vote against the government in non-essential votes. In terms of policy positions the different patterns found with regard to these opposition parties can easily be explained. New Zealand First and United Future are centre parties between Labour and National. Therefore, it is rational for them to support a Labour Government in exchange for policy concessions. Labour's coalition partner on the left under different names (Alliance, Progressive Coalition, Jim Anderton's Progressive Party) has nothing in common with National, the largest opposition party. The Greens are in a similar situation. In their case, however, there is some distance between Labour's policy preferences and their own regarding non-socioeconomic, post-materialist issues. A qualified support of the government from the outside gives the Greens the opportunity to continue to portray themselves as fully independent whilst achieving important policy concessions with regard to environmental issues and the budget.[37] Finally, to the right of National, we find ACT, a small neo-liberal party in a similar situation as the Greens on the left. It seeks to establish a compromise between their cooperation with National, the 'official opposition', and maintaining an independent policy profile.

The case of New Zealand reveals, in particular, that understanding 'the opposition' only through its institutional opportunities does not make much sense. Since it will not coordinate its activities based on a coherent set of policy aims, 'the opposition' as a collective actor simply cannot exist. Under minority governments, the different non-governmental parties experience extremely divergent possibilities to affect legislative decision-making. Legislative support parties become highly influential; the 'official opposition' has to accept a status of powerlessness.

Finally, an aspect not addressed so far is parliamentary party cohesion. The traditional approach to the government–opposition dualism takes unitary actor behaviour for granted. However, empirical findings in recent years have shown that this is not always the case. Normally, parliamentary leaderships successfully aim at finding intra-party compromises. If not, this intra-party mode[38] of legislative behaviour becomes evident to the public. In Britain and in Canada, dissenting behaviour of MPs has increased in recent decades, and in the latter case it usually results in the exclusion of the dissenting MP from the party caucus.[39] Consequently, it would be rational for opposition parties to try to aggravate internal divisions in the government party or parties. Whether this actually happens is an under-researched question so far. Party dissension is less of a problem for the government, or an option for the opposition, in Australia and New Zealand.

INSTITUTIONAL VETO POINTS EXTERNAL TO EXECUTIVE–LEGISLATIVE RELATIONS IN THE FIRST CHAMBER

Thus far, the analysis has focused on the combination of institutional opportunities for opposition parties and their policy-based behaviour relative to other parties in the first chamber. Regarding this, opposition parties in Australia seem to have the least influence and those in New Zealand the most influence on parliamentary decision-making. In the next step, institutional veto points external to the first chamber are taken into account. We will see that institutional arrangements such as federalism or bicameralism can, to a large extent, offset the powerlessness of non-government parties.

As already argued by Robert Dahl, the whole institutional regime of a political system is relevant for analysing the patterns of opposition politics. Central to this is the identification of situations or 'sites', as Dahl terms them, where oppositional actors are able to influence policy directly. 'The situation or circumstances in which an opposition employs its resources to bring about a change might be called a *site* for encounters between opposition and government'.[40] The proto-typical constellation in a Westminster system is that there is only one such site available – the parliamentary election. As there is a minimal chance to change the government's legislation during the term, the opposition concentrates on maximising votes in order to get elected. Regarding the four countries studied here, however, this pure constellation cannot normally be found, as the last two sections have already demonstrated. If we include other 'sites' in addition to executive–legislative relations in the first chamber, the findings differ even more from the textbook Westminster model.

Lijphart's second dimension (see Table 1) can serve as a first approximation for the relevance of these institutional veto points. The values for Australia and Canada differ considerably from those for New Zealand and Britain. New Zealand is a unitary country with a unicameral parliament.[41] Therefore, opposition parties cannot employ any sites except the House of Representatives if they want to affect policy by conventional means. Of course, they can and do try to influence public opinion via the media, interest groups or demonstrations. In the case of Britain, changes are observed through the constitutional reforms of the Blair governments in recent years. The House of Lords, every now and then the object of reform discussions, has always been a more relevant site for placing pressure on government policy than one would expect, based on its weak formal powers.[42] After decades of a built-in Conservative majority that Labour governments had to cope with, the change towards a predominantly appointed second chamber in 1999, where the two main parties now enjoy almost equal membership, but which also includes a large group of non-affiliated cross-benchers, has led to a situation where both Labour and Conservative governments have to face the possibility that the House of Lords utilises its delaying powers. Since time is a scarce resource in legislation one should not underestimate the role of Britain's second chamber as a 'site' for bringing about change to government policy.[43] The devolved parliamentary assemblies in Wales and, especially, in Scotland may become more important in the future, depending on how intergovernmental relations will develop.

Proper federalism, as found in Australia and Canada, is even more interesting for opposition parties as an institutional veto site. Carl J. Friedrich notes that 'federalism may be looked upon as a method for institutionalizing opposition alternative to the British parliamentary system. . . . Federalism and opposition mutually strengthen and support each other'.[44] Its functions in the context of opposition politics are twofold. Firstly, opposition parties on the federal level may simultaneously function in government at the sub-national level. This is exactly what we find in both Australia and Canada. So, for example, at the time of writing, the Australian Labor Party, the 'official opposition' in the federal House of Representatives holds the governments in all six states and two territories. In Canada, the Liberal Party governs in four provinces on a majority and in one province on a minority basis.[45] In addition, the New Democratic Party holds a majority government in two provinces. Secondly, controlling sub-national governments allows these parties not only public visibility and policy influence in those areas where legislative powers lie with the provinces and states, it also places them in an influential position regarding intergovernmental relations.[46] Although both federal systems are of a dual type, with powers strictly divided between the two levels of government, there is still a large area of voluntary cooperation, which can be used to arrive at substantial policy compromises.

In the Australian case, the Senate, the federal second chamber, is even more important as a veto point for opposition parties. The two chambers differ with regard to the electoral system with which their members are elected. Whereas the House of Representatives utilises alternative vote – a majoritarian system where voters have one vote but can rank candidates in order of preference – Senate elections are based on the proportional single transferable vote system also used in Ireland. Senate seats are distributed proportionally between parties according to their vote shares and small parties are represented. Consequently, since the early 1960s, neither the government nor the 'official' opposition in the House of Representatives has commanded a majority in the second chamber.[47] Hence, 'federal politics has two party systems, one for the Senate and one for the House of Representatives. ... Even if the same parties are involved, the dynamics of competition and the pattern of representation are quite different, just as the dynamics of parliamentary politics are different in each chamber'.[48] This bicameral constellation leads to a situation where small parties and independents hold the balance. These are mostly moderate centre parties such as the Australian Democrats or the Greens. Extreme Senators such as the single representative of the right-wing populist One Nation group who sat in the Senate from 1999 to 2005 are rare. As the Senate undoubtedly is one of the most powerful second chambers in the world – with coequal powers except for money and taxation bills – the small parties become pivotal whenever the government and 'official' opposition parties confront each other in legislative decision-making. Governments have no other choice than to bargain and seek policy deals.[49] This, again, illustrates that the policy influence of opposition parties does not necessarily depend on their strength in terms of seats but more on a combination of institutional opportunities and policy positions relative to other parties. In Canada, the Senate is far less relevant as an institutional veto point for opposition parties. It has fewer powers and is not directly elected. Although there has been a reform debate for a long time, Senators are still appointed by the Governor-General on a nomination by the federal Prime Minister.[50]

Taking into account institutional veto points, which opposition parties may use, changes the comparative account of opposition influence on legislative decision-making considerably. Regarding this, it is in Australia where opposition parties can have the most power. However, it is small, Senate-only parties, not the 'official' opposition, that profit the most. In addition, federalism in Australia and Canada creates opportunities for opposition parties actually to govern on the sub-national level and use intergovernmental relations for influencing policy-making on the federal level. Needless to say, these additional institutional opportunities come at a price. To achieve a cohesive political strategy of politicians from the same party in multilevel politics – in the two chambers but also on the two territorial levels – increases coordination costs considerably. In this regard, there is a clear difference between Australia and Canada. Whereas vertical integration of Australian parties is relatively high, the opposite is true for most Canadian parties.[51]

CONCLUSION

There is no such thing as a Westminster pattern of parliamentary opposition. Taking institutional opportunity structures, parties' policy positions, and veto points such as bicameralism and federalism into account, both in a comparative perspective and over time, we find an astonishing variety of constellations that characterise the behaviour of opposition parties. In institutional terms, the Westminster systems are still at the bottom of the league table when it comes to opposition influence on parliamentary decision-making. Coordinated behaviour between non-governmental parties is often difficult due to large policy distances. Especially in New Zealand, small, centrist parties can, as legislative support parties of minority governments, become influential beyond their sheer parliamentary strength. Federalism in Australia and Canada opens up the possibility for federal opposition parties to win office at the sub-national level and to use intergovernmental relations to affect policy-making. Finally, Australian bicameralism permits a constellation where small Senate-only opposition parties become important players in federal politics. Finally, over time there has been a clear trend towards strengthening the role of opposition parties, mainly as a consequence of reforms of parliamentary committee structures.

Thus, we have to distinguish between small opposition parties that may exploit favourable constellations of executive–legislative relations, and large opposition parties, the 'official' opposition, which can only criticise the government and hope for the next general election. However, government alternations occur less regularly than we would expect from the textbook version of majoritarian democracy.[52] Rather, the opposite seems to be the case in recent decades. In Australia, the Labor Party governed without interruption from 1983 to 1996 when it was replaced by a coalition government that is still in office at the time of writing. Earlier, in the post-war years, a coalition government was in power for as long as 23 years. In Canada, there have traditionally been very long periods of Liberal dominance, from 1935 to 1957, from 1963 to 1979, and more recently from 1993 to 2006. Alternation patterns in Britain are also characterised by long periods of dominance by one party. The Conservatives were in power from 1951 to 1964 and from 1979 to 1997. It is an open question how long the Labour Party, elected into government in 1997, will be able to stay in office. Similar patterns of long reigns by one party could be observed in pre-electoral reform New Zealand. Hence, the notion of the 'government in waiting' is not too comforting for the 'official' opposition. This may pose a significant reason why majoritarianism has come under pressure in the Anglo-Saxon world in recent decades.

NOTES

1. R.A. Dahl, 'Patterns of Opposition', in R.A. Dahl (ed.), *Political Oppositions in Western Democracies* (New Haven, CT and London: Yale University Press, 1966), pp.332–47.
2. A. Lijphart, *Patterns of Democracy. Government Forms and Performance in Thirty-Six Countries* (New Haven, CT and London: Yale University Press, 1999).
3. This comparatively high number includes the Northern Ireland parties.
4. In addition, there is one Country Liberal Party MP from the Northern Territory. This party is a fusion of the Liberal and National Parties on the national level and sits with these in the House of Representatives. There have been independent MPs in the British and Canadian Houses of Commons as well as in the Australian House of Representatives from time to time. Interest-ingly, with the introduction of proportional representation in New Zealand political entrepre-neurs have preferred to found their own parties instead; see T. Brechtel and A. Kaiser, 'Party System and Coalition Formation in Post-Reform New Zealand', *Political Science*, 51 (1999), pp.3–26.
5. The Laakso–Taagepera index measures the relative or effective number of parties by weigh-ing parties according to their seat shares.
6. This has early been predicted as the most likely pattern after the change to proportional rep-resentation; see J. Boston, *Governing under Proportional Representation: Lessons from Europe* (Wellington: Institute of Policy Studies, 1998).
7. An actor-centred analysis of opposition politics is not opposed to institutionalism. On the con-trary, it adds policy preferences and interaction to institutional opportunity structures. Hence, this distinction is different from the one between an institutional and a cooperation hypothesis made in L. Helms, 'Ansätze einer Handlungstheorie der politischen Opposition', *Österrei-chische Zeitschrift für Politikwissenschaft*, 26 (1997), pp.423–35.
8. A. Potter, 'Great Britain: Opposition with a Capital "O"', in R.A. Dahl (ed.), *Political Opposi-tions in Western Democracies* (New Haven, CT and London: Yale University Press, 1966), pp.3–33.
9. Dahl, 'Patterns of Opposition', p.333.
10. N. Michaud, 'Designating the Official Opposition in a Westminster Parliamentary System', *Journal of Legislative Studies*, 6 (2000), pp.69–90.
11. M. Laver and N. Schofield, *Multiparty Government: The Politics of Coalition in Europe* (Ann Arbor, MI: University of Michigan Press 1998), pp.114–17.
12. Dahl, 'Patterns of Opposition', p.332.
13. See F. Christiansen and E. Damgaard, this volume.
14. The exceptions are the long-standing cooperation of the Liberal and National parties in Australia and a few coalition experiments on the sub-national level in Australia and Canada (Tasmania 1989, Saskatchewan 1999). After the introduction of proportional rep-resentation, New Zealand has switched between different formats: majority coalition, min-ority coalition, and single-party minority government. See below on New Zealand's parliamentary opposition in minority government constellations; also E. McLeay and

J. Uhr, 'The Australian and New Zealand Parliaments: Context, Response and Capacity', *Australian Journal of Political Science*, 41 (2006), p.263, and T. Bale and T. Bergman, 'A Taste of Honey is Worse than None at All? Coping with the Generic Challenges of Support Party Status in Sweden and New Zealand', *Party Politics*, 12 (2006), pp.189–209. It remains to be seen whether the formation of stable coalition governments will become the norm in Scotland and Wales. For a preliminary analysis see B. Seyd, *Coalition Government in Scotland and Wales*, Report No. 110 (London: The Constitution Unit, 2004).

15. On actor-centred institutionalism generally see F. Scharpf, *Games Real Actors Play. Actor-Centered Institutionalism in Policy Research* (Boulder, CO and Oxford: Westview Press, 1997).

16. A. King, 'Modes of Executive–Legislative Relations: Great Britain, France, and West Germany', *Legislative Studies Quarterly*, 1 (1976), pp.11–36.

17. G. Powell, *Elections as Instruments of Democracies. Majoritarian and Proportional Visions* (New Haven, CT and London: Yale University Press, 2000), pp.102–9; K. Strøm, *Minority Government and Majority Rule* (New York: Cambridge University Press, 1990).

18. H. Döring, 'Parliamentary Agenda Control and Legislative Outcomes in Western Europe', *Legislative Studies Quarterly*, 26 (2001), pp.145–66; H. Döring, 'Worauf gründet sich die Agenda-Setzer Macht der Regierung? Theoretische und vergleichende Perspektiven auf den deutschen Fall', in S. Ganghof and P. Manow (eds.), *Mechanismen der Politik. Strategische Interaktion im deutschen Regierungssystem* (Frankfurt: Campus, 2005), pp.109–48.

19. For empirical findings on the last amendment power, see W.B. Heller, 'Making Policy Stick. Why the Government Gets What it Wants in Multiparty Parliaments', *American Journal of Political Science*, 45 (2001), pp.780–98.

20. A. Kaiser, *Mehrheitsdemokratie und Institutionenreform. Verfassungspolitischer Wandel in Australien, Großbritannien, Kanada und Neuseeland im Vergleich* (Frankfurt: Campus, 2002), pp.138–40, 494–7.

21. Inter-Parliamentary Union, *Parliaments of the World. A Comparative Reference Compendium* (London: Macmillan, 1976); Inter-Parliamentary Union, *Parliaments of the World. A Comparative Reference Compendium* (Aldershot: Gower, 2nd edn., 1986).

22. K.-U. Schnapp and P. Harfst, 'Parlamentarische Informations- und Kontrollressourcen in 22 westlichen Demokratien', *Zeitschrift für Parlamentsfragen*, 36 (2005), pp.348–70.

23. M. Laver and W.B. Hunt, *Policy and Party Competition* (New York: Routledge, 1992), p.125.

24. Schnapp and Harfst, Parlamentarische Informations – und Kontrollressourcen.

25. For instance, Powell uses the expert survey data to externally validate his own government control index in research on how well majoritarian and proportional electoral democracies achieve their self-proclaimed goals in terms of representativeness and responsiveness. See Powell, *Elections as Instruments of Democracy*, pp.107–9.

26. R. Salmond, 'Parliamentary Question Times. How Legislative Accountability Mechanisms Affect Mass Political Engagement', Conference paper, http://rsalmond.bol.ucla.edu/questiontimes.pdf (accessed 9 Sept. 2007); R. Salmond, 'Grabbing Governments by the Throat: Question Time and Leadership in New Zealand's Parliamentary Opposition', *Political Science*, 56 (2004), pp.75–90. See also E. Penner, K. Blidook and S. Soroka, 'Legislative Priorities and Public Opinion: Representation of Partisan Agendas in the Canadian House of Commons', *Journal of European Public Policy*, 13 (2006), pp.1006–20.

27. Formally, this is not the case in the British House of Commons. However, it can be circumvented since follow-up questions can be asked that may surprise the minister.

28. Salmond, *Parliamentary Question Times*, p.35.

29. Salmond, 'Grabbing Governments by the Throat', pp.87–90.

30. Kaiser, *Mehrheitsdemokratie und Institutionenreform*, p.493.

31. The Australian equivalent to an election manifesto is the party leader's policy speech at the outset of an election campaign. This is published in major newspapers. See I. McAllister and R. Moore (eds.), *Party Strategy and Change. Australian Political Leaders' Policy Speeches Since 1946* (Melbourne: Longman Cheshire, 1991).

32. Unfortunately, these data are only available until 2003, except in the British case where data for the 2005 election could be incorporated. For data and technical details, see I. Budge, H.-D. Klingemann, A. Volkens, J. Bara and E. Tanenbaum, *Mapping Policy Preferences. Estimates for Parties, Electors, and Governments 1945–1998* (Oxford: Oxford University Press, 2001); H.-D. Klingemann, A. Volkens, J. Bara, I. Budge and M. Macdonald, *Mapping Policy Preference II: Estimates for Parties, Electors and Governments in Eastern Europe, the European Union and the OECD, 1990–2003* (Oxford: Oxford University Press, 2006); S. Franzmann and A. Kaiser, 'Locating Political Parties in Policy Space. A Reanalysis of Party Manifesto Data', *Party Politics*, 12 (2006), pp.163–88.

33. Bale and Bergman, 'A Taste of Honey is Worse than None at All?', p.189.

34. A.T. Russell and E.A. Fieldhouse, 'Identifying an Attitudinal Heartland of Liberal Democrat Support in the 1997 General Election: An Exploration of Equidistance, Constructive Opposition and Third Party Politics', in P. Cowley, D. Denver, A. Russell and L. Harrison (eds.), *British Elections and Parties Review*, Vol. 10 (London: Frank Cass, 2000), pp.172–97.

35. An encompassing left–right dimension greatly simplifies the multidimensional character of Canadian politics, including the constitutional dimension (Quebec question, Senate reform). However, in principle one can extract as many dimensions from the Comparative Manifesto data set as one wishes. See Franzmann and Kaiser, 'Locating Political Parties in Policy Space', pp.166–74.

36. For details see R. Miller, 'Preparing for MMP: 1993–1996', in R. Miller (ed.), *New Zealand Politics in Transition* (Auckland: Oxford University Press, 3rd edn., 1997), pp.37–48; Brechtel and Kaiser, 'Party System and Coalition Formation', pp.18–24.

37. In fact, the Greens had in 2005 been willing to enter government, but New Zealand First and United Future refused to support a government with Green ministers in the cabinet.

38. King, 'Modes of Executive–Legislative Relations'.

39. P. Norton, 'The United Kingdom. Exerting Influence from Within', in K. Heidar and R. Koole (eds.), *Parliamentary Party Groups in European Democracies. Political Parties Behind Closed Doors* (London: Routledge, 2003), pp.39–56; D.C. Docherty, 'Parliament. Making the Case for Relevance', in J. Bickerton and A.-G. Gagnon (eds.), *Canadian Politics* (Peterborough, ON: Broadview Press, 4th edn. 2004), pp.163–83.

40. Dahl, 'Patterns of Opposition', p.338.

41. New Zealand switched to a unicameral legislature in 1950. For the reasons behind the dissolution of the Legislative Council, the second chamber, and its consequences, see A. Kaiser, 'Die Zweite Kammer in Neuseeland. Funktionsprobleme, Auflösung und Folgewirkungen', in G. Riescher, S. Ruß and C. Haas (eds.), *Zweite Kammern* (Munich and Vienna: Oldenbourg, 2000), pp.368–80.

42. A. Kaiser, 'House of Lords and Monarchy: British Majoritarian Democracy and the Current Reform Debate about its Pre-Democratic Institutions', in P. Catterall, W. Kaiser and U. Walton-Jordan (eds.), *Reforming the Constitution. Debates in Twentieth-Century Britain* (London: Frank Cass, 2000), pp.97–128.

43. For a formal model of bicameral negotiations that includes time as an 'impatience factor', see G. Tsebelis and J. Money, *Bicameralism* (Cambridge: Cambridge University Press, 1997). On the relevance of parliamentary time for government and opposition strategies in general, see H. Döring, 'Time as a Scarce Resource: Government Control of the Agenda', in H. Döring (ed.), *Parliaments and Majority Rule in Western Europe* (Frankfurt and New York: Campus/St Martin's, 1995), pp.223–47.

44. C.J. Friedrich, *Trends of Federalism in Theory and Practice* (New York: Praeger, 1968), pp.58, 67.

45. Things are, however, complicated by the fact that some of the provincial Liberal Party organisations are not formally affiliated to the party on the federal level.

46. N. Bolleyer, 'Federal Dynamics in Canada, the United States, and Switzerland: How Substates' Internal Organization Affects Intergovernmental Relations', *Publius: The Journal of Federalism*, 36 (2006), pp.471–502.

47. The exceptions are the second half of the 1970s and since 2005.
48. C. Sharman, 'The Representation of Small Parties and Independents in the Senate', *Australian Journal of Political Science*, 34 (1999), p.360.
49. So, for instance, in the early 1990s the pivotal senators and independents successfully traded their votes in favour of the Australian Labor Party government's budget for the government's acceptance of a substantial strengthening of Senate committee powers. See L. Young, 'Minor Parties and the Legislative Process in the Australian Senate: A Study of the 1993 Budget', *Australian Journal of Political Science*, 34 (1999), pp.7–27; J. Uhr, 'Generating Divided Government: The Australian Senate', in S. Patterson and A. Mughan (eds.), *Senates. Bicameralism in the Contemporary World* (Columbus, OH: Ohio State University Press, 1999), pp.93–119.
50. Stephen Harper, the Conservative Prime Minister at the time of writing, has promised to consult provincial voters before nominating candidates for Senate seats.
51. R. Dyck, 'Relations Between Federal and Provincial Parties', in B. Tanguay and A.-G. Gagnon (eds.), *Canadian Parties in Transition* (Toronto: Nelson, 1996), pp.160–89.
52. A. Kaiser, M. Lehnert, B. Miller and U. Sieberer, 'The Democratic Quality of Institutional Regimes: A Conceptual Framework', *Political Studies*, 50 (2002), pp.313–31.

APPENDIX

TABLE A1
INSTITUTIONAL OPPORTUNITY STRUCTURES FOR OPPOSITION PARTIES

(a) On the basis of three indicators

		1970s		
	(1)	**(2)**	**(3)**	$\sum$
AUS	0	1	0.5	1.5
CAN	1	0.5	1	2.5
NZ	1	0	1	2
UK	0.5	0	0.5	1

Notes: (1) The number of committees dealing with legislation and/or monitoring ministries is: > 10 = 1 point, 10–6 = 0.5, ≤ 5 = 0.
(2) The committees' domains mirror the portfolios of ministries: yes = 1 point, predominantly = 0.5, no = 0.
(3) The committees have the right to summon ministers; summon witnesses; inspect documents: three times yes = 1 point, twice yes = 0.5, once yes or no = 0.
Source: Inter-Parliamentary Union, *Parliaments of the World. A Comparative Reference Compendium* (London: Macmillan, 1976), tables 37, 40.

		1980s		
	(1)	**(2)**	**(3)**	$\sum$
AUS	0.5	0.5	1	2
CAN	1	0.5	1	2.5
NZ	1	0	1	2
UK	1	0.5	1	2.5

Source: Inter-Parliamentary Union, *Parliaments of the World. A Comparative Reference Compendium* (Aldershot: Gower, 2nd edn., 1986), tables 20, 23; coding for indicator (2) modified by author.

	1990s			
	(1)	**(2)**	**(3)**	Σ
AUS	0.5	0.5	0.5	1.5
CAN	1	0.5	1	2.5
NZ	1	1	1	3
UK	1	0.5	1	2.5

Source: Written survey of clerks of first chamber by author in 1998.

(b) On the basis of all indicators available for time period

	1970s			
	(1)	**(2)**	**(3)**	Σ
AUS	0	1	0.5	1.5
CAN	1	0.5	1	2.5
NZ	1	0	1	2
UK	0.5	0	0.5	1

Notes: (1) The number of committees dealing with legislation and/or monitoring ministries is: > 10 = 1 point, 10–6 = 0.5, ≤ 5 = 0.
(2) The committees' domains mirror the portfolios of ministries: yes = 1 point, predominantly = 0.5, no = 0.
(3) The committees have the right to summon ministers; summon witnesses; inspect documents: three times yes = 1 point, twice yes = 0.5, once yes or no = 0.

Source: Inter-Parliamentary Union, *Parliaments of the World. A Comparative Reference Compendium* (London: Macmillan, 1976), tables 37 and 40.

	1980s							
	(1)	**(2)**	**(3)**	**(4)**	**(5)**	**(6)**	**(7)**	Σ
AUS	0.5	0.5	0	1	1	0	0	3
CAN	1	0.5	0	1	0	0	0	2.5
NZ	1	0	0	1	0	0	1	3
UK	1	0.5	1	1	0	0	1	4.5

Notes: (1) The number of committees dealing with legislation and/or monitoring ministries is: > 10 = 1 point, 10–6 = 0.5, ≤ 5 = 0.
(2) The committees' domains mirror the portfolios of ministries: yes = 1 point, predominantly = 0.5, no = 0.
(3) Committee chairs are distributed between parliamentary parties on a more or less proportional basis: yes = 1 point, no = 0.
(4) The committees have the right to summon ministers; summon witnesses; inspect documents: three times yes = 1 point, twice yes = 0.5, once yes or no = 0.
(5) Committee minorities have the right to present a minority report: yes = 1 point, no = 0.

(6) The parliamentary agenda is determined by a 'business committee', which is not controlled by the government and that seeks to make decisions by consensus: yes = 1 point, no = 0.

(7) The opposition parties have the right to control the parliamentary agenda on at least ten days: yes = 1 point, no = 0.

Source: Inter-Parliamentary Union, *Parliaments of the World. A Comparative Reference Compendium* (Aldershot: Gower, 2nd edn., 1986), tables 11, 19, 20, 21, 23, 33; coding for indicator (2) modified by author.

		1990s							
	(1)	**(2)**	**(3)**	**(4)**	**(5)**	**(6)**	**(7)**	**(8)**	$\sum$
AUS	0.5	0.5	0	0.5	1	0.5	0	0	3
CAN	1	0.5	0	1	0	0.5	0	1	4
NZ	1	1	0	1	1	0	1	1	6
UK	1	0.5	1	1	1	0	0	1	5.5

Notes: (1) The number of committees dealing with legislation and/or monitoring ministries is: > 10 = 1 point, 10–6 = 0.5, ≤ 5 = 0.

(2) The committees' domains mirror the portfolios of ministries: yes = 1 point, predominantly = 0.5, no = 0.

(3) Committee chairs are distributed between parliamentary parties on a more or less proportional basis: yes = 1 point, no = 0.

(4) The committees have the right to summon ministers; summon witnesses; inspect documents: three times yes = 1 point, twice yes = 0.5, once yes or no = 0.

(5) Committee minorities have the right to present a minority report: yes = 1 point, no = 0.

(6) The committee stage takes place before the major principles of a bill are determined in the plenary session, i.e. before the second reading: yes = 1 point, from time to time = 0.5, no = 0.

(7) The parliamentary agenda is determined by a 'business committee', which is not controlled by the government and that seeks to make decisions by consensus: yes = 1 point, no = 0.

(8) The opposition parties have the right to control the parliamentary agenda on at least ten days: yes = 1 point, no = 0.

Source: Written survey of clerks of first chamber by the author in 1998.

TABLE A2
PARLIAMENTARY SEAT SHARES AND GOVERNMENT FORMATION, 1990–2006

(a) Australia, house of representatives

	Election year					
	1990	**1993**	**1996**	**1998**	**2001**	**2004**
Australian Labor Party	**78**	**80**	49	67	65	60
Liberal Party of Australia	55	49	**75**	**64**	**68**	**74**
National Party of Australia	14	16	**19**	**16**	**13**	**12**
Country Liberal Party	0	0	0	0	**1**	**1**
Independents	1	2	5	1	3	3
Sum	148	147	148	148	150	150

(b) Canada: house of commons

	Election year				
	1993	**1997**	**2000**	**2004**	**2006**
Liberal Party	**177**	**155**	**172**	**135**	103
Bloc Quebecois	54	44	38	54	51
Reform Party	52	60			
New Democratic Party	9	21	13	_19_	29
Progressive Conservative Party	2	20	12		
Canadian Reform Conservative Alliance			66		
Conservative Party of Canada				99	**124**
Independents	1	1	0	1	1
Sum	295	301	301	308	308

(c) New Zealand: house of representatives

	Election year					
	1990	**1993**	**1996**	**1999**	**2002**	**2005**
National Party	**68**	**50**	**44**	39	27	48
Labour Party	28	45	37	**49**	**52**	**50**
New Labour Party	1	0	0	0	0	0
Alliance	0	2	13	**10**	0	0
New Zealand First Party	0	2	**17**	5	13	7
ACT New Zealand	0	0	8	9	9	2
United New Zealand	0	0	1	1	0	0
Green Party of Aotearoa	0	0	0	7	9	6
United Future New Zealand	0	0	0	0	8	3
Progressive Coalition Party	0	0	0	0	**2**	0
Maori Party	0	0	0	0	0	4
Jim Anderton's Progressive Party	0	0	0	0	0	**1**
Sum	97	99	120	120	120	121

(d) United Kingdom: house of commons

	Election year			
	1992	**1997**	**2001**	**2005**
Conservative Party	**336**	165	166	198
Labour Party	271	**419**	**413**	**356**
Liberal Democrats	20	46	52	62
Ulster Unionist Party (UUP)	9	10	6	1
Democratic Unionist Party (DUP)	3	2	5	9
Ulster Popular Unionist Party	1	0	0	0
Social Democratic and Labour Party (SDLP)	4	3	3	3
Scottish National Party (SNP)	3	6	5	6
Plaid Cymru	4	4	4	3
Sinn Féin	0	2	4	5
United Kingdom Unionist Party (UKUP)	0	1	0	0
Kidderminster Hospital and Health Concern	0	0	1	1
Respect Unity Coalition	0	0	0	1
Independent	0	1	0	1
Sum	651	659	659	646

Notes: Parties that form a government after the general election are bold. Parties that support the government without joining it are italic. In 2000 the Canadian Reform Party aligned with the Progressive Conservative Party as Alliance. Alliance was renamed Conservative Party of Canada in 2004. Although Speakers in some cases run as independents they are counted here according to the party they originally come from.

Source: Center on Democratic Performance Election Results Archive, http://cdp.binghamton.edu/era/index.html (accessed 9 Sept. 2007).

Parliamentary Opposition under Minority Parliamentarism: Scandinavia

FLEMMING JUUL CHRISTIANSEN and
ERIK DAMGAARD

In his seminal article on the Danish parliamentary oppositions, Mogens Pedersen tended to agree with Robert Dahl who, investigating the American case, stated that 'To say where the "government" leaves off and the "opposition" begins is an exercise in metaphysics'.[1] While there were no difficulties in identifying the 'government', it seemed impossible to put under one formula the behaviour of parties outside of government. Pedersen's conclusion was widely shared by other observers and the crucial problem was how to deal with parliamentary opposition parties that more or less supported the government in office in one way or another.

The conclusion drawn by Dahl in his edited volume, comprising ten liberal democracies, was clear: there is no single pattern of political opposition in the countries under investigation. Therefore one should rather look at various aspects of the role of oppositions, such as their concentration, competitiveness, choice of site for encounters, distinctiveness, goals and strategies.

In this article we shall have a fresh look at the parliamentary oppositions in the three Scandinavian countries of Denmark, Norway and Sweden that, at least until recently, have been governed by minority cabinets for a long time. The paper deals with four main aspects of opposition parties in such situations: their composition in terms of strength, ideology and fragmentation, their institutional setting, their role in the legislative process and, finally, their importance compared to non-parliamentary oppositions. We shall focus on the situations and developments over the last 15–20 years. First, however, we must deal with the question of how to conceptualise a (parliamentary) opposition. At the abstract definitional level Dahl's sensible reasoning is the following:

> Suppose that A determines the conduct of some aspect of the government of a particular political system during some interval. ... Suppose that during this interval B cannot determine the conduct of the government; and that B is opposed to the conduct of government by A. Then B is what we mean by 'an opposition'.[2]

As mentioned, there are several patterns of opposition and some of them are clearly relevant in the Scandinavian context. For example, the degree of organisational cohesion or concentration of the opponents is influenced by the multiparty systems and high levels of party discipline. And a high level of competitiveness concerning government formations does not preclude cooperation in law-making. But there are further ways of distinguishing between opposition parties, particularly if the government in office is of the minority type. Such a government by definition faces an opposition majority that may be more or less concentrated/dispersed, and more or less competitive. Thinking about the Scandinavian experience we thus presume that opposition parties can be 'support parties', 'legislative agreement parties', ad hoc coalition partners, and perhaps 'pure opposition' parties.

WHO IS THE PARLIAMENTARY OPPOSITION?

We may compare the three Scandinavian countries with each other and with other countries of Western Europe. An example of these procedures is found in Table 1, showing the average ideological complexion of governments over the 50-year era following the Second World War. The first column lists the average share of cabinet seats controlled by social democratic and left-wing parties over time. By implication, the remaining cabinet seats were therefore controlled by centre, right and other parties. The average percentages indicate that the former parties were most likely to be in government in Sweden (76.3), Norway (73.1), followed by Austria (60.7), while the balance of forces was more even in Denmark (50.7). In all other countries, the social democratic and left-wing parties tended to be in opposition most

TABLE 1

LONG-TERM IDEOLOGICAL COMPLEXION OF GOVERNMENTS IN WESTERN EUROPE

Country	% of cabinet seats controlled by social democrats and other left-wing parties, 1950–94	Mean left score of government, 1945–95
Sweden	76.3	4.1
Norway	73.1	4.0
Austria	60.7	3.4
Denmark	50.7	3.0
Finland	33.6	2.8
Iceland	31.7	2.3
Luxembourg	28.4	2.1
United Kingdom	28.1	2.3
Belgium	27.6	2.3
Spain	26.0	n.a.
Germany	24.8	2.0
France	24.5	2.0
Switzerland	23.8	1.9
Greece	19.7	n.a.
Netherlands	18.6	2.0
Italy	12.4	1.6
Ireland	9.7	1.5
Portugal	5.7	n.a.

Source: M. Gallagher, M. Laver and P. Mair, *Representative Government in Modern Europe* (New York: McGraw-Hill, 2006).

of the time. The data clearly show that the Scandinavian governments have traditionally been dominated by social democrats, especially in Sweden and Norway, whereas they tended to be in opposition in other Western European countries (except for Austria).

The second column of Table 1 presents an index of the ideological composition of governments. It scores 1.0 if a country was ruled by a right-dominated government during the entire period, and 5.0 if it was ruled by a left-dominated government for the entire period. It appears that the rank orders of the two columns in Table 1 are very similar and even identical for the Scandinavian countries (and Austria): The mean left score of governments was 4.1 (Sweden), 4.0 (Norway), 3.4 (Austria) and 3.0 (Denmark).

Another way to approach opposition party politics is to look at the types of cabinet formed, as the role and influence of opposition parties is likely to vary according to such types. Table 2 lists some main types of cabinets formed in Western Europe since the Second World War.

As Table 2 indicates, single-party majority cabinets are comparatively rare in Western Europe, but they nevertheless dominate in the United Kingdom, Greece and Malta. Previously they have also been formed by social

TABLE 2
TYPES OF GOVERNMENT IN WESTERN EUROPE, 1945–2003

Country	Single-party majority	Coalition majority	Minority	Minority government percentage
Denmark	0	4	27	87
Sweden	3	5	18	69
Norway	6	3	19	68
Spain	4	0	4	50
Italy	0	33	20	38
Portugal	2	5	4	36
Ireland	7	8	7	32
Finland	0	29	11	28
France	0	48	9	16
Iceland	0	22	2	8
Belgium	3	31	3	8
United Kingdom	20	0	1	5
Germany	0	22	1	4
Austria	4	18	1	4
Netherlands	0	19	0	0
Luxembourg	0	18	0	0
Greece	8	1	0	0
Malta	9	0	0	0
Total	66	266	127	
Percentage	14	58	28	

Source: M. Gallagher, M. Laver and P. Mair, *Representative Government in Modern Europe* (New York: McGraw Hill, 2006).

democratic parties in Norway and Sweden, whereas no party commanded a majority in Denmark. Majority coalitions, either minimal winning or surplus cabinet coalitions, are clearly the most frequent type of government. They are also known in Scandinavia (in the minimal winning form), but they are few in numbers. The most interesting observation in the present context has to do with minority governments, either single-party or coalition cabinets. In several countries minority governments are hardly known, but they constitute by far the largest percentages of governments in Scandinavia: Denmark (87.9), Sweden (69.2) and Norway (67.9).

It is generally assumed in the literature that the existence of minority governments provides fertile ground for opposition party influence.[3] Jointly, opposition parties constitute a majority, and the government needs the support of at least one opposition party to pass legislation and to make other important decisions. To obtain such support, and to stay in office, the government must give policy concessions to non-governmental parties, which thus can exert influence without entering a government and can even avoid the possible electoral blame for unpopular decisions. The causal link between minority governments and opposition party influence is probably quite complex, however: do minority governments cause opposition party influence, or do potential opposition parties create minority governments? Anyway, there is a strong connection between minority governments and opposition influence.

Based on data from Laver and Hunt, Gallagher *et al.* provided interesting information on the relationship between minority governments and the possible influence of opposition parties on government policy.[4] Experts in the various countries were asked to rate their countries in terms of opposition impact on government policy. The scores are shown in Table 3. Aside from Italy, the Scandinavian countries score highest on opposition party impact, and these countries also have the highest frequency of minority governments. Even if the instrument of measurement may be somewhat crude, the results strongly support the expectation of a positive relationship between minority government and opposition party influence.

Summing up so far, we may conclude that the opposition in Scandinavia has often or mostly consisted of non-socialist parties, that the type of government in the three countries has mainly been minority cabinets, and that minority governments tend to increase the influence of opposition parties. In the following we shall look more closely into the party composition of parliament and government in recent years.

TABLE 3
ESTIMATED IMPACT OF OPPOSITION PARTIES ON
GOVERNMENT POLICY

Country	Score
Italy	7.1
Norway	6.8
Denmark	6.5
Sweden	5.2
Finland	4.9
Iceland	4.8
Portugal	4.3
Austria	4.1
Ireland	4.1
Luxembourg	4.0
Netherlands	3.6
Germany	3.5
France	3.4
Malta	3.3
Belgium	2.6
Greece	2.2
Spain	2.0
Britain	2.0

Note: Mean scores at a scale ranging from 1 (low) to 9 (high).
Source: M. Gallagher, M. Laver and P. Mair, *Representative Government in Modern Europe* (New York: McGraw-Hill, 2006).

After the very first parliamentary elections in the twenty-first century the by then almost traditional forms of government/opposition relations were still in force. As shown in Table 4a, all three countries were ruled by minority governments that had to attract support from one or more opposition parties which jointly commanded a majority of votes in parliament. As Table 4a also indicates, however, the opposition was not united or concentrated. It was rather dispersed or divided in the sense that opposition parties could be found at both sides of the governing parties. In Sweden the governing Social Democrats were also facing opposition parties to the right (Centre Party, Christian Democrats, Liberals, and Conservatives) and left (Greens, Left Party). In Denmark the minority coalition of Liberals and Conservatives faced the Danish People's Party on their right, and five centre and left-wing parties on their left (Christian People's Party, Social Liberals, Social Democrats, Social People's Party, and Unity List). Finally, the Norwegian minority coalition of the Christian People's Party, Liberals and Conservatives faced opposition from the Progress Party on its right, and the Centre Party, Labour, and Socialist Left on its left.

It is worth noting that, according to Table 4a, the opposition was also dispersed in the sense that there was always more than one party to the left of the government, but not necessarily to the right of it (Denmark, Norway). It should further be noted that the left-wing and right-wing 'extremist' parties had not been included in any government at the time immediately following the elections of 2001 and 2002. By definition they had therefore been

TABLE 4A

PARTY COMPOSITION OF SCANDINAVIAN PARLIAMENTS AFTER 2001 AND 2002
ELECTIONS

Sweden	Riksdag 2002	Denmark	Folketing 2001	Norway	Storting 2001
Left Party	30	Unity List	4		
Greens	17	Socialist People's Party	12	Socialist Left	23
Social Democrats	*144*	Social Democrats	52	Labour	43
Centre Party	22	Social Liberals	9	Centre Party	10
Christian Democrats	33	Christian People's Party	4	*Christian People's Party*	22
Liberals	48	*Liberals*	*57**	*Liberals*	*2*
Moderates	55	*Conservatives*	*16*	*Conservatives*	*38*
		Danish People's Party	21	Progress Party	26
		Others	3*	Coastal Party	1
Total	**349**	**Total**	**179**	**Total**	**165**

Note: Cabinet parties in *italics*. *Four members elected in Greenland and Faroe Islands. One joined Liberals.

TABLE 4B
PARTY COMPOSITION OF SCANDINAVIAN PARLIAMENTS AFTER 2005 AND 2006
ELECTIONS

Sweden	Riksdag 2006	Denmark	Folketing 2005	Norway	Storting 2005
Left Party	22	Unity List	6		
Greens	19	Socialist People's Party	11	*Socialist Left*	*15*
Social Democrats	130	Social Democrats	47	*Labour*	*61*
Centre Party	*29*	Social Liberals	17	*Centre Party*	*11*
Christian Democrats	*24*			Christian People's Party	11
Liberals	*28*	*Liberals*	*52*	Liberals	10
Moderates	*97*	*Conservatives*	*18*	Conservatives	23
		Danish People's Party	24	Progress Party	38
		Others	4*		
Total	**349**	**Total**	**179**	**Total**	**169**

Note: Cabinet parties in *italics*. *Four members elected in Greenland and Faroe Islands.

opposition parties all the time. That does not necessarily mean that they were lacking influence. In fact they had increasingly been included in legislative decision-making with the established parties and they can certainly not be called anti-system opposition parties.[5]

After the most recent elections in 2005 and 2006, the picture begins to change (see Table 4b). To be sure, the Danish situation is basically unchanged, with a Liberal-Conservative minority coalition firmly supported by the Danish People's Party in the most important matters. But in Norway and Sweden the situations now look different. Thus, in Norway a centre-left majority coalition was formed after the election of 2005. It has no opposition parties to its left but four to its right (Christian People's Party, Liberals, Conservatives, Progress Party). In Sweden, a majority coalition of 'bourgeois' parties (Centre Party, Christian Democrats, Liberals, and Conservatives) was formed in 2006. It has no opposition on its right, but three parties to its left (Social Democrats, Greens, Left Party).

As far as Norway and Sweden is concerned we may conclude that the former opposition parties have now joined in a majority cabinet coalition, that the opposition is now less dispersed or divided, and that it presumably has lost influence. We shall return to these interesting developments below in the section on the role of parliamentary oppositions.

THE INSTITUTIONAL SETTING

In this article we shall only highlight some of the more important features of the institutional setting.[6] The Scandinavian countries are small unitary states, although with relatively strong local government sectors. Formally, they are also constitutional monarchies, although the monarchs lost their political influence a long time ago. The systems of government are better understood as parliamentary democracies with a fusion of powers rather than a separation of powers. This implies that the government is responsible to the parliament. The core principle is that a government must leave office or call new elections if it loses the confidence of a majority in parliament. In Norway, though, dissolution within the four-year term is not allowed by the constitution, and in Sweden an election due to dissolution only has effect for the remainder of the ongoing term, which makes dissolutions less attractive than in Denmark.

The 'negative' version of parliamentarism, practised in all three countries, means that minority governments are possible as long as they do not receive a motion of censure passed by a majority in parliament. In Scandinavia the formation of a government does not require a positive majority of investiture. In that respect the three countries differ from several other European countries. In Norway and Denmark no vote is required at all; in Sweden it must be proven by a vote that an absolute majority is not against the appointment of a designated new prime minister.

An important characteristic of the Scandinavian party system is multiple parties, as we have seen. The number of parties represented in parliament after the two most recent elections is almost identical in the three countries: Denmark 8–7, Sweden 7–7, and Norway 7–7. What matters in this respect is the proportional representation (PR) election system that assures a good fit between the shares of votes and seats of a party, provided that the threshold for representation has been surpassed (two per cent in Denmark, four per cent in Sweden and Norway). A relatively low threshold facilitates the representation of new parties – including of course opposition parties – which is not the case with the 'first past the post' plurality elections in single-member districts. Even rather small new parties therefore have a fair chance to establish themselves as opposition parties in the official scheme of political representation. Arguably this could reduce the incentive to get involved in some forms of non-parliamentary opposition activity. Seats in parliament provide a state funded platform, equipped with various resources and facilities, from which to promote certain interests and ideas, ranging from constituency service to views on problems of globalisation.

The Scandinavian countries have unicameral parliaments. With the same number of parties represented in the three parliaments, the Swedish party groups are generally larger than their counterparts in Denmark and Norway, as the Swedish Riksdag has a much higher number of members (349) than the Danish *Folketing* (179) and the Norwegian *Storting* (169). One might also say that members of the smaller Danish and Norwegian party groups have to carry a heavy workload compared to Swedish party group members.

Aside from government ministers, the party groups are the most important actors in the Scandinavian parliaments.[7] They are organised with a leadership group and specialisation in terms of committee assignment and spokesperson for the party in a certain policy area. The cohesion or discipline of the party groups is very high, but that does not prevent cooperation across party lines in many areas.[8] The emphasis on the primacy of party is well founded. However, it is also obvious that the committee system in parliament plays an important role.

All three parliaments have a system of permanent, specialised committees with a division of labour that roughly mirrors the jurisdictions of government ministries. MPs have different preferences concerning committee membership, but they cannot all get what they want. Still, member preferences explain a great deal of the committee assignments, but seniority and party loyalty is also part of the explanation.[9]

MPs in Norway and Sweden reported that the influence of committees matched the influence of party leaders, whereas Danish MPs thought that the influence of party leaders was significantly greater than the influence of committees. In interpreting the figures one should remember that committees are composed of members who primarily consider themselves to be party representatives. However, in Hagevi's words:

> the committee system is the core of internal party group specialisation in all of the Nordic parliaments. Such specialisation means that MPs holding a position on a standing committee gain recognition as party spokespersons within a particular policy area. As such, they can affect their party's standpoint in that area, especially if they serve as committee chairman.[10]

Legislative research scholars probably agree that control of the executive is a major function of parliaments, or perhaps rather of the parliamentary opposition party groups. Many of them might also agree that the control activities – involving monitoring of ministers and possibly invoking sanctions – are most effective when they are least needed, and vice versa. In other words, ministers of strong majority governments can resist attacks from the parliamentary minority opposition, whereas ministers of weak minority governments cannot do so by means of their own votes.

Instruments of parliamentary control are numerous in the Scandinavian countries.[11] They include debates on bills and resolutions, various forms of questions and interpellations, committees of various types, and institutions such as the Ombudsman and the National Auditing Office. To this could be added non-parliamentary actors seeking to check and scrutinise the government, as we shall discuss below in a brief section on non-parliamentary oppositions.

THE ROLE OF PARLIAMENTARY OPPOSITIONS

Parliamentary government in Scandinavia can be argued to represent a distinct model of executive–legislative relations that differs from parliamentary models characterised by majority government.[12] Minority governments simply need support from opposition parties for majority-building. This mathematical necessity is fundamental for assessing the legislative role of the opposition in Scandinavia. It creates bargaining situations between government and opposition parties in which the latter can attain political influence in return for support to the government. In this section we explore how opposition parties get involved in legislative coalitions under various structures of 'minority governance' identified in the three countries.[13]

Opposition parties may influence legislation indirectly if governments anticipate their reactions and adjust their policies. Direct influence may come in at least two different forms: 'alternative majorities' or negotiated agreements. If opposition parties approve legislative initiatives against the votes of the government, and if the latter nevertheless accepts its defeat without resigning, then we have rule by alternative majority. More often, political influence of opposition parties results from negotiated agreements with the government. Such agreements may either be based on permanent external support parties or on shifting majorities in a more or less ad hoc fashion.[14] The involvement of opposition parties in legislative coalitions may vary in size (minimal winning or 'oversized'), scope (few or many topics), and duration (long term or short term).[15] When bargaining between political parties results in legislative agreements these may be formalised as written documents (published or not) and vary in length and detail.[16] We do not claim that involvement is equal to influence, but we do think that forms or 'modes' of opposition affect the conditions for opposition party influence.[17]

In the following subsections we use the variables mentioned above to assess how Scandinavian opposition parties have been involved in the legislative process. We point out how bargaining has been conducted in different forms and find a development away from shifting majorities towards more integrated relations between minority governments and support parties. This reflects that minority governments today use majorities within their own 'bloc' to a larger extent than used to be the case. During minority government, state budgets have developed into a major marketplace for legislative exchange, and reforms of the procedures concerning their approval have affected the conditions for involvement of opposition parties. Increased integration is also found between the opposition parties that do not support the government. In fact, the three Scandinavian government constellations of 2007 are all essentially results of pre-electoral coalitions.

Sweden

The involvement of opposition parties in Sweden during minority government seem to have changed in the recent decade from shifting – and often broad – agreements, to closer integration between the government and one or more opposition parties. The Social Democrats have dominated Swedish politics for decades. Thus, since 1982 the bourgeois parties only held a majority from 1991 to 1994 and again from 2006. The rest of the time Social Democratic minority governments stayed in office. In the 1980s the Social Democrats could usually rely on the support of the Left Party Communists[18] without offering the latter party major policy concessions in return.[19] The governments still often formed a broad majority even though an increasing number of 'reservations' from opposition parties and more bloc politics in general could also be observed.[20] In addition the Left Party Communists began to break out of 'captivity' and demand concessions, illustrated by an incident occurring in 1990 when the party voted against an economic crisis solution, which the government had explicitly turned into a vote of confidence; the government resigned, but soon after it took office again.[21] The bourgeois government 1991–94 did not have its own majority either but was dependent on the party New Democracy not voting against it taking office. However, in a major compromise in 1992 the government and the Social Democrats dealt with the severe economic crises that struck Sweden at the time.[22]

Majority-building under the Social Democratic governments 1994–2006 has changed compared to the classic situation of more or less passive support from the Left Party before 1990. A form of party cooperation has evolved that Aylott and Bergman name 'contract parliamentarism'.[23] Bale and Bergman define the concept as an explicit, written contract that commits the partners beyond a specific deal or a temporary commitment. It must be available to the public, and it may include representatives to serve in the central administration.[24]

It all began in 1995 with an oral agreement of cooperation for two years between the government and the Centre Party. As part of the agreement, the Centre Party appointed one political advisor (*politisk sakkunnig*) to the Ministry of Finance and one to the Ministry of Defence. These were the two policy areas covered by the oral agreement. The two parties stated as their motivation for the arrangement that a safe majority was needed in order to deal with the evidently severe economic problems of the country.[25]

After the election of 1998, the Social Democrats turned to the Greens and the Left Party and found an agreement on five specific areas: economy and state budget, employment, distributive justice, gender equality and environment. The parties did not commit each other to cooperation on other issues but stated their intention to work together for a full electoral period. This was published in a press release only, and there was no written joint programme. Neither were there appointments of political advisors as there had been in the cooperation with the Centre Party. The party leaders did meet occasionally, however, and a group of cooperation, the SAMS,[26] was established. So was a group of coordination regarding economic policies, the SVAMP.[27] The SAMS consisted of the deputy leaders of the three parties. It took care of problems in the cooperation that had not been solved on a lower level, and information was also channelled through this organ. The SVAMP was the real site of the annual state budget negotiations, and it prepared the agenda and solved minor difficulties in advance of the final budget negotiations at party leader level. The group also coordinated other budget matters and worked with surveillance of the common economic policies. It met twice per month and its members were the junior minister in the Ministry of Finance, the party spokespersons on finance, and a few other representatives from the parties, but only occasionally the minister.[28]

Even though especially the Greens wanted cabinet seats after the 2002 election the Social Democrats refused to offer this. Instead, the result was another agreement with the Social Democrats, Greens and the Left Party.[29] The agreement, called 'The 121 points', was nothing less than a political programme for cooperation between three parties. The programme was intended to last for four years with a renegotiation that took place in the autumn of 2004. The document was published, and its 121 points did cover a whole range of domestic policy areas, not least economy and budget.[30] There were over 4,200 words in the agreement, making it longer than many coalition agreements.[31] It contained a mix of declarations of more or less specific intents and initiatives to be taken. The EU and defence and foreign policy were explicitly excluded.[32]

The 121 points also specified a number of procedural and organisational arrangements. The details were further elaborated in a separate agreement on the 'forms of cooperation' between the three parties.[33] The stated purpose of the organisational arrangements was to guarantee influence and insight for the cooperating parties.[34] As in the agreement between the government and Centre Party 1995–97, the support parties appointed political advisors, up to eight each to be deployed according to their own choice.[35] Their main function was to control the implementation of the common programme on behalf of their parties.

In the Ministry of Finance, two special coordination offices were established to take care of relations between the parties, coordination with the political advisors in the departments, and the implementation of the 121 points.[36] In addition, the agreement upheld the two coordination groups, the SAMS and the SVAMP. Every second month the SAMS evaluated the current state of implementation of the 121 points programme. The '121 points' also set up three coordination committees (on public administration, integration of foreigners and health issues) in order to develop coordination among the departments involving the cooperation parties. Other political coordination groups were established temporarily when needed, often including parliamentarians as well as a political advisor.[37] The party leaders, including the prime minister, met for lunch each month.[38] Finally, the '121 points' document specified common press conferences on common initiatives.

The cooperation between the governing Social Democrats and the party's two partners came close to a coalition government in many regards. Not only did the parties have a common programme, and a declared intention to share credit (and perhaps even blame) in public, but they also arranged procedures to monitor the realisation of it. The lack of cabinet seats for the two small parties makes the arrangement different from Cabinet committees and other coordinating devices common in coalition governments, also in Sweden. The Bildt government 1991–94 had an office in the Ministry of Finance with the purpose of coordination between ministers of different parties.[39] The novelty in Sweden after 1998 was central government offices coordinating policies of the entire cabinet with selected opposition parties.

Denmark

In the past two decades only one Danish government controlled a majority (1993–94). The bourgeois minority coalition government of 1984–87 could rely on support from the Social Liberals in economic policies, but it had to live with 'alternative majorities' on a number of other questions.[40] Since 2001, the Liberal-Conservative minority governments have enjoyed support from the Danish People's Party for most major initiatives. This cooperation is not formalised in an overarching support agreement like the ones described above for Sweden.

In general support agreements are not common in the *Folketing*, but another significant form of committing legislative coalition is frequent. In these 'forlig' Danish governments and opposition parties agree on certain policies to which they bind each other for a period, either fixed in the agreement or running until they are terminated.[41] Policies may cover a single topic or a number of topics. 'Forlig' may concern bills or other proposals already introduced to parliament, or they may contain provisions for the government to initiate legislation. A 'patchwork agreement' is a set of agreements among different coalitions of parties together constituting a whole. 'Forlig' may be valid beyond general elections or government turnovers. At least they run until all agreed elements have been passed. A party can give notice prior to a general election that after the election it will no longer commit itself to the agreement in which it has taken part. As long as an agreement is valid, the parties are not permitted to support changes to what has been agreed without unanimous consent among the other parties. This veto power is a defining characteristic of 'forlig'. Parties are expected to remain loyal to the agreement in public. Norms concerning this type of agreement can be traced back in detail more than 100 years in Danish parliamentary life.[42] With frequent minority governments, they have played a role ever since and have continued to institutionalise.

When a policy area is covered by a valid 'forlig', political responsibility is shared by the group of parties that take part in it. Party representatives – typically the spokespersons for the policy area – and the minister who holds the relevant portfolio are the relevant actors who may decide on outstanding issues or approve legislation to be introduced according to the agreement. The minister enjoys support from a majority in the *Folketing* and can expect less public critique from the opposition. This comes at the price of allowing informal veto power – and, possibly, giving concessions – to opposition parties, which enjoy a quasi-governmental position as 'share holders' in a binding legislative agreement.[43] This behaviour may blur the ideological profile of an opposition party, however, and prolong the life of the government by giving it an easier ride.

A written document is often attached to a 'forlig'. Like coalition agreements – of governments – their likely purpose is to cement together a group of different political parties in order to prevent them reneging on what has been agreed by committing themselves in text. Such 'contracts' commit the parties to certain formulations, thereby reducing the uncertainty of the deal.[44] Also like coalition agreements but with a narrower scope, the content of the documents attached to the 'forlig' are mainly concerned with substance and less with procedure. The older ones, especially, were plain statements of specific points the parties had agreed to, sometimes supplemented with a brief motivation. Today, the texts are often very detailed and contain more elaborate declarations of intent as well as points to be decided at a later stage. Accordingly, the size of the documents has increased[45] – in 1984–87 12 texts had an average length of about 550 words whereas in 1998–2001 40 texts had an average length of about 2,650 words.

Legislative agreements are not officially recorded. To get an idea of their frequency, information on 'forlig' has been registered from a number of sources, including written agreements, annual yearbooks, and historical overviews.[46] An identification of legislative agreements, like the one that the figures in Table 5 are based upon, can never be completely exhaustive. However, it does give an impression of the frequency of this phenomenon in Danish politics. It comes as no surprise that a significantly smaller volume of approved legislation is covered by a legislative agreement when

TABLE 5
PERCENTAGES OF ENACTED LAWS COVERED BY LEGISLATIVE AGREEMENTS IN
THE FOLKETING 1984–2001 AND PERCENTAGES OF PARTICIPATION FROM
DIFFERENT TYPES OF OPPOSITION PARTIES

Period	Gov. seats %	Bills cov. by accom. %	Laws enacted	Gov. bloc. extr. %	Centre parties %	'Main-stream' opp. %	Non-gov. extr. %
1984–87	44	20	653	0	90	42	2
1987–88	39	23	94	0	100	73	0
1988–90	38	22	415	43	61	54	19
1990–93	34	27	491	20	96	81	22
1993–94	51	6	400	60	NA	92	16
1994–96	42	21	527	55	NA	65	2
1996–98	40	22	255	77	65	40	4
1998–2001	40	29	789	72	66	45	1

Source: Own data. NA means 'Not applicable'.

there is a majority government. During minority government between 20 and 30 per cent of the approved bills were results of legislative agreements. A majority (57 per cent) of the approved bills covered by the 'forlig' have been 'oversized' in party composition, 38 per cent were 'minimal winning', and, finally, five per cent were 'undersized'. Those bills needed and achieved the support of parties not endowed with the procedural rights of the 'forlig'. In Table 5 different types of opposition parties are singled out as extreme parties of the government bloc, centre parties, 'mainstream parties' of the non-government bloc, and extreme parties of the non-government bloc. During most of the period centre parties took part in the highest number of approved bills that were a covered by 'forlig'. The extreme parties within the bloc of the government participated to an increasing extent, whereas broad cooperation with the 'mainstream' parties of the non-government bloc declined, albeit from a high level to begin with. Except for 1988–94 extreme parties of the non-government bloc were barely represented. The results indicate that ideological position is important.

Since 2001 the Liberal-Conservative minority government has primarily relied on the support of the Danish People's Party. A number of major decisions, like municipality reform and Danish participation in the war in Iraq, have been carried through with the sole support of this party. In addition the party has supported the general economic policy of the government. In exchange for support the Danish People's Party has achieved various concessions from the government and succeeded in influencing tight immigration policies. Legislative agreements in the form of 'forlig' have still been the primary framework for cooperation. The most important unresolved issue between the government and its external support party seems to be attitudes towards the European Union. On this question, the government is supported by other opposition parties.

Legislative agreements provide one of the major channels for Danish opposition parties to gain influence. They achieve a veto right regarding the specific policies to which they have agreed. The 'governing' parties shift from one policy area to another. Today, all parties in the *Folketing* occasionally participate in these types of agreement. However, when an agreement has been reached, opposition parties that do not take part in it become more or less sidelined from the decision-making process.

Norway

Before 2005 Norway had rather weak minority governments for two decades, alternating between single-party Labour cabinets (1986–89, 1990–97 and 2000–2001) and bourgeois coalitions (the remaining years). Throughout the period the non-socialist parties held a majority of seats, but they were often too divided internally to govern. With no 'bloc majority', Labour single-party governments needed the support of at least one of the non-socialist parties. The bourgeois minority coalitions needed the support of Labour or of other non-socialist parties. Both types of cabinets used shifting coalitions for majority-building and did not develop a permanent support arrangement. However, in the years preceding, Norwegian minority governments have begun to involve themselves in pre-negotiated agreements with opposition parties on certain legislative measures – a behaviour otherwise rare in the *Storting*.[47]

Shifting coalitions imply that several opposition parties from time to time take part in important legislation and perhaps obtain concessions in the form of amendments during the legislative process. Traditionally such majorities have been established in the decentralised committee structure of the *Storting*. However, Narud and Strøm point out that an increasingly complex bargaining environment and a centralised internal structure of the Progress Party, has meant that many critical deals are now struck directly between party leaders.[48] The government may also consult non-cabinet parties before presenting its proposals in the legislature with the aim of exploring what can be passed. Allegedly, this form of adaptation behaviour has occurred mostly under minority governments with a weak parliamentary basis.[49] In the 1990s the *Storting* amended and defeated a higher number of government proposals than used to be the case. These observations correspond with an increasing number of committee reservations in the same period.[50] In addition, the *Storting* have more often used a right to instruct the government on details.[51] However, it must be stressed that the most important legislation has been proposed by the government.[52]

The three-party government formed in 2001 needed the support of the Progress Party to topple the incumbent Labour government that would only step down if asked to by a majority. The Progress Party first rejected the formation of a single-party Conservative government. Next, it asked 50 questions regarding the political intentions of the proposed coalition government. The three parties answered those questions. After consideration, the Progress Party nodded, the Labour government resigned, and the new government could be formed.[53] Through this manoeuvring, the Progress Party formed a majority with the government and reinforced that it was a vital part of the government's parliamentary basis. In spite of their impact on government formation, the 50 questions and their answers cannot be characterised as a general formal agreement. The parties in government stated that they did not want to tie their hands but to pursue majorities on an ad hoc basis.[54] Nevertheless the three parties had committed themselves politically when they answered the questions. In addition they made written agreements with the Progress Party twice on the annual state budget and once gained its support by turning the approval of the budget into a confidence vote.

So, to a limited extent Norwegian minority governments have also 'integrated' with opposition parties. Since the 2005 election, three parties have taken the full step into a majority coalition government, obviously reducing the significance of the opposition parties on the passing of legislation.

Dynamics of Change in Opposition Involvement

In each of the three countries majority-building has become less ad hoc and instead takes place in more integrated arrangements between the governments and specific opposition parties. In Sweden integration has gone furthest with elaborate support arrangements whereas the Norwegian case is still predominantly characterised by majority-building from issue to issue. The Danish case falls somewhere in between with binding agreements between more or less shifting groups of parties. These different levels affect the conditions for opposition party influence. A high level of integration between a group of parties, either through coalition government or a support arrangement between a minority government and one or more support parties, corresponds with a high level of interdependence between these parties, while other opposition parties become less important. A higher number of opposition parties become relevant when majorities are built issue by issue.

Strøm and Damgaard both assess executive–legislative relations under minority government.[55] Strøm points out that ad hoc coalitions give minority governments an opportunity to pick the least expensive coalition partner available, while support agreements add to the viability of a government – they are 'the recourse of risk averse parties'.[56] Thus, there is a trade-off for minority governments between security and flexibility. Damgaard regards the dynamics of executive–legislative relations as the result of inter-party relations on a general level. He proposes three factors causing change in inter-party relations, and ultimately changes in the influence of opposition parties: institutional reforms, election results, and change in party strategies.[57] The remainder of this section analyses the dynamics of opposition party integration. In the rest of this sub-section we analyse party-related explanations. In the following sub-sections we turn to the question of institutional reform in a discussion of the state budgets. In the final sub-section we discuss how opposition parties in recent years have formed pre-electoral coalitions.

We can point to two significant changes concerning the composition of the Scandinavian parliaments. First, over the years the social democratic parties have lost some of their electoral support and previous dominant position, especially in Norway but less so in Sweden, while the Danish Social Democrats have also lost support but from a lower level to begin with. Second, as we have seen, each of the parliaments now has seven parties compared to the traditional Scandinavian five-party systems.[58]

The new parties are no longer just challengers to the existing parties but have become integrated into legislative decision-making.[59] Scandinavian governments now utilise their bloc majority in their strategy, meaning that 'legislation is passed with support of left- or right-wing parties only'.[60] The reduced dominance of social democrats has increased the likelihood of forming governments within the bourgeois bloc. The possibility of bloc politics has made majorities across the centre less necessary for a minority government, even though it does not preclude broad majorities – perhaps even the contrary – but then agreements will reflect that the opposition parties of the 'non-governmental bloc' do not possess any veto power.[61] So, a minority government is stronger when it is able to use bloc majorities. However, the more a minority government relies on its bloc majority the less attractive this state of affairs is to the opposition parties of the non-governmental bloc. Therefore, we expect these parties to take initiatives in order to get into the cabinet themselves by defeating the government in the upcoming election. In this dynamic process the government becomes ever more dependent on its own bloc. Still, it may be difficult for support parties to advance in status and receive cabinet seats.[62]

Involvement of Opposition Parties in Bargaining over State Budgets

Bargaining concerning the annual state budget has become an ever more important arena for legislative exchange between parties in government and in opposition in the last two decades in each of the Scandinavian countries.

Meanwhile, the formal or informal procedures for approval of the state budgets have changed profoundly and we consider these to be the most important institutional changes that have affected the conditions for influence of opposition parties. The three governments now need to show once a year that they can mobilise a majority for the total state budget. If the government's state budget proposal is rejected, the effect is most likely de facto similar to a vote of no confidence. We expect this to increase the propensity of cabinet parties to engage in arrangements offering them security. In return for such support, a minority government may offer concessions to specific opposition parties or involve them in legislative agenda-setting, leaving the other opposition parties outside this process. Below we describe the reforms and their consequences for parliamentary majority-building.

In Sweden, the Riksdag approved a new procedure for the state budget in 1995.[63] Until the reform, the Riksdag did not at any point decide on the budget in its totality. Instead, individual posts added up to become a full budget. Since the reform, the Riksdag decides on the state budget in a top-down process. Expenditures are divided into 27 areas. A budget proposal contains an economic ceiling and the frames for each expenditure area. Next, the standing committees work with appropriations, approximately 20 for each expenditure area, with each area covered by only one committee.

Budget matters have been a cornerstone of the three support agreements between parties in governments and opposition. Each year, budget negotiations have taken place between the cooperating parties, and not always without difficulties.[64] Nevertheless, after the reforms agreements have always been reached (see Table 6).[65] The political advisors in the Ministry of Finance, as well as the permanent involvement of the partners of the government in economic planning and surveillance in the SVAMP coordination group, have most likely contributed to this process. Concessions have included a large number of environmental-related initiatives.[66] Another example was an amnesty for a number of refugee seekers in return for Green support for the 2006 Budget.[67] The new majority government utilised its own votes to pass the 2007 Budget.

The Danish government must present a 'finance bill' each year. Government as well as opposition parties can propose amendments to the bill. In the final vote, the *Folketing* either approves or rejects the amended bill. This formal framework has not changed for decades but in the 1980s informal norms changed. A government could no longer rely on almost automatic support for the Finance Bill in the final vote, with no regard to its content, from a number of 'responsible' parties.[68] Since then the governments have had to certify that a sufficient number of parties would support the passing of the budget. To this end they work out negotiated agreements with opposition parties. During this process the governments may offer concessions to

TABLE 6

BUDGET COALITIONS IN SCANDINAVIA 1988–2007

Budget year[a]	Sweden	Denmark	Norway
1988	S + LP + shifting	CO, LI, CD, CPP + S, SL	LA + CPP, SP
1989	S + shifting	CO, LI, SL + shifting	LA + CPP, SP
1990	S + shifting	CO, LI, SL + PP, CD, CPP	H, CE, CPP + PP
1991	S + LI + shifting	CO, LI + CD, SL, CPP	LA + CPP, CE
1992	M, LI, CE, CD + shifting	CO, LI + S, CD, SL, CPP	LA + CPP, CE
1993	M, LI, CE, CD + S + +shifting	CO, LI + S, CD, SL, CPP	LA + CPP, CE
1994	M, LI, CE, CD + S + shifting	S, CD, SL, CPP	LA + CPP
1995	S + CE + shifting.	S, SL, CD + LI, CO	LA + CPP, SL
1996	S + CE	S, SL, CD + CO	LA + shifting
1997	S + CE	SD, SL, CD + SP, UL[b] + shifting	LA + CPP, CE, LI
1998	S + CE	SD, SL + SP, CD, ind. + shifting	CP, CE, LI + CO, PP
1999	S + LP, GR	SD, SL + LI, CO, CD, CPP	CP, CE, LI + CO, PP
2000	S + LP, GR	SD, SL + SP, CD + shifting	CP, CE, LI + LA
2001	S + LP, GR	SD, SL + SP, CD[c], UL[d] + shifting	LA + CP, CE, LI
2002	S + LP, GR	LI, CO + DPP	CP, CO, LI + PP[e]
2003	S + LP, GR	LI, CO + DPP + shifting	CP, CO, LI +PP
2004	S + LP, GR	LI, CO + DPP + shifting	CP, CO, LI +LA
2005	S + LP, GR	LI, CO + DPP + shifting	CP, CO, LI +PP
2006	S + LP, GR	LI, CO + DPP + shifting	LA, SL, CE
2007	M, CE, LI, CD	LI, CO + DPP + shifting	LA, SL, CE

Notes:Cabinet parties in *italics*. Parties mentioned in Tables 4a and 4b, except: PP (Denmark) Progress Party.
[a]Calender year, except in Sweden until 1996. Until then 1988 equals 1987/88 etc. Thus, the 'half' budget year 1996 in Sweden falls out.
[b]The Unity List abstained, thereby securing the majority of the government in the final vote.
[c]CD supported only limited parts of the finance bill amendments, but it did support the total bill.
[d]The Unity List supported important amendments and took part in a number of agreements but voted against the finance bill in the final vote.
[e]The government declared approval of the state budget with a vote of confidence and was supported by the Progress Party.
Sources: Political yearbooks, *European Journal of Political Research*; L. Bille, *Fra valgkamp til valgkamp. Dansk partipolitik 1998–2001* (Copenhagen: Jurist- og Økonomforbundets Forlag, 2002); L. Bille, *Det nye flertal. Dansk partipolitik 2001–2005* (Copenhagen: Jurist- og Økonomforbundets Forlag, 2006); I. Mattson, *Förhandlingsparlamentarism. En jämförande studie av Riksdagen och Folketinget* (Lund: Lund University Press, 1996); H.M. Narud and H. Valen, *Demokrati og ansvar. Politisk representasjon i et flerpartisystem* (Oslo: N.W. Damm & Søn, 2007), at p.223; P. Overgaard, 'Finanslovene – kontinuitet eller forandring? 1965–1999' (Unpublished thesis, Aarhus: Department of Political Science); own data.

opposition parties. Agreements have also been reached on major or minor political reforms and other legislation, not necessarily related to the budget in a strict sense.[69] In addition, it has become common to make agreements on expenditure areas for a number of years, for instance regarding police, defence or theatres.

In connection with the Danish agreements, written documents have been issued.[70] They have increased in size over time; the 2007 budget agreements contain about 37,000 words, compared to about 14,000 words in the 1997 agreements, and about 3,000 words in the 1990 agreement. The written agreements occasionally include detailed remarks about various earmarked initiatives, often concessions to a specific opposition party. In the last decade Danish budget agreements have usually been of the 'patchwork' type. In Table 6 we seek to identify the Danish budget coalitions. We find that shifting coalitions became more common in the 1990s even though a number of 'core' parties could usually be identified. Until 2001 the minority governments built different coalitions almost every year. Since 2001, the Liberal–Conservative government has cooperated closely with the Danish People's Party concerning the Finance Bill. In return it has put its label on various initiatives, for example a special check for the elderly.

In 1997, the *Storting* followed the Swedish example and approved a state budget reform.[71] Until the reform, each parliamentary committee suggested an expenditure level for its own area. Next, the state budget went through a round of 'balancing the account' on the floor of the *Storting*. The process was characterised as very fragmented and detail-oriented.[72] Weak minority governments in the 1990s often gave in to pressure for increased spending, and also accepted occasional defeats.[73] After the reform, the *Storting* decides on the size of revenues and expenditures and their distribution in a package vote on 21 expenditure frames. Next, the standing committees specify the distribution of expenditures for each frame.[74]

Except for the 2002 Budget, when the government made the approval of the state budget a vote of confidence, almost every approved budget, pre-reform or post-reform, has been the result of negotiated agreements (see Table 6). Coalitions have often shifted, except for the present majority government. However, the Bondevik coalition government 2001–5 relied on its parliamentary basis, the Progress Party, for three out of its four state budgets. In addition the government each year took its first round of negotiations with the Progress Party.[75] In recent years, written budget agreements have been issued and published.[76] They are brief documents – only a few pages long. These written agreements contain support for the budget proposal of the government – with a number of amendments agreed to – and they list a number of legislative initiatives that the government is expected to take. Examples hereof from the 2003 Budget Agreements include support for 'free choice' between private and public schools and hospitals as well as harsher punishments for violence-related crimes. The agreements end with a 'Musketeer's oath' in which the parties commit themselves to secure a majority for the agreed proposals and only to enter alternative majority constellations with the approval of the partners in the budget agreement.

Following formal and informal institutional changes, Scandinavian minority governments now negotiate annual budget agreements with non-cabinet parties. To an increasing extent these agreements have been made within the 'bloc majority' of the government. The highest degree of institutionalisation of such arrangements is found in Sweden, but pre-negotiated agreements are now even observed in Norway where such agreements apparently have not been common otherwise. The Norwegian agreements tend to be more short-sighted – primarily covering votes in the *Storting* and its committees – whereas the Danish agreements reach out at least for one budget year and usually cover a higher number of other legislative decisions than their Norwegian counterparts.

The reforms and informal changes have affected the conditions for involvement of opposition parties in legislative decision-making.[77] In Sweden and Norway, and to some extent in Denmark, an opposition party seeking policy influence now needs to be ready to support the total state budget and thereby prolong the life of the government. In return for the support it may be offered significant political concessions. In the patchwork agreements it is possible for a Danish opposition party only to support parts of a state budget. In Sweden and Norway this is also theoretically possible at committee level, but the necessity to decide the frames in advance seems to have had the effect that minority governments agree with one or more opposition parties on total state budgets. An opposition party supporting a total state budget risks losing some of its political profile. As a consequence of the reforms, opposition parties that do not form part of the parliamentary basis for the government can be expected to be more reluctant about supporting the state budget or to demand more for their eventual support.

We consider the formal or informal institutional changes regarding the approval of the state budget to be – at least – a partial explanation of the increased 'integration' between parties in government and opposition in most recent years. Especially in the Swedish and Norwegian cases, where reforms seem to have made shifting majorities redundant, we also consider the changes to have made it more attractive for political parties to share cabinet seats, thereby enhancing the likelihood of majority governments such as those recently formed.

Pre-electoral Coalitions: Integration among Opposition Parties

We have noted above that the 'other' opposition parties have become less necessary for majority-building, when minority governments in recent years have made arrangements with permanent external support parties. Meanwhile, opposition parties in Sweden, Denmark and Norway appear to have formed more 'pre-electoral coalitions'.[78] Sona Golder suggests that a pre-electoral coalition exists 'when multiple parties choose to coordinate their electoral strategies rather than run for office alone', but we tend to agree with Allern and Aylott that, 'the "coordination of party strategies" must have the explicit aim of forming a post-election executive coalition'.[79] As of May 2007 the government constellations in each country are identical to pre-electoral coalitions formed while the parties were still in opposition. Below we briefly describe these cases and consider why Scandinavian opposition parties enter this strategy.

In 2004 the four non-socialist opposition parties represented in the Riksdag presented themselves in a common document as the 'Alliance for Sweden', with the aim of taking over power at the 2006 elections.[80] This five-page document (about 2,000 words) stated a number of policy positions and it described the establishment of a number of committees. The committee chairmen and the party leaders soon came to be considered as a kind of 'shadow cabinet'.[81] The four parties did not elect a common candidate for prime minister to begin with, but as the election approached, the leader of the Moderates was recognised as such by all of the parties. The alliance parties issued various joint policy documents during their two years in opposition, and they no longer individually made any major agreements with the government.[82] Consequently, the Social Democratic government was not able to renew its defence settlement with the Centre Party in 2004 but opted for a majority with its two support parties (instead of a broad agreement with all of the alliance parties).

A few months before the 2001 *Folketing* election, Liberals and Conservatives presented a short document (about 800 words), which listed a number of common policies but no procedural arrangements.[83] The two parties publicly declared their intention to form a common government but at the time it was not ruled out as an option that one or two centre parties could be included as well.

In 2004 Labour, the Socialist Left and the Centre Party in Norway publicly declared that they worked together with the intention of forming a common government after the 2005 election.[84] Two months before the election, this 'red–green coalition' presented a list of 155 points of policy agreement (about 3,500 words).[85] Thereby Labour no longer sought to form a single-party government. The new strategy was defended by its party leader with the argument that the problems of minority government were greater than those of coalition government in spite of the differences between the three parties.[86]

The three cases illustrate that pre-electoral coalitions among opposition parties come in more or less institutionalised forms, more so in Sweden than in Denmark and Norway. Such coalitions appear with a higher frequency than previously. Pre-electoral coalitions limit individual parties from pursuing an electoral strategy with a clear policy profile, which may disengage the party faithful and also could cost voters for individual parties in the coalition.[87] Furthermore, parties reduce their freedom to bargain with any other party after the election.[88] If opposition parties coalesce in this manner in spite of these collective action problems, it must be because they expect an increased likelihood of getting into cabinet either by vote maximising or otherwise.[89] According to the 'signalling hypotheses', some voters are only prepared to vote for a party in a coalition, and not a party standing alone, because they thereby feel more certain what its policies will be, but empirical evidence is mixed for this claim.[90] One may also raise the supposition that pre-electoral coalitions prepare the parties for overcoming some of the difficulties of governing together. Our observations further suggest that such coalitions reflect a dynamic among opposition parties similar to the 'integration' between minority governments and external support parties, and that pre-electoral coalitions reduce the manoeuvrability of the government, thereby underscoring the increased 'bloc' competition of Scandinavian parliamentary politics.

The formation of pre-electoral coalitions has become a common strategy among Scandinavian opposition parties, but as of May 2007 there are no current ones. In Sweden, the Social Democrats may still want to return to cabinet office alone. In Denmark, the leader of the Socialist People's Party has publicly proposed an alliance with the Social Democrats and the Social Liberals, but until now the two other parties have declined to take part.[91] In Norway, the differences between the Progress Party and the centre parties may prevent the formation of a united opposition bloc.

THE ROLE OF NON-PARLIAMENTARY OPPOSITIONS

A major international research programme introduced the concept of 'external constraints' on the parliamentary chain of governance.[92] The leading idea is that a number of different actors and institutions, outside the formal system of parliamentary policy-making, may limit the actual power of parliamentary actors. It seems obvious that such actors can also in many cases be considered to be 'non-parliamentary' oppositions competing with the regular parliamentary opposition. While this is certainly not true for Scandinavian heads of state (monarchs), and only to a limited extent true for constitutional courts and central banks, it does make sense for certain other organisations and institutions.

Thus, in his chapter on Norway in Dahl's edited volume, Stein Rokkan argued convincingly that there was not only a parliamentary channel of influence and opposition, but also a corporate channel in which the big interest groups of labour, farmers and business could negotiate with each other, and with the government, to protect and promote their interests.[93] In Rokkan's often quoted words: 'Votes count but resources decide.' In fact Norway and Sweden, and to a lesser degree Denmark, have traditionally been ranked very high on various indexes of corporatism proposed in the literature.[94] However, there seems to be general agreement on a decline of corporatism in Scandinavia and elsewhere since the 1980s.[95] It has been shown that the links between parties and interest groups have been reduced in Scandinavia.[96] The literature also indicates that interest groups have adjusted to minority rule and relatively strong opposition parties in order to influence policy-making. There is more lobbyism or pluralism in Scandinavian politics.[97] These developments notwithstanding, it is safe to conclude that although one can observe a relative decline of interest organisations, including the major groups of public employees, many of them are still active as possible opposition forces to be taken seriously. The latter also applies to the associations of sub-national governments which represent local and regional governments in negotiations with the national government.

Generally speaking, social movements do not play as big a role as they did in the 1970s. But they are still used to mobilise opposition against membership of the European Union and further integration in Europe. Thus they played a decisive role when Norway twice rejected EU membership in a referendum (which by itself is a non-parliamentary institution), whereas they were not successful in the cases of Denmark and Sweden. However, the movements in Denmark and Sweden have obtained representation in the European Parliament. As they do not run for national offices, they may be considered as a hybrid of parliamentary and non-parliamentary opposition. Referendums in Denmark and Sweden rejected membership of the European Monetary Union. In Denmark the Maastricht Treaty was also originally rejected but then approved with some opt-outs in the so-called Edinburgh Agreement. The 'yes' side also prevailed in referendums on the Internal Market and the Amsterdam Treaty.

Membership of the EU per se entails a delegation of powers to the supranational level that constrains the national parliamentary government. However, it is also true that member states (or certain groups and interests) may gain from supranational decisions which could not have been made and implemented by the national actor acting alone.[98] Although Norway is not a member of the EU, its membership of the European Economic Area (EEA) entails similar constraints on the country.[99]

The mass media also qualify as a potential actor or arena for non-parliamentary opposition. The development in this respect is almost the opposite of that for interest groups: the mass media have become more important in the political process. Both a Danish and a Norwegian power and democracy project thus concluded that mass media have become more independent of parties and institutions over recent decades.[100] In the process the media have developed their own news criteria to which politicians must adapt if they want to get their message through to the electorate.

The Danish study looks systematically at the mass media in relation to the political agenda, public opinion, and the political decisions made. It illustrates that the media can indeed play a role in agenda-setting. It also finds that they, at least in the short run, can affect political attitudes. However, it appears that the media only rarely are able to shape the actual decisions made by parties and parliament. Nevertheless, one might conclude that the mass media may function as increasingly important non-parliamentary opposition actors.

The study warns against too firm conclusions in this respect. The media has considerable influence in several respects, but they have not usurped power. Perhaps a distinction between the media as an actor versus the media as an arena can be helpful in understanding the role of the mass media. While the media can be influential actors in some cases, they are perhaps best understood as political arenas: 'The media constitute the arena in which the political fights between other actors are fought. Politicians are rarely just victims of the media. Most often they are conscious co-players in the fight about attention.'[101] In sum, even if interest organisations, the media, referendums and EU affairs may channel non-parliamentary opposition in several cases, this brief survey gives no reasons to challenge the general view that parliamentary opposition is the most important form of political opposition in Scandinavia.

CONCLUSION

The Scandinavian countries have been known for their relatively strong social democratic parties facing opposition from non-socialist parties. They have also been known for their propensity to form minority governments aiming at survival and stability in an exchange process with opposition parties that can exert considerable political influence. The involvement of opposition parties may differ in form in the three countries. However, in recent years Scandinavian minority governments have increasingly relied on permanent external support parties instead of finding majorities on an ad hoc basis, more so in Sweden than in Norway, with Denmark somewhere in between. In addition, such arrangements have become institutionalised commitment devices with written texts and various procedural arrangements. Permanent support parties primarily benefit the opposition parties that are involved, but still they are not on an equal footing with the parties in government. In this process other opposition parties become less important for decision-making. Finally, we have observed that these have also begun to integrate by entering pre-electoral coalitions to defeat incumbent governments. We noted that parliamentary opposition is predominant even though various forms of extra-parliamentary opposition – like interest groups and mass media – have also played roles as actors and arenas.

Coalition governments, support agreements, 'forlig', ad hoc coalitions and 'alternative majorities' all reflect choices made by political parties on when and how to cooperate or compete; these choices are affected by factors internal to the party, a point that needs to be elaborated more upon in future works. Opposition involvement may be considered as a democratic virtue, as a check on the executive power. However, minority governments may also be quite weak and therefore not able to address policy problems effectively. The Scandinavian political systems are highly adaptive and have developed forms of cooperation under minority government.

We should always be cautious when interpreting developments and trends. Earlier, Damgaard argued that an 'ebb and flow' perspective probably is the most sensible way to describe developments in Scandinavian executive–legislative relations.[102] Right now Sweden and Norway have majority governments, and the Danish government has a secure majority with its support party. This situation is markedly different from the situation with weak minority governments found in the three countries 15 or 20 years ago. However, electorates with high levels of volatility may shake up the present party composition and again produce situations without possibilities for a clear majority. Nevertheless, the reforms of the state budget procedures in Sweden and Norway, and to a lesser extent the informal changes in Denmark, seem to have more permanently promoted integration of opposition parties in decision-making.

NOTES

1. M.N. Pedersen, 'Consensus and Conflict in the Danish Folketing 1945–65', *Scandinavian Political Studies*, 2 (1967), pp.143–66; R.A. Dahl, 'The American Oppositions: Affirmation and Denial', in R.A. Dahl (ed.), *Political Oppositions in Western Democracies* (New Haven, CT: Yale University Press, 1966), p.34.
2. Dahl, *Political Oppositions in Western Democracies*, p.xviii.
3. For example, K. Strøm, *Minority Government and Majority Rule* (Cambridge: Cambridge University Press, 1990).
4. M. Laver and W.B. Hunt, *Policy and Party Competition* (New York: Routledge, 1992); M. Gallagher, M. Laver and P. Mair, *Representative Government in Modern Europe* (New York: McGraw-Hill, 2006).
5. F.J. Christiansen, 'The Inclusion of Challenger Parties into Legislative Accommodations in Danish Parliamentary Politics' (Paper, ECPR Conference, Marburg, Sept. 2003).
6. Useful descriptive information on the institutional setting in which parliamentary opposition parties operate may be found in the individual contributions on the Scandinavian countries in G.T. Kurian (ed.), *World Encyclopedia of Parliaments and Legislatures* (Washington, DC: Congressional Quarterly, 1998) – E. Damgaard on Denmark, D. Arter on Norway, and D. Olson and M. Hagevi on Sweden. Also, a number of interesting comparative aspects are dealt with by P. Esaiasson and K. Heidar (eds.), *Beyond Westminster and Congress. The Nordic Experience* (Columbus: Ohio State University Press, 2000).

7. K. Heidar, 'Parliamentary Party Groups', in Esaiasson and Heidar (eds.), *Beyond Westminster and Congress. The Nordic Experience*, pp.183–209.
8. T. K. Jensen, 'Party Cohesion', in Esaiasson and Heidar (eds.), *Beyond Westminster and Congress*, pp.210–36.
9. M. Hagevi, 'Nordic Light on Committee Assignments', in Esaiasson and Heidar (eds.), *Beyond Westminster and Congress. The Nordic Experience*, pp.237–61.
10. Hagevi, 'Nordic Light on Committee Assignments', p.238.
11. E. Damgaard (ed.), *Parliamentary Change in the Nordic Countries* (Oslo: Scandinavian University Press, 1992); E. Damgaard 'Developments in Danish Parliamentary Democracy: Accountability, Parties and External Constraints', *Scandinavian Political Studies*, 27 (2004), pp.115–31; H.M. Narud and K. Strøm, 'Norway: Madisonianism Reborn', *Scandinavian Political Studies*, 27 (2004), pp.175–201; T. Bergman, 'Sweden: Democratic Reforms and Partisan Decline in an Emerging Separation-of-Powers System', *Scandinavian Political Studies*, 27 (2004), pp.203–25; M. Wiberg (ed.), *Parliamentary Control in the Nordic Countries. Forms of Questioning and Behavioural Trends* (Helsinki: Finnish Political Science Association, 1994).
12. A. Sannerstedt, 'Negotiations in the Riksdag', in L.-G. Stenelo and M. Jerneck (eds.), *The Bargaining Democracy* (Lund: Lund University Press, 1996), pp. 17–58; D. Arter, *Scandinavian Politics Today* (Manchester: Manchester University Press, 1999).
13. T. Bale and T. Bergman, 'Captives No Longer, but Servants Still? Contract Parliamentarism and the New Minority Governance in Sweden and New Zealand', *Government and Opposition*, 41 (2006), pp.422–49.
14. Strøm, *Minority Government and Majority Rule*.
15. D. Arter, *Democracy in Scandinavia. Consensual, Majoritarian or Mixed?* (Manchester: Manchester University Press, 2006), p.20.
16. Christiansen, 'The Inclusion of Challenger Parties into Legislative Accommodations in Danish Parliamentary Politics'.
17. Cf. A. King, 'Modes of Executive–Legislative Relations: Great Britain, France and West Germany', *Legislative Studies Quarterly*, 1 (1976), pp.11–36.
18. In 1990 the Left Party Communists was renamed as the Left Party.
19. Bale and Bergman, 'Captives No Longer, but Servants Still?', p.432.
20. A. Sannerstedt and M. Sjölin, 'Sweden: Changing Party Relations in a More Active Parliament', in Damgaard (ed.), *Parliamentary Change in the Nordic Countries*, pp.99–149.
21. Bale and Bergman, 'Captives No Longer, but Servants Still?'; Arter, *Scandinavian Politics Today*, p.208.
22. I. Mattson, *Förhandlingsparlamentarism. En jämförande studie av Riksdagen och Folketinget* (Lund: Lund University Press, 1996), p.169.
23. N. Aylott and T. Bergman, 'Almost in Government, But Not Quite: The Swedish Greens, Bargaining Constraints and the Rise of Contract Parliamentarism' (Paper, ECPR joint sessions of workshops, Uppsala, April 2004).
24. Bale and Bergman, 'Captives No Longer, but Servants Still', p.424.
25. Cf. A. Lagercrantz, *Över blockgränsen. Samarbetet mellan centerpartiet och socialdemokraterna 1995–1998* (Stockholm: Gidlunds, 2005).
26. The name probably plays with a Swedish word for agreeing.
27. An acronym of the three Swedish party names.
28. The information on SAMS and SVAMP stems from: A. Ullström, *Samarbetskanslierna – Vårtor på, länkar till eller delar av Regeringskansliet? Om den demokratiska styrningskedjan och samarbetskansliernas organisering* (Stockholm: Score, 2005), p.19.
29. Aylott and Bergman, 'Almost in Government, But Not Quite'.
30. *Hundratjugoen punkter för ett tryggare, rättvisare och grönare Sverige. Överenskommelse mellan Socialdemokraterna, Vänsterpartiet och Miljöpartiet* (Regeringen, 2002).
31. Cf. K. Strøm and W.C. Müller, 'The Key to Togetherness: Coalition Agreements in Parliamentary Democracies', *Journal of Legislative Studies*, 5 (1999), pp.255–82.
32. In addition to the '121 points', the Social Democrats and the Left Party published a short 'Declaration of Intent' in which the parties state to have common values concerning a

number of points: *Avsiktsförklaring mellan vänsterpartiet och socialdemokraterne* (Socialdemokraterna och Vänsterpartiet, 2002).

33. *Överenskommelse om samarbetsformer och rutiner mellan Socialdemokraterna, Vänsterpartiet och Miljöpartiet* (Konstitutionsutskottet, 2002/03:KU30, Bilaga A5.2).

34. *Hundratjugoen punkter för ett tryggare, rättvisare och grönera Sverige. Överenskommelse mellan Socialdemokraterna, Vänsterpartiet och Miljöpartiet.*

35. The Greens had four advisors in the Ministry of Finance, two in the Ministry of Trade, one in the Ministry of Environment, and one in the Ministry of Agriculture. The Left Party had three positions in the Ministry of Finance, two and a half in the Ministry of Trade, one in the Ministry of Environment, one in the Ministry of Education, and one-half in the Ministry of Justice according to Ullström, *Samarbetskanslierna – Vårtor på, länkar till eller delar av Regeringskansliet?*, p.17.

36. *Överenskommelse om samarbetsformer och rutiner mellan Socialdemokraterna, Vänsterpartiet och Miljöpartiet.*

37. Ullström, *Samarbetskanslierna – Vårtor på, länkar till eller delar av Regeringskansliet?*, p.20.

38. *Hundratjugoen punkter för ett tryggare, rättvisare och grönera Sverige. Överenskommelse mellan Socialdemokraterna, Vänsterpartiet och Miljöpartiet.*

39. T. Bergman, 'Sweden: When Minority Cabinets are the Rule and Majority Coalitions the Exception', in W.C. Müller and K. Strøm (eds.), *Coalition Governments in Western Europe* (Oxford: Oxford University Press), pp.212–13.

40. E. Damgaard and P. Svensson, 'Who Governs? Parties and Policies in Denmark', *European Journal of Political Research*, 17 (1989), pp.731–45.

41. Christiansen, 'The Inclusion of Challenger Parties into Legislative Accommodations in Danish Parliamentary Politics'.

42. H.H. Pedersen, 'Politiske forlig i dansk politik 1850–2001. En analyse af sammenhængen mellem mindretalsparlamentarisme og forekomsten af forpligtende lovgivningskoalitioner' (Unpublished thesis, Aarhus: Department of Political Science, 2005).

43. R. Klemmensen, 'Forlig i det danske folketing', *Politica*, 37 (2005), pp.440–52.

44. Strøm and Müller, 'The Key to Togetherness: Coalition Agreements in Parliamentary Democracies', p.268; A. Timmermans, 'Standing Apart and Sitting Together. Enforcing Coalition Agreements in Multiparty Systems', *European Journal of Political Research*, 45 (2006), pp.263–83.

45. We are thankful to The Library and Archive of the Danish Folketing for access to its collection of such written legislative agreements.

46. The procedure for collection of the data is described by: F.J. Christiansen, 'Aftaler på tværs af sektorer i Folketinget', *Politica*, 37/4, pp.423–39.

47. T. Nordby, *I politikkens sentrum. Variasjoner i Stortingets makt 1814–2004* (Oslo: Universitetsforlaget, 2004), p.156.

48. Narud and Strøm, 'Norway: Madisonianism Reborn', p.179.

49. Nordby, *I politikkens sentrum. Variasjoner i Stortingets makt 1814–2004*, p.152.

50. H. Rommetvedt, *The Rise of the Norwegian Parliament* (London: Frank Cass, 2003), p.51.

51. Nordby, *I politikkens sentrum. Variasjoner i Stortingets makt 1814-2004*, pp.146–7.

52. Narud and Strøm, 'Norway: Madisonianism Reborn', p.179.

53. T. Aalberg, 'Norway', *European Journal of Political Research*, 44 (2005), pp.1140–46.

54. N. Bolin, 'Samarbete, stöd eller opposition? Majoritetsbyggande i Skandinavien' (Unpublished Thesis, Umeå: Department of Political Science, 2004).

55. Strøm, *Minority Government and Majority Rule*; E. Damgaard, 'The Strong Parliaments of Scandinavia: Continuity and Change of Scandinavian Parliaments', in G.W. Copeland and S.C. Patterson (eds.), *Parliaments in the Modern World: Changing Institutions* (Ann Arbor, MI: University of Michigan Press, 1994), pp.85–103.

56. Strøm, *Minority Government and Majority Rule*, p.109.

57. Damgaard, 'The Strong Parliaments of Scandinavia'.

58. Cf. S. Berglund and U. Lindström, *The Scandinavian Party System(s)* (Lund: Studentlitteratur, 1978).

59. Christiansen, 'The Inclusion of Challenger Parties into Legislative Accommodations in Danish Parliamentary Politics'.
60. C. Green-Pedersen and L. Hoffmann-Thomsen, 'Bloc Politics vs. Broad Cooperation. The Functioning of Danish Minority Parliamentarism', *Journal of Legislative Studies*, 11 (2005), p.157.
61. Green-Pedersen and Hoffmann-Thomsen, 'Bloc Politics vs. Broad Cooperation', p.165.
62. Cf. Aylott and Bergman, 'Almost in Government, But Not Quite'; Bale and Bergman, 'Captives No Longer, but Servants Still'.
63. P. Molander, 'Budgeting Procedures and Democratic Ideals: An Evaluation of Swedish Reforms' *Journal of Public Policy*, 21 (2001), pp.23–52.
64. Cf. A. Widfeldt, 'Sweden', *European Journal of Political Research*, 41 (2002), pp.1089–94.
65. Coalition behaviour concerning state budgets in Sweden and Denmark 1971–95 is covered by Mattson, *Förhandlingsparlamentarism. En jämförande studie av Riksdagen och Folketinget.*
66. T. Bale and T. Bergman, 'A Taste of Honey Is Worse Than None at All? Coping with the Generic Challenges of Support Party Status in Sweden and New Zealand', *Party Politics*, 12 (2006), pp.189–209.
67. A. Widfeldt, 'Sweden', *European Journal of Political Research*, 45 (2006), pp.1270–74.
68. E. Rasmussen, 'Finanslovsforkastelse i dansk parlamentarisme: Normer og konsekvenser – En historisk – politologisk debatanalyse 1894–1984', *Historie – Jyske Samlinger*, Ny række XVI (1985), pp.56–118.
69. J. Loftager, *Politisk offentlighed og demokrati i Danmark* (Århus: Aarhus University Press, 2004); C.A. Larsen and J.G. Andersen, *Magten på borgen. En analyse af beslutningsprocesser i større politiske reformer* (Århus: Aarhus University Press, 2004).
70. 'Aftaler om finansloven' (Finansministeriet, Several years).
71. B.E. Rasch, *Budsjettbehandlingen i Stortinget. Bør alternativ votering benyttes?* (Oslo: Makt- og demokratiutredningen 1998–2003, 2001).
72. B.E. Rasch (ed.), *Symbolpolitikk og parlamentarisk styring* (Oslo: Universitetsforlaget, 1993).
73. Nordby, *I politikkens sentrum. Variasjoner i Stortingets makt*, pp.223–25.
74. L. Helland, 'Minority-Rule Budgeting under a De Facto Constructive Vote of No Confidence: A Cure for the Norwegian Illness?', *Scandinavian Political Studies*, 27 (2001), pp.391–401.
75. Bolin, *Samarbete, stöd eller opposition?*
76. *Avtaler om statsbudsjettet* (Finansdepartementet, Several years).
77. The reforms appear to have had positive fiscal effects: J. Wehner, 'Budget Reform and Legislative Control in Sweden', *Journal of European Public Policy*, 14 (2007), pp. 313–32; R.J. Hagen, *Finanspolitisk tvangstrøye eller keiserens nye klær? Reformen af Stortingets budsjettbehandling i lys av nyere teori og empiri* (Bergen: Stiftelsen for samfunns- og næringslivsforskning, 1999).
78. Compared to the publicly available data at Sona Golder's webpage: http://homepages. nyu.edu/%7Esln202/#research, under replication materials (downloaded 22 May 2007).
79. S.N. Golder, 'Pre-Electoral Coalition Formation in Parliamentary Democracies', *British Journal of Political Science*, 36 (2006), p.195; E.H. Allern and N. Aylott, 'Overcoming the Fear of Commitment: Pre-Electoral Coalitions in Norway and Sweden' (Paper presented at Political Science Association Conference, Bath 2007).
80. *Allians för Sverige. Samverkan för maktskifte 2006*, www.maktskifte06.se, Högforsdokumentet (downloaded 22 May 2007).
81. Widfeldt, 'Sweden', p.1272.
82. May 2006 the Alliance issued its common electoral platform, *Fler i arbete – mer at dele på. Valmanifest 2006*, Allians för Sverige, www.maktskifte06.se.2006, Valmanifest (downloaded 22 May 2007).
83. Its title was 'The first 100 days with a new liberal-bourgeois government': 'De første 100 dage med en ny liberal-borgerlig regering', reprinted in *Dagbladet Information*, 16 Aug. 2001.
84. T. Aalberg and T. Brekken, 'Norway', *European Journal of Political Research*, 45 (2006), pp.1221–30.
85. The 155 points have been downloaded from: www.dna.no/index.gan?id=34609&subid=0 (24 May 2007).
86. Aalberg and Brekken, 'Norway', p.1223.

87. In the Scandinavian cases the parties still appear as separate lists on the ballot and electoral alliances between lists are not an option. Low thresholds and highly proportional electoral systems imply that with the same number of votes there would be none, or very limited, rewards from combining lists.

88. Pre-electoral coalitions increase the proportionality of portfolio allocations in government formations, indicating that the bargaining power of individual parties is affected: R. Carroll and G.W. Cox, 'The Logic of Gamson's Law: Pre-Election Coalitions and Portfolio Allocations', *American Journal of Political Science*, 51 (2007), pp.300–313.

89. Cf. Allern and Aylott, 'Overcoming the Fear of Commitment'.

90. S. N. Golder, 'Pre-Electoral Coalitions in Comparative Perspective: A Test of Existing Hypotheses', *Electoral Studies*, 24 (2005), pp.643–63.

91. The left-wing party, the Unity List, is not supposed to be part of such a coalition.

92. K. Strøm, W.C. Müller and T. Bergman (eds.), *Delegation and Accountability in Parliamentary Democracies* (Oxford: Oxford University Press, 2003).

93. S. Rokkan, 'Norway: Numerical Democracy and Corporate Pluralism', in Dahl (ed.), *Political Oppositions in Western Democracies*, pp. 70–115, quotation from p. 105.

94. L. Lewin, *Samhället och de organiserade intressena* (Stockholm: Norstedts, 1992).

95. Damgaard 'Developments in Danish Parliamentary Democracy'; Narud and Strøm, 'Norway: Madisonianism Reborn'; Bergman, 'Sweden: Democratic Reforms and Partisan Decline in an Emerging Separation-of-Powers System'.

96. E.H. Allern, N. Aylott and F.J. Christiansen, 'Social Democrats and Trade Unions in Scandinavia: The Decline and Persistence of Institutional Relationships', *European Journal of Political Research*, 46 (2007), pp. 607–35.

97. A. Binderkrantz, 'Strategies of Influence: How Interest Organizations React to Changes in Parliamentary Influence and Activity', *Scandinavian Political Studies*, 26 (2003), pp.287–306; P. M. Christiansen and H. Rommetvedt, 'From Corporatism to Lobbyism? Parliaments, Executives, and Organized Interest in Denmark and Norway', *Scandinavian Political Studies*, 22 (1999), pp.195–220; P.M. Christiansen and A.S. Nørgaard, *Faste forhold – flygtige forbindelser. Stat og interesseorganisationer i Danmark i det 20. århundrede* (Århus: Aarhus University Press, 2003).

98. T. Bergman and E. Damgaard (eds.), *Delegation and Accountability in European Integration. The Nordic Parliamentary Democracies and the European Union* (London: Frank Cass, 2000).

99. Bergman and Damgaard (eds.), *Delegation and Accountability in European Integration*.

100. L. Togeby, J.G. Andersen, P.M. Christiansen, T.B. Jørgensen and S. Vallgårda, *Magt og demokrati i Danmark. Hovedresultater fra magtudredningen* (Århus: Aarhus University Press, 2003); Ø. Østerud, F. Engelstad and P. Selle, *Makten og demokratiet. En sluttbok fra Makt- og demokratiutredningen* (Oslo: Gyldendal, 2003).

101. Togeby *et al.*, *Magt og demokrati i Danmark*, p.229 (authors' translation).

102. Damgaard, 'The Strong Parliaments of Scandinavia', p.103.

Parliamentary Opposition in Post-Consociational Democracies: Austria, Belgium and the Netherlands

RUDY B. ANDEWEG, LIEVEN DE WINTER and
WOLFGANG C. MÜLLER

'Any form of political opposition necessarily involves some kind of competition. The reverse does not hold true: political competition does not necessarily involve opposition.'

This dictum by Otto Kirchheimer is from his chapter on Germany in Dahl's famous *Political Oppositions in Western Democracies*.[1] Does it also apply to Austria, Belgium and the Netherlands – the countries to which this paper is devoted? Austria, Belgium and the Netherlands have commonly been labelled consociational democracies. Arend Lijphart has defined a consociational democracy as 'government by elite cartel designed to turn a democracy with a fragmented political culture into a stable democracy'.[2] A fragmented political culture means that civil society is segmented into mutually hostile pillars (*zuilen* in Dutch), camps (*Lager* in German) or sociological worlds, divided by ethnic, linguistic, religious, class, or ideological cleavages, that encapsulate citizens from the cradle to the grave within their subcultures. Government by elite cartel can take many forms, but the four characteristics offered by Lijphart that are most commonly used are: grand coalition, proportionality, segmental autonomy and mutual (minority) veto.[3] What these characteristics indicate is that political decision-making is not based on a victory by a majority, but on a consensus involving all, or at least as many as possible, of the opposing segments. In other words: in a consociational democracy there is no shortage of ideological opposition, but, contradicting Kirchheimer, this opposition involves some kind of elite cooperation rather than competition.

Although few theorists of consociational democracy have focused on the relations between government and parliamentary opposition, we can deduce the following hypotheses from the theory:[4]

a) In order to facilitate cooperation and accommodation, governments will tend to include all or most of the pillar parties, and thus will be oversized or 'grand' coalitions rather than aiming at minimum size.

b) Hence, the parliamentary opposition tends to be small in size, and mainly composed of parties that do not represent a particular pillar and its constituent organisations. Often the parties in the parliamentary opposition will have an anti-establishment or even anti-system profile, given the 'closed' or 'blocked' nature of their political system.

c) Elections will tend to be only mildly competitive as, on the one hand, citizens will not vote for a party not representing their own pillar, and the campaign primarily serves to mobilise the party's natural constituency. On the other hand, election results also do not strongly influence a party's chances to enter government. Good relations with the other pillar parties are more important to get access to offices, policies and public goods.

d) The parliamentary opposition, especially the non-pillar parties, will be powerless vis-à-vis the cartel of pillar parties in government that may have installed oligopolistic parliamentary rules that constrain the opposition role of small parties.

e) The opposition is not only weak in parliament, but neither is it capable of mobilising large sections of the population for extra-parliamentary opposition activities, unless a pillar party in opposition decides to mobilise the members of its pillar's organisations and media when it feels that other pillar parties do not respect the rules of the consociational game.

f) As the media, interest groups, and 'old' social movements are to a large extent also pillarised, and the latter have privileged access to pillar elites in the political as well as the corporatist arenas, they do not tend to engage in extra-parliamentary opposition activities, unless a pillar party in opposition decides to mobilise the members of its pillar's organisations and media.

Before confronting these theoretical expectations with the empirical reality in Austria, Belgium and the Netherlands, we should note that in all three countries some forms of de-pillarisation have been observed, in varying degrees, and with different take-off, transition, and consolidation periods. De-pillarisation means that the effective orientation of individuals towards their pillar weakens, and that cross-pillar membership increases. Organisationally, de-pillarisation means that the depth and width of the penetration of pillar organisations in society declines, that pillar organisations de-ideologise, that cross-pillar mergers may take place, that new non-pillarised parties and organisations emerge, and that the structural bonds between pillar parties and pillar organisations weaken. In terms of periodisation, there is a consensus that the three countries were still in the heyday of consociationalism by the end of the 1950s and early 1960s. De-pillarisation seems to have progressed furthest, and is by now all but completed in the Netherlands.[5] In Belgium the situation is complicated by the fact that there is still ongoing de-pillarisation along the religious and class cleavages, accelerating in the last decade, while segmentation along the linguistic cleavage has increased considerably.[6] In Austria, a creeping de-pillarisation had already begun in the 1960s, but did not gain momentum before the 1980s.[7]

Consociational theory is largely silent on the implications de-pillarisation might have for patterns of opposition and government. It seems inevitable that the de-alignment brought about by de-pillarisation results in elections that have now become truly competitive, but is there still opposition? In his early writings, Lijphart warned against continued elite cooperation in a de-pillarised society. When he launched his typology of democratic systems in 1968, Lijphart noted then that social cleavages in Europe were beginning to erode.[8] According to consociational theory, this reduced the need for elite cooperation to safeguard democratic stability, but Lijphart actually observed a trend towards more elite cooperation: 'The model democracy of the New Europe is characterised both by cultural homogeneity and by consociational patterns of government'.[9] However, there is an important difference between consociational democracy and this new 'depoliticised democracy': 'The abandonment of strictly competitive politics in consociational democracies is a deliberate response to the tensions of a fragmented society, whereas the adoption of grand coalition politics in depoliticised democracy is in response to the convergence of ideologies.'[10] We argued above that consociational theory belies Kirchheimer's suggestion that opposition always involves competition, but it would seem that there is no such disagreement with the second part of Kirchheimer's dictum: that competition does not necessarily involve opposition. Has de-pillarisation in consociational countries such as Austria, Belgium and the Netherlands produced a shift from opposition without competition to competition without opposition?

The answer to that question is complicated by the fact that Lijphart feared that continued elite cooperation in a de-pillarised society would create its own anti-system opposition and he referred to Dahl's concluding chapter to *Oppositions in Western Democracies*. Dahl suggested that in 'high-consensus European systems' people might come to reject the 'new Leviathan' as 'too remote and bureaucratized, too addicted to bargaining and compromise, too much an instrument of political elites and technicians with whom they feel slight identification', and that this could lead to a new form of structural opposition.[11] In Lijphart's view, after de-pillarisation the voters, liberated from their sub-cultural confinement, are able to make a real choice, but continued collusive behaviour of the elites would deprive them from meaningful alternatives to choose from. The danger would be that dissatisfied voters would have no option but to vote for anti-system parties. One could only hope that prudent elites would recognise the danger in time and shift towards a more competitive style. If they did, de-pillarisation resulted in a 'normalisation' of the relations between government and opposition and most of our hypotheses about opposition under consociationalism would no longer hold. If the elites did not heed the warning, however, the only hypothesis that would have been affected by de-pillarisation is the one about the absence of real electoral competition. But in that case we may add a new hypothesis:

g)   The very absence of opposition within a de-pillarised but still elite-cartel system leads to opposition against the system.[12]

In the remainder of this article, we will assess to what extent the role of the opposition in Austria, Belgium and the Netherlands corresponded to the theoretical expectations of opposition during consociationalism, and to what extent de-pillarisation has modified this role in the expected direction. With regard to some aspects of the functioning of opposition we can provide factual evidence but other aspects are more open to interpretation.

IDENTIFYING THE OPPOSITION

This is not the place for a lengthy introduction to the political history of our three countries, but it is important to identify the main players. Initially, post-war Austria by all standards was a deeply divided society. The country's first encounter with fully-fledged democracy, the First Republic (1918–34), had ended in civil war between Social Democrats and Catholic Conservatives, and the establishment of a dictatorship. The Catholic-conservative authoritarian regime gave way to Nazism in 1938, when Austria was made part of the German Reich. Under Nazi rule both Social Democrats and Catholic Conservatives were oppressed and prosecuted, and defections from these two camps had swollen the traditional German-national constituency, leaving post-war Austria with more than half a million card-carrying members of the Nazi party. Post-war politicians hence faced the legacy of two dictatorships, Allied occupation leading to the zoning of the country, the latent threat of a Communist takeover, and severe problems of scarcity. This challenge was met by the development of consociationalism with the two protagonists being the People's Party (ÖVP) and the Socialist Party (SPÖ) that will be referred to as 'pillar parties' in this article.[13]

In Belgium the organisation of ideological segments of society had already started in the late nineteenth century, first by the socialist 'world' and, in reaction to this, by the Catholics, although the Liberal notables were the first to organise themselves into a political party. Thus Belgium came to be divided by three social cleavages: between Catholics and Liberals (later joined by Socialists) over the relationship between Church and state (in particular concerning schools), between Socialists (plus the Catholic Left) and Liberals (plus the Catholic Right) over social class issues, and, initially to a lesser extent, between the French-speaking and the Dutch-speaking communities with the Catholics getting most of their parliamentary seats in the Flemish constituencies, and the Socialists getting their seats in the French-speaking Walloon constituencies. Consociational practices developed hesitantly during the inter-bellum period, partly as a reaction to external threats (the First World War, the internal menace of pro-fascist movements, the Second World War). After the Second World War consensus politics was interrupted from 1946 to 1959 when, first, the question of the return of the King polarised relations between Catholics on the one hand, and Socialists and most Liberals on the other in the 1945–50 period, and, subsequently, this same polarisation was reinforced around the financing of Catholic vs. public educational networks between 1950–58. Consociational practices resumed by the conclusion of a School Pact, negotiated outside parliament by the elites of the three pillars.

In the Netherlands, orthodox Protestants, Catholics and Social Democrats gradually organised themselves during the latter half of the nineteenth century in emancipation against dominant Liberals. They were divided by the issues of state subsidies for religious schools (Protestants and Catholics vs. Liberals), by class issues (Social Democrats vs. Liberals), and by the struggle over universal suffrage (Socialists, Catholics, and some Protestants vs. Liberals). In the early twentieth century each of these groups developed its own network of sub-cultural organisations, each with its own political party, although the Protestants had two political parties (divided primarily by allegiance to one of the two main Dutch Protestant denominations of the time). The issues of school financing and general suffrage were resolved in a package deal known as the 'Great Pacification of 1917' and this marks the beginning of consociational practices.

For each country we present in a summary table the party complexion of the government–opposition divide (see Tables 1a–c). We first report a number of party system indicators: electoral net volatility based on votes (the Pedersen index), the effective number of parliamentary parties (based on seats, with no aggregation of parties), and government status. We distinguish four types of government. The first is minimum-winning (mw) or close to minimum-winning (mw+). The latter category tries to adapt Riker's intuition to the real world of party politics. According to Riker a minimum-winning government is the majority cabinet with fewer seats than any alternative majority government that could be formed in the present parliament. Yet in practical terms a few seats more often do not really make a difference in terms of bargaining power, and they may indeed only provide what Riker called a 'working majority'.[14] We then need an operational definition of what we still count as close to the minimum-winning mark: we count every government having an advantage of no more than 10 per cent of the seats over the minimum-winning alternative as 'mw+'. This, of course, is an arbitrary threshold but the governments we classify in that category indeed were generally not considered grossly 'oversized' in their countries. Consequently, we label all cabinets 'oversized' that control more parliamentary seats than 'mw+' governments. We also report on the requirement of government parties for majority status. Governments that contain a party that was not required for the cabinet in order to achieve majority status (50 per cent plus one seat) are classified 'surplus majority' ('sm'). Note that governments can be oversized with or without surplus parties and 'mw+' governments (but not minimum-winning cabinets in the strict sense) can contain surplus parties. Finally, we identify minority governments, those being cabinets consisting of parties that collectively command less than 50 per cent of the parliamentary seats. The tables also allow us to distinguish between single-party governments (seats of only one party in bold) and coalitions (seats of two or more parties in bold). The tables provide the Left–Right orientation of the parties, as we place them from left to right. Our unit of observation is a government (defined by the criteria 'party composition' and 'between elections', hence each change in the party composition and each election brings about a new government).

From these tables it is clear that not all of our theoretical expectations are borne out: the occurrence of 'grand coalitions', one of the defining characteristics of consociationalism, was less regular than might have been expected. It is not

R.B. ANDEWEG, L. DE WINTER AND W.C. MÜLLER

TABLE 1A
GOVERNMENT AND OPPOSITION IN AUSTRIA, 1945–2007

Year	Government	Elect. volatility	% Pill. Parties (votes)	Effective no. leg. Parties (N2)	Government Status	Seats Pillarised Parties	Government strength		KPÖ	GA	SPÖ	ÖVP	VdU/FPÖ	BZÖ	LF
							Seats	% of Seats							
1945	Figl I		94.40	2.09	o	161	165	100	**4**		*76*	*85*			
1947	Figl II		82.75		o	161	161	97.5	4		*76*	*85*			
1949	Figl III	12.2	83.37	2.54	o	144	144	87.2	5		*67*	*77*	16		
1953	Raab I	4.0	89.00	2.47	o	147	147	89.0	4		*73*	*74*	14		
1956	Raab II	5.7	88.98	2.22	o	156	156	94.5	3		*74*	*82*	6		
1959	Raab III	3.0	89.43	2.20	o	157	157	95.1			*78*	*79*	8		
1963	Gorbach II	1.7	90.91	2.20	o	157	157	95.1			*76*	*81*	8		
1966	Klaus II	6.2	93.11	2.18	mw	159	85	51.5			*74*	*85*	6		
1970	Kreisky I	6.7	93.15	2.15	min	159	81	49.0			*81*	*78*	6		
1971	Kreisky II	2.0	93.37	2.21	mw	173	93	50.8			*93*	*80*	10		
1975	Kreisky III	0.4	92.93	2.21	mw	173	93	50.8			*93*	*80*	10		
1979	Kreisky IV	1.3	90.87	2.22	mw	172	95	51.9			*95*	*77*	11		
1983	Sinowatz	4.8	84.41	2.26	mw+	171	102	55.7			*90*	*81*	**12**		
1987	Vranitzky II	10.0	74.85	2.63	o	157	157	85.7		8	*80*	*77*	18		
1990	Vranitky III	10.1	62.59	2.99	o	140	140	76.5		10	*80*	*60*	33		
1994	Vranitzky IV	15.4	66.35	3.07	o	117	117	63.9		13	*65*	*52*	42		11

1996	Vranitzky V	4.0	66.35	3.48	o	124	124	67.7	9	71	53	40	10
2000	Schüssel I	8.9	60.06	3.41	mw	117	104	56.8	14	65	52	52	
2002	Schüssel II	21.0	78.81	2.88	mw+	148	97	53.0	17	69	79	18	7
2007	Gusenbauer	10.2	69.67	3.40	o	134	134	73.2	21	68	66	21	

Note: Number of seats 1945–70: 165, from 1971: 183.

Party placement from left to right.

Italics = pillarised parties.

Bold = governing parties

Coalition status:

mw = minimum winning.

mw+ = close to minimum winning (i.e. not oversized).

o = oversized (operationally defined as having at least 10% more seats than the minimum-winning alternative).

sm = surplus majority (contains at least one party that was not required for majority status).

min = minority (less than 50% of the seats).

Parties:

K = KPÖ = Kommunistische Partei Österreichs (Communist Party of Austria).

GA = Grüne Alternative (Green Alternative).

S = SPÖ = Sozialdemokratische (Sozialistische) Partei Österreichs (Social Democratic [Socialist until 1991] Party of Austria).

V = ÖVP = Österreichische Volkspartei (Austrian People's Party).

VdU = Verband der Unabhängigen (League of Independents).

F = FPÖ = Freiheitliche Partei Österreichs (Freedeom Party of Austria).

B = BZÖ = Bündnis Zukunft Österreich (Union for the Future of Austria).

LF = Liberales Forum (Liberal Forum).

TABLE 1B
GOVERNMENT AND OPPOSITION IN BELGIUM, 1946–2007

Year	Government	Elec. Volatility (Votes)	% Pill. Parties (Votes)	Eff. no. leg. Parties (N2)	Govt. Status	Seats Pill. Parties	Govt. strength Seats	Govt. strength % of Seats	PCB/KPB	PSB/BSP (a) PS	SP	E	A	RW	FDF	PSC/CVP (b) PSC	CVP	VU	PLP/PVV (c) PRL	VLD	UDRT	FN	VB	Other
1946	Spaak I		88.1	2.91	min	178	69	34.2	23	69							92			17				1
1946	Van Acker III		88.1		mw	178	109	54.0	23	69							92			17				1
1947	Spaak II		88.1		o	178	161	79.7	23	69							92			17				1
1949	Eyskens I	8.1	94.4	2.75	mw	200	134	63.2	12	66							105			29				
1950	Pholien	8.9	96.7	2.49	mw	205	108	50.9	7	77							108			20				
1954	Van Acker IV	6.9	97.2	2.63	mw	206	111	52.4	4	86							95			25				1
1958	Eyskens II	5.0	98.6	2.45	min	209	104	49.1	2	84							104	1		21				
1958	Eyskens III		98.6		mw+	209	125	59.0	2	84							104	1		21				
1961	Lefèvre	5.0	94.3	2.69	o	200	180	84.9	5	84							96	5		20				1+1
1965	Harmel	15.8	89.1	3.59	o	189	141	66.5	6	64							77	12		48				
1966	Van den Boeynants I		89.1		mw+	189	125	59.0	6	64				2	3		77	12		48				
1968	Eyskens IV	6.0	82.5	4.97	mw+	175	128	60.4	5	59				2	3	19	47	20		47				
1972	Eyskens V	6.9	76.4	5.85	mw+	162	128	60.4	5	61				5	7	20	47	21	20	14				
1973	Leburton		76.4		o,sm	162	162	76.4	5	61				14	10	20	50	21	20	14				
1974	Tindemans I	3.3	75.9	5.80	min	161	102	48.1	4	59				13	9	22	50	22	9	21				3
1974	Tindemans II		75.9		mw+	161	115	54.2	4	59				13	9	22	50	22	9	21				
1977d	Tindemans III		77.3	5.81	min	164	105	49.5	4	59				10	9	22	50	22	12	21				
1977	Tindemans IV	6.4	81.6	5.24	o,sm	173	172	81.1	2	62				5	10	24	56	20	14	17				2
1979	Martens I	6.2	83.0	6.80	o,sm	176	151	71.2	4	32	26			4	11	25	57	14	14	22	1		1	1
1980	Martens II		83.0		o,sm	176	140	66.0	4	32	26			4	11	25	57	14	14	22	1		1	
1980	Martens III		83.0		o,sm	176	177	83.5	4	32	26			4	11	25	57	14	14	22	1		1	
1980	Martens IV		83.0		o,sm	176	140	66.0	4	32	26			4	11	25	57	14	15	22	1		1	
1981	Martens V	14.4	82.1	7.62	mw+	174	113	53.3	2	35	26	2	2	2	6	18	43	20	15	28	3		1	
1985	Martens VI	9.8	84.0	7.00	mw+	174	115	54.2	0	35	32	5	4	0	3	20	49	16	24	22	1		1	
1988	Martens VII	4.3	85.8	7.13	o,sm	182	150	70.8	0	40	32	3	6	0	3	19	43	16	24	25	0		2	
1991	Martens VIII		85.8		o,sm	182	134	63.2	0	40	32	3	6	0	3	19	43	16	23	25	0		2	
1992	Dehaene I	12.4	78.3	8.41	mw+	166	120	56.6	0	35	28	10	7	0	3	18	39	10	23	26	0	1	12	
1995	Dehaene II	6.7	80.7	8.03	mw+	121	82	54.7	0	21	20	6	5	0	(e)	12	29	5	20	21	0	2	11	
1999	Verhofstadt I	10.9	70.7	9.05	sm,o	106	94	62.7	0	19	14	11	9	0	(e)	10	22	8	18	23	0	1	15	3

2003	Verhofstadt II	12.7	84.0	7.03	o	126	97	64.7	0	**25**	**23**	4	0	0 (e)	8	21	1	**24**	**25**	0	1	18
2007	?	?	76.7	7.91	?	115	?		0	20	14	8	4	0 (e)	10	30	0	23	18	0	1	17	5(d)

Notes: Number of seats 1946: 202; 1949–91: 212; from 1995: 150.

(a) From 1973 to 1979, the Brussels PLP (PVV/PLP) seceded and changed the name of the Brussels PLP into PLPD (*Parti Libéral Démocrate et Pluraliste* - Liberal Democratic and Pluralistic Party). It was further renamed PL/LP (*Parti Libéral/Liberale Partij*) in June 1974. Their MPs (three in 1974, two in 1977 and one in 1978) did not support the three Tindemans governments in which the Walloon and Flemish Liberals were part. The Brussels Liberals re-united the Walloon Liberals in May 1979 when the PRL was created.

(b) In November 1976, the PLP was renamed PRLW (*Parti des Réformes et de la Liberté de Wallonie*, Reforms and Freedom Party of Wallonia, which became PRL in 1979), and three MPs from the RW joined the party. Hence, when in March 1977 the RW was ejected from the Tindemans II government, the number of seats controlled by the next government (Tindemans III) went down to 105 instead of 102 as the Tindemans I government controlled, even though these two governments consisted of the same coalition of parties. In effect, the number of MPs of the PRLW was then 12 instead of nine (without any election being held) and the number of remaining RW MPs was ten.

(c) The party still exists, but in a federation with the French-speaking Liberals. The "new party" is currently named MR (Mouvement Reformateur).

(d) Lijst De Decker (right wing populist).

Party placement from left to right.

Italics = pillarised parties

Bold = governing parties

Coalition status:

mw = minimum winning.

mw+ = close to minimum winning (i.e. not oversized).

o = oversized (operationally defined as having at least 10% more seats than the minimum-winning alternative).

sm = surplus majority (contains at least one party that was not required for majority status).

min = minority (less than 50% of the seats).

Parties:

PCB/KPB = Parti Communiste Belge/Kommunistische Partij België (Belgian Communist Party.)

BSP/PSB = Until 1978, the [Flemish] and French-speaking Socialist parties (SP and PS) were united in the unitary Belgian Socialist Party [BSP/PSB].

SP = Socialistische Partij ([Flemish] Socialist Party) (the party was called 'Belgian' Socialist Party [BSP] until the 'B' was dropped in March 1980, a bit more than one year after the split of the Belgian Socialist Party [BSP/PSB]).

PS = Parti Socialiste ([French-speaking] Socialist Party) (the party was called 'Belgian' Socialist Party [PSB] until the 'B' was dropped in December 1978, when the unitary Belgian Socialist Party])

A = AGALEV = Anders Gaan Leven (Another Way of Living [Flemish Ecologists]) (now called *Groen!*).

E = ECOLO = Ecologistes Confédérés pour l'Organisation de Luttes Originales (Confederated Ecologists for the Organisation of Original Struggles [French-speaking Ecologists]) (The full name is a play on words in order to get the acronym. It is never used and hardly known.)

RW = Rassemblement Wallon (Walloon Rally).

FDF = Front Démocratique des Francophones (French-speakers' Democratic Front).

CVP/PSC = Before 1968, the Flemish and the French-speaking Christian Democratic parties (CVP and PSC) were united in the unitary Belgian Christian Democratic Party [CVP/PSC].

CVP = Christelijke Volkspartij (Christian People's Party [Flemish]).

PSC = Parti Social-Chrétien (Christian Social Party [French-speaking]).

VU = Volksunie (People's Union [Flemish Nationalists]).

PVV/PLP = Before 1972, the Flemish and the French-speaking Liberal parties (VLD and PRL) were united in the unitary Belgian Liberal Party [PVV/PLP]. Before 1961, the Liberals used to be called LP/PL (Liberale Partij/Parti Libéral [Liberal Party]).

VLD = Vlaamse Liberalen en Democraten (Flemish Liberals and Democrats [Flemish Liberals]), known as the PVV = Partij voor Vrijheid en Vooruitgang (Freedom and Progress Party) from 1972 to 1992.

PRL = Parti Réformateur Libéral (Liberal Reform Party [French-speaking Liberals]), known as the PLP = Parti de la Liberté et du Progrès (Freedom and Progress Party) from 1972 to 1976, then PRLW (Parti des Réformes et de la Liberté de Wallonie [Reforms and Freedom Party of Wallonia]) from November 1976 to May 1979 when the PRL was created.

UDRT = Union Démocrate pour le Respect du Travail (Democratic Union for the Respect of Work [Poujadist Party]).

FN = Front National (National Front).

VB = Vlaams Blok (Flemish Block, Vlaams Belang since 2004).

TABLE 1C
GOVERNMENT AND OPPOSITION IN THE NETHERLANDS, 1945–2007

Year	Government	Elect. Volatility	% Pill. Parties (votes)	Eff. no leg. Parties (N2)	Govt. Status	Seats Pill. Parties	Govt. Strength Seats	Govt. Strength % of Seats	SP	Small Left	PvdA	D66	ARP	KVP	CHU	CDA	Orth rel	VVD	Pop Right	Other
1946	Beel I	–	86.2	4.47	o	88	61	61.0		10	29		13	32	8		2	6		
1948	Drees I	5.6	86.9	4.68	o,sm	89	76	76.0		8	27		13	32	9		3	8		
1952	Drees III	6.3	86.7	4.65	o,sm	90	81	81.0		6	30		12	30	9		4	9		
1956	Drees IV	4.1	91.5	4.07	o,sm	140	127	84.7		7	50		15	49	13		3	13		
1958	Beel II				mw+	140	77	51.3		7	50		15	49	13		3	13		
1959	De Quay	5.9	91.7	4.15	o,sm	142	94	62.7		5	48		14	49	12		3	19		
1963	Marijnen	5.0	87.5	4.51	o,sm	135	92	61.3		8	43		13	50	13		4	16	3	
1965	Cals				o,sm	135	106	70.7		8	43		13	50	13		4	16	3	
1966	Zijlstra				min	135	63	42.0		8	43		13	50	13		4	16	3	
1967	De Jong	10.8	78.8	5.71	mw+	123	86	57.3		9	37	7	15	42	12		4	17	7	
1971	Biesheuvel I	12.0	71.6	6.40	mw+	113	82	54.7		10	39	11	13	35	10		5	16	1	10; incl DS70:8
1972	Biesheuvel II				min	113	74	49.3		10	39	11	13	35	10		5	16	1	10
1973	Den Uyl	12.6	73.0	6.42	o,sm	113	97	64.7		16; incl PPR:7	43	6	14	27	7		6	22	3	6
1977	Van Agt I	14.4	83.6	3.70	mw	130	77	51.3		6	53	8				49	4	28	1	1
1981	Van Agt II	9.6	76.4	4.29	o	118	109	72.7		9	44	17				48	6	26		
1982	Van Agt III				min	118	65	43.3		9	44	17				48	6	26		
1982	Lubbers I	9.3	82.9	4.01	mw	128	81	54.0		3	47	6				45	6	36	1	
1986	Lubbers II	10.2	85.3	3.49	mw+	133	81	54.0		3	52	9				54	5	27	1	
1989	Lubbers III	8.4	81.8	3.75	o	125	103	68.7		6	49	12				54	6	22		
1994	Kok I	22.2	66.2	5.42	o	102	92	61.3	2	5	37	24				34	7	31	1	
1998	Kok II	15.1	72.1	4.81	o,sm	112	97	64.7	5	11	45	14				29	8	38	3	
2002	Balkenende I	30.0	58.4	5.79	o	90	93	62.0	9	10	23	7				43	6	24	28; incl LPF:26	7
2003	Balkenende II	16.6	73.8	4.74	mw+	114	78	52.0	9	8	42	6				44	5	28	8	
2006	Balkenende III				min	114	72	48.0	9	8	42	6				44	5	28	8	
2007	Balkenende IV	17.2	62.4	5.54	mw+	96	80	53.3	25	7	33	3				41	8; incl CU:6	22	9	2

Note: Number of seats: 1946–52: 100; from 1956:150.

Party placement from left to right.

In Italics = pillarised parties.

In Bold = governing parties

Coalition status:

mw = minimum winning.

mw+ = close to minimum winning (i.e. not oversized).

o = oversized (operationally defined as having at least 10% more seats than the minimum-winning alternative).

sm = surplus majority (contains at least one party that was not required for majority status).

min = minority (less than 50% of the seats)

Parties:

SP   Socialist Party.

Small left   since 1989 Green Left; before: CPN (Communist), PSP (Pacifist-Socialist), PPR (Radical), EVP (Evangelical Left).

PvdA   Labour Party.

D66   Democrats 66.

ARP   Anti-Revolutionary Party (protestant).

KVP   Catholic People's Party.

CHU   Christian Historical Union (protestant).

CDA   Christian Democratic Appeal (merger of ARP, KVP and CHU).

Orthodox   GPV (Reformed Political Alliance), RPF (Reformed Political Federation (since 2000 these two parties form CU, Christian Union), SGP (Political Reformed Party), KNP (Catholic National Party), RKPN (Roman Catholic Party of the Netherlands).

VVD   Liberal Party.

Populist Right   BP (Farmers Party), RVP (Rightist People's Party), CP (Centre Party), CD (Centre Democrats), LN (Livable Netherlands), LPF (List Pim Fortuyn), PVV (Freedom Party).

Other   NMP (Retailers Party), DS70 (Democratic Socialists '70), AOV (Pensioners' Party), Unie 55+ (55+ Union), PvdD (Animal Rights).

true that most governing coalitions included more parties than necessary for a majority, or even all parties. With one exception (the first Austrian post-war cabinet) no all-party cabinets existed, and only in the Netherlands do we see a dominance of surplus-majority coalitions until the onset of de-pillarisation in 1966. In Austria, the ÖVP could have formed a single-party majority cabinet before 1949 but did not. For the two decades after 1966, Austrian governments were largely single-party majority cabinets (plus one single-party minority and one 'mw+' coalition). In Belgium, before the linguistic split of the major parties in the late 1960s and 1970s, most governments were also 'mw' or 'mw+' with a few single-party minority governments. If the governments in these countries were 'grand', they were so in terms of the number of seats they commanded, and even in this respect there were exceptions. In Austria the percentage of seats in the hands of the governing parties regularly approached 100 per cent before the first single-party government took office in 1966. In Belgium we see huge governing majorities whenever Christian Democrats and Social Democrats joined in a coalition, but more moderate majorities for the coalitions of Christian Democrats and Liberals. In the Netherlands we see large majorities of 75 per cent of the seats until the end of the 1950s when Social Democrats and Liberals started to exclude each other as coalition partners. Although non-pillar parties were rarely represented in government it is not true that all pillar parties were always included. Even in the period of classic consociationalism this is true only for Austria (until 1966); in Belgium and the Netherlands at least one of the main pillar parties usually joined the opposition.

Looking at the opposition, it is true that it was small and largely consisted of non-pillar parties. Immediately following the Second World War, the Communists were strong in all three countries, and were included in a governing coalition both in Austria and Belgium, but with the advent of the Cold War, the Communists were first excluded from government and later reduced to just a few seats in Belgium and the Netherlands and they disappeared altogether from parliament in Austria. In Belgium no other opposition parties won significant (more than one seat) representation in parliament until the breakthrough of linguistic parties in the mid 1960s. In Austria, the League of Independents (the Freedom Party from 1956) joined the Communists as non-pillar opposition, but after initial success in 1949, it declined and remained small until the late 1980s. The situation in the Netherlands was slightly more complicated. In 1959 the Communists were joined by a small, equally anti-system Pacifist-Socialist party. These two parties can also be regarded as ideological competitors of the main Social Democrat party. Similarly, the main Protestant parties received ideological competition from small orthodox parties SGP (Staatkundig Gereformeerde Partij, already before the Second World War) and GPV (Gereformeerd Politiek Verbond, since 1963). Similar competition for the Catholics tended to be short-lived, as the bishops intervened. All these small parties formed a more or less permanent parliamentary opposition in the three countries, usually in addition to a more temporary opposition role of one of the pillar parties.

As an (imperfect) indicator of electoral competitiveness, our tables present figures on electoral volatility. There is no objective standard for classifying volatility as high or low, but during the heyday of consociationalism, before 1965, average volatility was 5.2 in Austria, 5.4 in the Netherlands, and 7.3 in Belgium. This is considerably lower than in Germany, Italy or France during the same period, but no lower than, for example, in the UK or the Scandinavian countries.[15] From 1965 onwards, we expect de-pillarisation to result in an increase in electoral volatility. The figures in Table 1c show that this has certainly been the case in the Netherlands where post-1965 figures have consistently been much higher than the pre-1965 figures, culminating in a net volatility of 30 in the 2002 elections. This fits the general pattern of de-pillarisation in the Netherlands that started abruptly around 1965 and proceeded rapidly. In line with the slower pace of de-pillarisation in Austria until the 1980s, Table 1a shows small increases in volatility in 1966 and 1970, followed by record low volatility in the remainder of the 1970s, with clearly increasing volatility again since the 1980s. In Table 1b we see a somewhat similar pattern for Belgium: the 1965 elections clearly marked the end of consociationalism's heyday with a volatility of 15.8, followed by electoral stability until the 1980s when a period began in which high and low volatility seem to alternate. For the Belgian case it is important to recall that religious and class de-alignment were accompanied by a deepening linguistic cleavage. This also led to a complete split of the party system into parallel systems of Dutch-speaking and French-speaking parties (although, with the exception of the largest constituency of the capital Brussels-Halle-Vilvoorde, voters are confronted with only one of these party systems on their ballot).

If de-pillarisation has also led to more competitiveness outside the electoral arena, we might expect less cooperation in cabinets and hence more minimum-winning coalitions and single-party governments. We do see such a development in the Netherlands, where the once customary surplus-majority cabinets (including parties not necessary for providing the government with a parliamentary majority) have become exceptional. Although real, this change should not be overestimated. To some extent it can be explained by the merger of the Catholic and two main Protestant parties into the Christian Democratic Appeal in 1977. Assuming that the relative strengths of the three parties in this merger have not changed since then, some of the more recent 'mw+' coalitions would have been surplus majority had the merger not taken place (or, alternatively, some of the oversized coalitions of the 1950s and 1960s would have been 'mw+' had the merger taken place earlier). Austria, as we saw, did not have surplus-majority cabinets after 1949. There was a shift from coalitions to single-party governments from 1966 to 1983, but since then coalition government has resumed as no party could win a majority. In Belgium surplus-majority coalitions have actually been formed more frequently after de-pillarisation started than before, but this might be interpreted as an artefact, caused by the split into two party systems: the Constitution demands linguistic parity in cabinet and, until 2007, Belgian parties have not entered a federal coalition without their ideological sister party from across the language border, even if that was not necessary for obtaining a parliamentary majority. In addition, surplus majorities most often occurred in periods when constitutional reforms requiring approval by a two-thirds majority were high on the political agenda.

The opposition has grown in size since de-pillarisation, but its composition has also become more varied. In Austria the Greens first entered parliament in 1986, clearly presenting itself as a non-pillar party. We have already mentioned the Freedom Party as an earlier anti-consociational party. After 1986 it transformed itself into a right-wing populist party, reaching out quite effectively to the de-pillarised electorate. This change also led to a split-off, the Liberal Forum, which was represented in parliament from 1993 to 2000 as Austria's third non-pillar party. In 2006 another split-off from the Freedom Party, the Bündnis Zukunft Österreich (BZÖ), won seats in parliament. In Belgium the virtual absence of non-pillar opposition parties came to an end with the growing representation of linguistic parties: with the growth of the Flemish *Volksunie* in the 1960s and the emergence of the French-speaking *Rassemblement Wallon* and FDF. In the 1980s they were joined on the Left by two Green parties (*Agalev* and *Ecolo*) and on the Right by the populist French-speaking UDRT and later the Front National, and the Dutch-speaking *Vlaams Blok*, now *Vlaams Belang* (Flemish Interest). The Netherlands already had a variety of small non-pillar parties, but after de-pillarisation more new ones entered parliament. Many of them were short-lived, and linking that fact to the decay of the pillarised system, the authors of a Dutch text wrote about 'new parties that came and went like mushrooms in the Autumn of Dutch politics'.[16] There were parties of the populist Right, such as the Farmers' Party that entered parliament in 1963, the Centre Democrats in the 1980s, or most famously the List Pim Fortuyn (LPF) that was founded in 2002, soon splintered, and eventually disappeared. Single-issue parties for retailers or pensioners suffered the same fate. Other new parties eventually merged with older non-pillar parties into the current Green Left and Christian Union parties. D66, founded in 1966 in direct opposition to the non-democratic character of Dutch consociational politics, and the populist Left SP are the only new non-pillar parties that have neither disappeared nor merged.

Not all of these non-pillar parties have remained on the opposition benches. What has also changed since the 1960s is that the door to government has opened to non-pillar parties. Even after de-pillarisation the pillar parties continue to dominate the governments of our three countries, but in the Netherlands in 1971 the first non-pillar party, the now defunct DS70, entered a short-lived five-party coalition, followed by D66 and by PPR (the latter now merged into Green Left) in 1973, D66 again in 1981, 1982, 1994 and 1998, the right-wing populist LPF in 2002, and the orthodox Protestant Christian Union in 2007. In Austria's more compact party system, non-pillar government participation is confined to the Freedom Party (FPÖ), first in coalition with the Socialists in 1983, and, after its populist transformation, with the People's Party in 2000 and 2002. Interestingly, the very rise of the non-pillar opposition had first led to a return of the grand coalition of the Social Democrats and the People's Party in 1987 as these two parties deemed neither the Greens nor Haider's populists *koalitionsfähig* (fit for coalition) yet. The monopoly of the pillar parties for government participation in Belgium was broken, not surprisingly, by the new linguistic parties, by the *Rassemblement Wallon* in 1974, the FDF in 1977 and 1979, and the *Volksunie* in 1977 and 1988. In 1999 Belgium's two Green parties were accepted as coalition partners. So far, the right-wing populist VB, now the largest non-pillar party in Belgium, has been excluded from government participation at all levels (national, regional, provincial and local) through a *cordon sanitaire* agreement between the democratic parties. We shall return to this interesting contrast with the Austrian and Dutch experience later in this article.

OPPORTUNITIES FOR OPPOSITION

It might be expected that during consociationalism, the governing elite cartel would have engineered the institutional rules so as to protect itself against oppositional activity in parliament. However, there is very little evidence that this has actually been the case. All three countries operate electoral systems that are highly proportional. For Belgium, according to the Gallagher index of disproportionality, the average was 3.23 for the 1945–90 period, whereas the score for the Netherlands was 1.29 before 1956, and 1.32 since then.[17] Even in the most disproportional of the three systems, Austria – until the 1970 electoral system reform – the average score was just 3.61. This is quite low: for all electoral systems together, Gallagher calculates the average disproportionality at 6.2, and even for all systems of proportional representation (PR), the average is still 4.4.[18] In other words, the electoral systems of our three countries are towards the proportional end even among PR systems. This need not surprise us: after all, PR was introduced in these countries because it was useful for the pillar parties themselves. That it also offers relatively easy access to the parliamentary arena for non-pillar parties was merely an unintended side effect. Yet such an aggregated view does not distinguish between the pillar parties and their competitors. On closer inspection, in the Austrian case the electoral system worked in favour of the large parties – the pillar parties sharing government office – until the 1970 reform. As long as no non-pillar party achieved a major electoral breakthrough the system was strong enough to marginalise them in parliament (see below) or even prevent them from crossing the threshold of representation.[19] The 1970 reform (bringing down the Gallagher index to 1.43 for the 1971–90 period) was the product of alliance formation beyond the consociational parties that became politically possible after the end of the grand coalition. This system was again changed in 1992 by the revived grand coalition that introduced a four per cent national threshold and de facto switched over to the d'Hondt system that is generally considered the least proportional of the main PR variants (with the consequence of the Gallagher index rising to 1.86 for the 1994–2006 period).

Turning to the opportunity structure within parliament, all three countries have structures that are generally favourable for strengthening parliament vis-à-vis government and all subscribe to the principle of proportionality (rather than privileging the majority). Strong parliamentary committees are generally regarded as a useful opportunity for opposition parties to influence policies. In all three countries most parliamentary committees are permanent and special-ised in a particular policy area, usually corresponding to a ministerial depart-ment; and are relatively small (with a maximum of around 25 members); they deliberate before the plenary stage; minority reports are allowed; and the allo-cation of committee chairs to parties is proportional. Nothing relevant has changed since the heyday of consociationalism with respect to these features. The committees in these three countries are quite autonomous, although in different ways: according to Mattson and Strøm, Dutch parliamentary com-mittees have almost complete control over their own agenda, but are low on drafting authority (rewriting government bills and suchlike), whereas the opposite is true for Belgium, with Austria in between.[20]

With regard to the instruments available to opposition parties, we see con-siderable variation between the countries and over time. Belgium and the Netherlands until the 1970s had systems more open to the use of important parliamentary instruments by the opposition, that were a function of both the formal parliamentary rules and the size of the opposition and its individual com-ponents. In Belgium, there were and are hardly any limitations on the rights of initiative of the individual MP: a single MP can introduce a private member bill (or amendment) at any moment of the legislative process, can introduce an inter-pellation, ask oral or written questions, can introduce a motion of censure against a minister or the government, and make a personal statement after a vote. The main constraint is time, and usually the Conference of Group Presidents decides consensually on the number of speakers and on the time that should be allotted for each debate, interpellation or oral question. There are also formal time rules for the latter two activities. When many oral questions deal with a common current problem an *actualiteitsdebat* can be organised. For most activities, each group can mandate one speaker, independent from the size of the group. Support of a fifth of the MPs is required for holding an emergency debate. For asking legal advice of the Council of State on a bill or amendment the support of a third of MPs is needed, while a majority is required for launching a committee of investigation. Parliamentary scrutiny over the budget was increased in 1989. Since 1993, at the introduction of the general budget in September, the PM delivers a 'State of the Union' speech which provides a new opportunity for the opposition to challenge the government's general policy agenda.

As in Belgium, introducing a private member bill or asking a written question was and is the prerogative of each individual MP in the Netherlands. Proposing a parliamentary resolution or even a censure motion requires only five signatures. Starting an emergency debate needed the support of a majority in parliament, but even at the heyday of consociationalism it was considered undemocratic for the governing majority to refuse a minority request. Since de-pillarisation started the support requirement was reduced to 30 MPs in 2003 and an annual Accountability Day was added to the parliamentary agenda in 2000: a day of debate in which the government's performance is scrutinised.

Austria distinguishes itself from Belgium and the Netherlands by having had fewer minority-friendly rules throughout the consociational period and more substantial changes since then.[21] Until today, most parliamentary instruments require a minimum of support of MPs. Individual MPs can only make plenary speeches. Questions to ministers need the signatures of five MPs. Establishing a committee of investigation requires majority support. These rules have remained unchanged. For a long time introducing private member bills or amendments required the support of eight MPs, asking urgent questions required 20. Thus, during the first period of grand coalition government, opposition parties were too small to make use of the most basic parliamentary instruments in some of the parliamentary terms and the instrument of the urgent question remained practically dormant until the end of grand coalition government in 1966. Oral questions were not introduced before 1961. Moreover, the parliamentary rules left the government much leeway with regard to answering questions. It was only in 1975, after both pillar parties had spent at least one parliamentary term in opposition, that more effective means of control were introduced: the parliament's right to receive proper answers to questions were shaped and two important minority rights were introduced: direct appeal to the Constitutional Court in the case of legislation and the minority order to the Audit Office to scrutinise government branches (both instruments requiring one-third of MPs and the latter being rationed). It was the return to grand coalition government in 1987 that triggered a substantial strengthening of minority rights in 1988: the support requirement for private member bills, amendments and other proposals was reduced to five MPs (to make these instruments available to the then smallest opposition party, the Greens) and several new instruments were created: the topical hour, short debates on procedural matters, and special parliamentary committees (*Enquete-Kommission*) as means of collecting information and forming opinions on important questions. At the same time, responding to opposition attempts at filibustering, urgent questions and plenary time were rationed (the latter required specific decisions to be made by a two-thirds majority before the beginning of the debate – at that time the grand coalition commanded that majority). In 1993, responding to more attempts at opposition filibuster, plenary time was further rationed, but other control devices improved (parliamentary question rights extended and the ration for minority orders to the Audit Office increased). While the grand coalition was in command of a two-thirds majority at that time, it just failed to renew it in 1994. As Austria's EU accession in 1995 required opposition support, a package deal gave parliament the most extensive rights to scrutinise EU affairs and check the ministers of all Member States. In 1996 a further rationing of plenary time and of extra meetings of parliament (when in recess) was introduced, as a response to the FPÖ's extensive use of these instruments. These changes were balanced by introducing the new instruments of urgent proposals and short debates on proposals for establishing a scrutiny committee (both rationed) that won the support of the opposition parties other than the FPÖ.

Some of the instruments mentioned in the paragraphs above are primarily designed to provide the opposition with publicity for its concerns and proposals. This can also be provided by giving the public better access to the deliberation and decision-making process beyond the plenary meeting. In all three countries committee meetings used to take place behind closed doors in the period of classic consociationalism. In the Netherlands some parliamentary committees unofficially opened their doors in the 1970s and in 1980 the rules were changed to stipulate that all committee meetings are public, with the exception of meetings to discuss procedural matters. In Belgium (from 1985) and Austria (from 1988) parliamentary committees gradually opened their meetings to the public, facilitating the dissemination of the opposition's critique on the government.

Finally, opposition capacity depends on its human and financial resources. Due to its access to the machinery of the state the government will always be in an advantageous position, but the gap can be smaller or greater. In the Netherlands MPs' salaries have increased since de-pillarisation, which has made membership of parliament a full-time job. In Austria and Belgium

MPs' salaries have always allowed full-time concentration on parliamentary work (yet many MPs prefer not to become full-time politicians). In the Netherlands the support structure for MPs and parliamentary parties has also improved significantly. Yet Austria and Belgium have gone further in that direction.

The picture is similar with regard to party and parliamentary group finance. In Austria parliamentary groups consisting of a minimum of five out of 183 MPs (out of 165 before 1971) have received subsidies since 1963. In the 1970s state subsidies to the party academies and eventually the political party organisations were introduced. The latter, in election years, are also available to non-parliamentary parties who poll a minimum of one per cent of the vote. Over the years party finance has been increased considerably. Public funds are allocated proportionally but small parties are somewhat favoured as all parties receive a fixed minimum. In election years more funds are available. In 2002, an election year, €46.8 million were allocated to the parties; in 2003, a non-election year, it was €35.7 million.[22]

In Belgium since 1989 parliamentary groups – parties comprising at least five out of 150 MPs since 1995 (three out of 212 MPs before that) – are entitled to receive increasingly generous funding on the basis of proportionality. A comprehensive system of public financing of the extra-parliamentary parties at the national level was introduced in the same year. It provides a lump sum for each party (with at least one MP in each chamber) and an additional sum for each voter at the last legislative elections.[23] Both schemes were substantially extended in the 1990s, leading to a total amount of public party finance of about €54 million for all parties in 2004. The basic rule of allocation is proportionality, with a slight bias for the smaller parties given the small fixed minimum each party gets. Parties not represented in parliament are not subsidised but get a minimal amount of time on public media to present their programme. As a consequence, most of the party income (80 per cent) now comes from the state.

In the Netherlands the parties have gradually received more money and, since 1998, face fewer restrictions on its use. The amount was always roughly proportional to parliamentary strength. Since 2006 a complex formula is used that also takes into account the number of members – €176,580 + (€51,217 x number of seats won by party) + ((€193,345/total number of party members of all parties) x number of members in party). In total an overall amount of €15 million is available for these subsidies annually (not including money for parliamentary party staff). There is no distinction between election years and non-election years. The only 'subsidy' affected by the election cycle is TV and radio time on the public channels. Parties not yet represented in parliament also get the same amount of time on air during the campaign period with a lottery to decide the allocation of time slots.

In sum, the structure of parliamentary opportunities has not changed much in the Netherlands since the height of consociationalism, it has changed moderately in Belgium and significantly in Austria. While an open opportunity structure had always existed in the Netherlands and Belgium, this was not the case in Austria. Yet subsequent reforms have levelled these differences. This is also clear from the somewhat dated snapshot comparison from the early 1990s by Herbert Döring, suggesting that the opportunity structure is quite open for opposition parties in all three countries.[24]

OPPOSITION PARLIAMENTARY BEHAVIOUR

We have no truly comparative data on the actual use that was made by opposition parties of these opportunities both before and after de-pillarisation. However, we can outline the developments in our three countries by drawing on a variety of national studies. In general, parliamentary instruments were more actively used in all three countries in the latter period.

In the Netherlands the average number of amendments went up from fewer than 150 per year before 1966 to more than 1,000 per year since then (while the number of government bills remained relatively constant). The average number of written questions and parliamentary motions also rose spectacularly from the start of de-pillarisation. Of special interest are Parliamentary Inquiries. In the nineteenth century they were held to investigate urgent problems (contagious cattle disease, child labour, and so on) that needed the government's attention. They then fell into abeyance until they were rediscovered in the 1980s as an instrument to investigate government fiascos. Starting in 1982, eight Parliamentary Inquiries have been held into government interference in the shipbuilding industry, the failure to develop a tamper-proof passport, suspected fraud with government building contracts, the Srebrenica disaster, and more. The increase in Inquiries took place although attempts to make them possible without majority support always failed.[25]

In Austria, the level of parliamentary activity significantly increased from the first grand coalition period to that of single-party governments.[26] The number of written questions rose from 384 in 1962–66 to 1570 in 1966–70 and remained at roughly 2,500 in each full parliamentary term until 1986. From there the number of questions rose further and exceeded the 6,000 mark in each full parliamentary term from 1986 – when the Greens entered parliament, the FPÖ turned populist, and a fifth parliamentary party was in the game for part of the time. The breakdown of the questions clearly shows that opposition parties are much more active in that respect and that government parties in grand coalitions are more active than those approaching the minimum-winning criterion.[27] While only one parliamentary committee of inquiry was set up before the end of the first grand coalition in 1966, nine were established during the period of single-party governments (until 1983), and five more under the different coalitions in office since then (including those established in 2007, when the outgoing ÖVP–FPÖ government was still in office as a caretaker government but had lost its parliamentary majority).[28]

In general, the Belgian parliament has also become more active, although the development is less pronounced than in the Netherlands and Austria, and the rate of activity fluctuates considerably. Thus, the number of written parliamentary questions increased considerably after the 1960s, with the all-time high in the late 1970s and early 1980s. The number of oral questions is still growing, while interpellations peaked in the 1990s. Also, the number of private member bills (introduced and passed), show upward trends until the beginning of this decade. While only nine Parliamentary Inquiries were set up in the entire 1880–1988 period, since then on average one is set up each year. They have developed into an alternative instrument of parliamentary oversight gaining considerable publicity, mostly captured by opposition MPs.

Most empirical evidence (although there are no longitudinal time series available) shows that in the three countries the parliamentary opposition makes disproportionate use of the parliamentary opportunities open to them. But even if we were to assume that there is no difference between the governing majority and opposition in this respect, the opportunities for opposition MPs to influence public policy may have the paradoxical effect that the distinction between government and opposition is blurred when it comes to voting behaviour in parliament. Empirical evidence for this is rare with regard to the Netherlands, but we do have some exceptional figures. According to Visscher's detailed study of some 3,000 bills processed by the Dutch parliament between 1963 and 1986, the Liberals voted against eight per cent of all bills when in opposition, and Labour voted against 12 per cent of all bills in opposition (the Christian Democrats were in government during the entire period). Even the most oppositional of opposition parties, the Communist Party, voted against only 16 per cent of all government bills. And the other way around, amendments introduced by the opposition are not all doomed to failure: during this period the government disapproved strongly of 68 per cent of opposition amendments, but it registered no objections to 13 per cent of those amendments and even adopted seven per cent of them. When it came to a final vote 11 per cent of opposition amendments received majority support. Since de-pillarisation, opposition amendments seem to have become even more successful: under the 1963–65 Marijnen government, for example, 5.4 per cent of opposition amendments received majority support (against 13.9 per cent of amendments by governing parties) and under the 1982–86 Lubbers I government 16.1 per cent of opposition amendments were supported by a majority in parliament (against 21.4 per cent of governing parties' amendments).[29]

The reason for this partial blurring of the distinction between governmental majority and opposition is probably that Dutch opposition MPs are not successful because they belong to an opposition party, but because they are respected as experienced parliamentarians specialised in a particular policy area, despite sitting on the opposition benches. For much of the legislative process, parliament is not so much an arena for the struggle between government and opposition (King's inter-party mode), but rather a marketplace where policy advocates make deals with each other, regardless of their belonging to the government or opposition blocs (King's cross-party mode).[30]

In Belgium, in the period from 1954–65, nearly half of all final plenary votes followed the consensus pattern, while the majority/opposition pattern prevailed in more than one out of four votes (and was dominant for votes on budgets, amendments, and articles of legislative proposals).[31] In the 1980s, consensus patterns on final votes became rare.[32] In the 1990s, one out of three votes was clearly majority vs. opposition, while one out of eight was unanimous (consensus) votes. Hence, on average the majority parties are supported by at least one opposition party. Dissident voting is a bit more frequent and common in opposition than among the majority parties. To conclude, consensus voting seems to be in decline, but this is partially also the result of the skyrocketing fragmentation of the party system, which makes it more likely that at least one opposition party will not share the consensus amongst the other parties.

Austrian parliamentary voting patterns were registered only after the end of grand coalition government in 1966. Under first single-party governments and then the SPÖ–FPÖ coalition in each parliamentary term the vast majority of legislation was passed unanimously (the minimum was 72 per cent in the 1966–70 term, the maximum 85 per cent in the 1971–75 term) and the mean support level for new legislation was above 90 per cent of the parliamentary votes. Thus, a high degree of consensus was maintained. This changed dramatically in 1986, with the Greens entering parliament and the FPÖ turning to a populist strategy. Since then unanimous consent in legislative voting has dropped below the 50 per cent mark (with a minimum of 27 per cent in the 1996–2000 term). Yet the mean support level of legislation only once dropped below 80 per cent (79.4 per cent under the ÖVP–FPÖ government in the 2000–2002 term). Of course, such aggregates include many technical laws that win the support of all parties and are driven up by the vast majorities of grand coalition governments (see Table 1a).[33]

The distinction between government and opposition is not only blurred by the opposition supporting government proposals and vice versa, but also by governing parties opposing proposals from government parties, sometimes even if they have gone through the clearing house of the cabinet. This has been noted first for the Austrian case. As we saw, the grand coalitions of the ÖVP and SPÖ left little room for parliamentary opposition by opposition parties, but opposition to policies promoted by ÖVP ministers came from the coalition partner SPÖ, and vice versa.[34] To a large extent, this *Bereichsopposition* is practised within the cabinet or within the coalition committee, with junior ministers of one party being appointed as watchdogs in the departments of the other party's cabinet ministers, or with the unanimity rule within the coalition providing each party with a veto over the policies proposed by the other party. Some of the *Bereichsopposition* takes place in parliament, and is used by each of the coalition parties to mark its own position for the benefit of its voters. This takes the form of asking critical parliamentary questions of the coalition partner's ministers, as opposed to friendly questions to ministers of one's own party.[35] A few parliamentary inquiries have been held when a coalition party teams up with the opposition to examine a scandal in a policy area dominated by its coalition partner.[36] *Bereichsopposition* also includes the presentation of policy alternatives in the form of legislative bills. While introducing these bills was consistent with the coalition agreements, under these rules the coalition parties were not allowed to join forces with the opposition in parliamentary voting. Therefore, many of these bills were never voted upon. Yet, this practice could also cause inconvenience to the relevant government party when an opposition party generally in agreement with the direction of the proposed change pressed for a vote and the government party was committed to prevent the enactment of its own proposal. Kirchheimer even saw *Bereichsopposition* as an alternative for more traditional forms of opposition after the 'waning of oppositions' that he predicted[37]. However, this type of opposition is severely constrained, the restriction being that the survival of the coalition should not be jeopardised.[38] The practice as described here has characterised all grand coalitions to date. If anything, *Bereichsopposition* has become stronger and extended to areas such as government relations with mass media that were less relevant in the period of classic consociationalism. In contrast, coalitions that were minimum-winning or close to that mark (SPÖ–FPÖ in the 1980s and ÖVP–FPÖ/BZÖ in the 2000–2006 period), while not exclusively cooperative, were characterised by a much downsized version of *Bereichsopposition*.[39]

There is no Dutch or French equivalent to the term *Bereichsopposition* in Belgium and the Netherlands, but similar practices can be observed in these countries as well: the appointments of junior ministers to departments that are headed by another party's minister (in the Netherlands on average two-thirds of all junior ministers) and attempts in the cabinet or coalition committee to influence the policies of other party's ministers, in particular if the coalition agreement is not clear on the issue. In parliament, during the heyday of consociationalism, the Dutch cabinet was deliberately kept somewhat aloof from party politics: the coalition agreement covered only a few major issues; most ministers were recruited from outside parliament, and more for their technical expertise than for their political experience; in most major parties that joined a governing coalition, the party leader remained in parliament rather than joining the cabinet; and coordination between a governing party's ministers and its MPs was generally frowned upon. This allowed a parliamentary party in the governing majority to go even further than in Austrian-style *Bereichsopposition*: to oppose unwelcome government proposals, even when such proposals were initiated by one of its own party's ministers. In the Netherlands, too, such opposition was not meant to put the cabinet's survival in danger, but occasionally clashes between a governing party and its ministers led to the resignation of an individual minister, and even to a few full-blown cabinet crises (1951, 1960). With de-pillarisation this oppositional behaviour by governing parties has gradually disappeared: as elections became more competitive, coalition politics became more politicised: the coalition agreement became more detailed; more ministers with a political rather than a technocratic profile were recruited; most party leaders accepted a post in the cabinet when their party joined the coalition; and weekly meetings of a party's ministers and parliamentary leaders are convened to help prevent open conflicts between MPs from governing parties and ministers.

In Belgium, most of the *Bereichsopposition* is played out in cabinet and coalition bodies rather than parliament. Given the fragile nature of cabinets that since the 1970s have consisted of four to six parties, the danger of government destabilisation by *Bereichsopposition* has been considered simply too great for carrying much of it into the parliamentary arena. Consequently, a wide variety of inter-party and intra-party monitoring devices have been developed, all aiming at reinforcing coalition cohesion. First, the government agreements have become more comprehensive and strictly binding and ministerial initiatives are carefully scrutinised with regard to their conformity with this 'coalition bible'. For that purpose several coordination mechanisms have been set up within the individual parties and the government. There is a demanding code of conduct enforcing the collective and collegial behaviour of ministers, but in case of very heterogeneous cabinets it is nevertheless often violated.

With coalition cohesion and stability constantly under threat by the opposing views of many parties in government, the autonomy of actors external to the government had to be seriously reduced. This holds for the majority parliamentary groups and MPs that very rarely rebel against the compromises found at government level.[40] It also holds for the party executive (and rank-and-file) where ministers and the party president play a predominant role.[41] This leaves no space for the intervention of opposition parties, of non-pillarised pressure groups,[42] or of citizens through referenda. Consequently, with very few exceptions (such as the law on abortion), no party sought support amongst opposition parties in order to push through its proposals against the will of another government party.

Bereichsopposition became quite pronounced in the two most recent cabinets (composed of Liberals, Socialists and, in the first one, also the Greens). In these six-party (or four-party) cabinets, characterised by major policy divides, coalition discipline was frequently violated by ministers and their supporting parties. In this 'open debate culture', the collective nature of cabinet decision-making declined, as ministers were allowed to 'score' in their specific policy fields. Nevertheless, the opposition was kept at bay.

Bereichsopposition in Belgium traditionally also had intra-party sources, in particular the factionalised nature of the Christian Democratic party that participated in most post-war cabinets.[43] Yet de-pillarisation has weakened the impact of these 'estates' amongst Flemish Christian Democrats (but only since the 1990s) and it has virtually vanished amongst the French-speaking ones (since the 1980s). Hence, while inter-party *Bereichsopposition* has increased, intra-party *Bereichsopposition* has lost relevance.

PARLIAMENTARY VS. EXTRA-PARLIAMENTARY OPPOSITION

Consociational practices were never confined to the political arena alone. Pillarisation implied the existence of integrated networks of organisations belonging to the same pillar: political parties, trade unions and employers' organisations, media, organisations for housing, public health, education and so on. For socio-economic policies in particular, separate institutions were set up such as the 'Chambers' and the 'Parity Commission' in Austria or the 'PBO boards' in the Netherlands. Thus, consociationalism and corporatism were strongly interrelated concepts in Austria, Belgium, and the Netherlands. In Austria and Belgium, leadership, or at least coordination, of the various organisations within the pillar was provided by its political party, in particular within the Socialist pillars in these countries.[44] In the Netherlands, by contrast, the parties were less central to their respective pillar. The parties acted more as the pillar's embassy in The Hague. Party patronage did not dictate appointments to leadership positions in pillarised interest groups, while representatives of these organisations were offered safe parliamentary seats by the pillar's party. This led Van Schendelen to conclude that, from 1917 to 1960, 'pillarised groups ran the parliament'.[45]

However, for the relationship between parliamentary and extra-parliamentary opposition, this does not make a difference: the strong links between parties and organisations within pillars usually prevented incongruence between their strategies. Non-pillar organisations were weak or deliberately weakened by excluding them from corporatist arrangements (as happened to the Communist trade union in the Netherlands shortly after the Second World War). Any potential that non-pillar organisations might have had for mobilising citizens into an extra-parliamentary opposition were dampened by the control that pillar parties had over the mass media. In all three countries, pillar parties controlled their own newspapers. In Austria and Belgium, the broadcasting and TV were state-controlled. In Belgium an informal agreement ensured that the three main pillar parties were proportionally represented in the executives and councils of the broadcasting system. Similarly, the Austrian broadcasting corporation until the mid-1960s was one of the prime examples of *Proporz* – dividing government spoils between the ÖVP and SPÖ and their reporting largely ignoring the opposition. In the Netherlands, pillar control over the media was achieved by distributing broadcasting time on the state-owned channels proportionally to pillarised broadcasting associations.

De-pillarisation has created more room for a disjunction between the parliamentary and the extra-parliamentary opposition. Many pillar organisations have de-emphasised their sub-cultural identity in an effort to attract a broader public, and they now often face competition from new non-pillar organisations. This has not resulted in an end to corporatist consultations but corporatism has changed in nature. Now that institutional ties between parties and pressure groups have weakened, the government is a much more independent actor in negotiations with pressure groups. This independence was reinforced by government participation of parties without a background in pillarisation and corporatism, such as the FPÖ in Austria and the regionalist and green parties in Belgium, and of parties that have transformed themselves into anti-consociational and anti-corporatist parties, such as the Flemish Liberals in Belgium. 'Parliament is becoming more influential in political decision-making; even the parties are beginning to emancipate themselves from their corporatist complements', writes Crepaz about Austria.[46] This trend has further strengthened under the ÖVP–FPÖ coalition[47] and given the financial collapse of the Trade Union Congress after unsuccessful financial speculations it is hard to see how corporatism could see another spring under the current grand coalition. Van Schendelen reaches a similar conclusion for the Netherlands: since 1960 'parliamentary parties rival with pressure groups'.[48] Also in Belgium, the pillarised groups no longer maintain 'exclusive' relations with the party, but 'privileged' relations, also seeking 'sympathetic ears' in other parties in government and parliament. This was especially the case within the Catholic pillar, as its party was pushed into opposition for the first time in 40 years (1999–2007). The result is that pressure groups can rely less on bridgeheads within parliament and more often address the government directly. Conflicts in this relationship can now more easily lead to oppositional activity outside parliament, such as strikes and demonstrations.

This tendency is reinforced by the greater independence of the media. The traditional party press has declined in all three countries and the remaining print media have become less partisan. In Belgium, in 1996, a new law significantly reduced political control over the broadcasting stations. In Austria all parties have fought hard to gain or maintain influence over the public broadcasting corporation since the 1960s, leading to several reforms and changes in key personnel and periods of more or less independence from the parliamentary majority. Yet even in periods of more government control, the opposition parties find much better opportunities for airing their messages than in the time of strict *Proporz* broadcasting. In all three countries, the public broadcasting system now has to compete with commercial broadcasting stations, reducing the impact of political control over or independence of the former. This development provides easier access to extra-parliamentary organisations or to political entrepreneurs, to mobilise public opinion in opposition to the government.

The structure of opportunities has also become more advantageous for extra-parliamentary opposition through institutional changes such as European integration. One of the effects of the EU membership of these three countries is that it has strengthened the role of the judiciary and court action is now used more frequently as a means to oppose government policies. In the Netherlands, the judiciary has also adapted the definition of an 'interested party', making it easier for interest groups to go to court. Referenda, such as the Belgian referendum on the return of the King (1950) and the Austrian referendum on nuclear power (1978) were occasions when the emphasis clearly shifted from the parliamentary to the extra-parliamentary arena. In practice, EU membership has also affected the use of the referendum: referenda on European integration in Austria, and recently also in the Netherlands provide an occasion to mobilise extra-parliamentary opposition. When a referendum was held on the EU constitutional treaty in the Netherlands in 2005, both the government and the main opposition party, the Social Democrats, were in favour of the European constitution (after all these parties had supported European integration from the very start). In parliament, opposition came primarily from small parties: SP on the Left, and the Christian Union in particular on the Right. These small parties successfully turned public opinion from indifference into opposition: with a turnout of over 63 per cent, the treaty was rejected by 61.5 per cent. In Belgium, the submittal of the Treaty to the population by referendum was also briefly discussed, but abandoned, for two reasons. First, the constitution does not allow it and a repetition of the disastrous results of the referendum on the King's Question (resulting in opposite results among Flemish and French speakers) could accelerate the disintegration of the Belgian state. Second, elites feared that the referendum would be abused by the *Vlaams Belang*, turning the question into a vote against Turkish accession.

FROM OPPOSITION WITHOUT COMPETITION TO COMPETITION WITHOUT OPPOSITION

Austria, Belgium and the Netherlands are treated together in this article because all three countries are generally known as classic cases of consociational democracy. From our reading of consociational theory, we derive a number of hypotheses concerning the composition of the government and the parliamentary opposition, the competitiveness of parliamentary elections, the institutional opportunities for parliamentary opposition and the use made of these opportunities, and the relation between the parliamentary and extra-parliamentary opposition. The common denominator of these hypotheses is that under consociationalism there was no lack of opposition, but this did not lead to real competition. From the 1960s onward, all three countries have experienced de-pillarisation in some form, and to some extent. From the perspective of consociational theory, de-pillarisation has reduced the need for consociational practices and we may find that our expectations concerning opposition in our countries are no longer valid. And if they continued to be valid despite de-pillarisation, we may expect the emergence of an anti-system opposition.

Not all our theoretical expectations derived from consociational theory found equal support in the political history of Austria, Belgium and the Netherlands. Even when social segmentation was still at its zenith, all-party coalitions were practically absent at the national level and although most governing coalitions could count on very safe margins in parliamentary votes, coalitions including more parties than strictly necessary for a parliamentary majority were less common than might be expected. Non-pillar parties were usually excluded from participation in government, but their opposition in parliament was often reinforced by one or two pillar parties, at least in Belgium and the Netherlands. Measured by electoral volatility, elections were not very competitive, but this was not that uncommon in Europe in those years. Any lack of active parliamentary opposition cannot be attributed to very restrictive parliamentary rules and institutions, though we have noted clear differences between the countries in this respect. Writing about opposition under consociationalism, Engelmann speaks of a 'pooling of opposition' in Austria, and Daalder refers to an opposition that 'dissolves into the system' in the Netherlands.[49] Such terms are appropriate when we realise that government ministers often met with opposition from MPs belonging to the other party in the coalition (*Bereichsopposition* in Austria), and that opposition MPs sometimes supported government proposals precisely because they had an opportunity to influence these proposals during parliamentary proceedings (especially in the Netherlands). Exceptions notwithstanding, the integration of many extra-parliamentary organisations and mass media into the pillarised networks did make it difficult to distinguish a parliamentary and an extra-parliamentary opposition in those days.

De-pillarisation has indeed caused changes in the patterns of opposition (or at least de-pillarisation and these changes are correlated) but often these changes were smaller and more gradual than might be expected. The coalition status of governments has not changed much except in the Netherlands, but its composition has. Although governments are still dominated by pillar parties, non-pillar parties have gained access to the governmental arena. The opposition is now also more varied in composition. Elections have become more competitive or at least more volatile but this has not been a linear development, especially not in Belgium. There are also signs of increased competition in parliament, with more frequent use being made of parliamentary instruments in the legislative process and parliamentary oversight. Finally, the disintegration of the pillarised networks has given extra-parliamentary organisations more freedom to initiate or join extra-parliamentary oppositions, and it has given any extra-parliamentary opposition more access to the mass media in order to mobilise public opinion.

Not surprisingly, political reality of opposition in Austria, Belgium and the Netherlands is more variegated than the stylised picture we inferred from consociational theory. Nevertheless, at the heyday of consociationalism, opposition in the three countries was not absent, but not very active or competitive, and since de-pillarisation began, competition has increased in elections, and in parliament. However, the ideological differences between the political parties have also become less pronounced since de-pillarisation. This is sometimes seen as the cause of de-pillarisation (citizens no longer feel a need to remain loyal to the pillar now that the pillars are ideologically less distinct), and sometimes as a result of de-pillarisation (dealignment forcing the party to adopt a catch-all strategy), but in either case the result is that competition may have increased, whereas ideological opposition has decreased. During the era of pillarisation we had distinct pillar parties forming a sometimes uneasy cartel, but now we see a development towards cartel parties.[50] This 'waning of oppositions'[51] is also visible in the relations between the major parties. Writing about current Dutch politics, Koole and Daalder observe: 'the present consensual atmosphere differs from that of the days of pillarisation, in that it is due to converging visions on many political issues rather than to negotiations among political elites despite their initial differences in principle. One could say, in somewhat exaggerated terms: compromises then, consensus now.'[52]

Koole and Daalder seem to echo Lijphart's misgivings a third of a century ago: 'The abandonment of strictly competitive politics in consociational democracies is a deliberate response to the tensions of a fragmented society, whereas the adoption of grand coalition politics in depoliticized democracy is in response to the convergence of ideologies.'[53] Has Lijphart's prediction that this would give rise to anti-system oppositions also come true? Lijphart and Dahl expected this new opposition to come from the radical Left, seeking to democratise and 'to reconstruct the Leviathan to a more nearly human scale'.[54] The rise of the Greens in Belgium and Austria might fit this prediction (the Dutch Greens are merely an amalgamation of pre-existing Leftist parties), but the most visible anti-system opposition that has developed in all three countries is coming from the populist Right. In Austria, Jörg Haider's transformation of the FPÖ and its subsequent electoral successes (becoming Austria's second largest party in the 1999 elections) have been linked with the party's attacks on consociationalism and corporatism.[55] In Belgium the steady growth of the VB (*Vlaams Blok*, now *Vlaams Belang*) has also profited from criticising the cosy cartel of the old pillar parties. In the Netherlands, the spectacular rise of Pim Fortuyn and his LPF has widely been interpreted as a sign of alienation from the ruling political class, or 'The Hague'.[56]

Admittedly, the success of the populist Right in the three countries cannot be attributed solely to anti-cartel sentiments. Interpreting the motives of voters for these parties is exceedingly difficult, not least because of the social stigma attached to supporting them. Populism is usually defined as a revolt of a 'pure and homogeneous people' against a 'corrupt political class'. In addition to disenchantment with the ruling elites, anxiety about a multicultural erosion of the 'Volk' will therefore play an important role for many voters. Moreover, country-specific motives, such as Flemish nationalism in Belgium, should not be discounted either. However, it remains reasonable to assume that the appeal of the populist Right is at least partly due to the fact that it offers an opposition to a system in which voters are not offered clear choices, either during the election campaigns or in terms of policies that the parties they voted for implement once in power.

In Belgium, the populist Right has been confined to the parliamentary opposition. So far, no other parties have defected from the tacit agreement to erect a *cordon sanitaire* around the VB.[57] This strategy for dealing with the new anti-system opposition differs radically from the one pursued in Austria and the Netherlands. In Austria, after the FPÖ's spectacular success in the 1999 elections, the party entered a coalition with the ÖVP in 2000. This new government was controversial within Austria, but even more so with other EU Member States, led by Belgium. EU sanctions, such as a freezing of bilateral contacts and a refusal to support Austrian candidates for positions in international organisations, were largely inconsequential. The sanctions were lifted after a few months. In the Netherlands, no political party ever made a more impressive debut than the LPF, becoming the second largest party in parliament in 2002. Its leader, Pim Fortuyn, had been assassinated by an animal rights activist a few days before the elections, plunging the country into unprecedented turmoil. In this situation, the decision to invite the LPF to join a governing coalition with Christian Democrats and Liberals was hardly controversial in the Netherlands, and the other EU Member States did not want to repeat the mistake they had made only two years earlier. In both Austria and the Netherlands, winning seats in government has proved to be a poisoned chalice for the populists.[58] Unable to meet the high expectations of their supporters, both the FPÖ and LPF quickly dropped in the polls: in the 2002 elections in Austria, the FPÖ dropped from 26.9 per cent to 10.2 per cent; in the 2003 elections in the Netherlands, the LPF dropped from 17 to 5.7 per cent, and in the 2007 elections the party disappeared from parliament. Internal conflicts contributed to the decline of these parties. In Austria, conflicts soon emerged between those who put a premium on government participation and those more interested in maintaining the party's radical agenda, eventually leading to a split into two parties: the FPÖ and BZÖ (*Bündnis Zukunft Österreich*, led by Haider). Being a new party, and having lost its leader, internal conflicts were even quicker to emerge in the Dutch LPF. Conflicts among its ministers, among its MPs, and in the party executive over policy, party finance, and above all over personality, were the order of the day. Deemed too unstable to be a governing party, the LPF was dropped from the coalition after only 87 days in office. These Austrian and Dutch experiences are regularly referred to by commentators who expect that the *cordon sanitaire* in Belgium will only serve to make the populist Right stronger and bigger, but so far this has not led to a change in the pattern of opposition in Belgium. The *cordon sanitaire* pushed the VB into its favourite role as underdog, boosting its scores at every election. This trend was (temporarily?) halted at the local, provincial, and general elections of 2006 and 2007. However, this was mainly due to the emergence of another right-wing, but non-racist, populist party – Lijst De Decker.

On the other hand, the deadly embrace of the Austrian and Dutch populists by the established parties may only give these political systems a temporary reprieve from anti-system challenges if it leads to a return to 'competition without opposition'. As post-consociational countries, Austria, Belgium and the Netherlands are all three still struggling, each in its own way, to find new patterns of government and opposition that make the governments of these countries truly accountable and provide the voters in these countries with a real choice. To the extent that a trend towards 'cartel parties' can be observed in Europe more generally, this quest is not peculiar to Austria, Belgium or the Netherlands, but given their history, the problem may be more acute in these three countries.

NOTES

1. O. Kirchheimer, 'Germany: The Vanishing Opposition', in R.A. Dahl (ed.), *Political Oppositions in Western Democracies* (New Haven, CT: Yale University Press, 1966), p.237.
2. A. Lijphart, 'Consociational Democracy', *World Politics*, 21 (1969), p.216

3. A. Lijphart, *Democracy in Plural Societies: A Comparative Explanation* (New Haven, CT: Yale University Press, 1977), pp.25–47.
4. See Lijphart, *Democracy in Plural Societies*; A. Lijphart, *Power-Sharing in South Africa* (Berkeley, CA: Institute for International Studies, 1985), pp.83–117; A. Lijphart, 'Democratic Political Systems: Types, Cases, Causes, and Consequences', *Journal of Theoretical Politics*, 1 (1989), pp.33–48; R.B. Andeweg, 'Consociational Democracy', *Annual Review of Political Science*, 3 (2000), pp.509–36.
5. R.B. Andeweg, 'Parties, Pillars and the Politics of Accommodation: Weak or Weakening Linkages? The Case of Dutch Consociationalism', in K.R. Luther and K. Deschouwer (eds.), *Party Elites in Divided Societies* (London: Routledge, 1999), pp.110–21.
6. K. Deschouwer, 'And the Peace Goes On? Consociational Democracy and Belgian Politics in the Twenty-first Century', *West European Politics*, 29 (2006), pp.895–911.
7. See F. Plasser, P.A. Ulram, and F. Grausgruber, 'The Decline of "Lager Mentality" and the New Model of Electoral Competition in Austria', in K.R. Luther and W.C. Müller (eds.), *Politics in Austria: Still a Case of Consociationalism?* (London: Frank Cass, 1992), pp.16–44.
8. A. Lijphart, 'Typologies of Democratic Systems', *Comparative Political Studies*, 1 (1968), pp.36–7.
9. Lijphart, 'Typologies of Democratic Systems', p.37.
10. Lijphart, 'Typologies of Democratic Systems', p.39.
11. R.A. Dahl, 'Epilogue', in Dahl (ed.), *Political Oppositions in Western Democracies*, p.400.
12. It should be added that Lijphart is now more optimistic about consensus government without deep social divisions. See R.B. Andeweg, 'Lijphart versus Lijphart: The Cons of Consensus Government in Homogeneous Societies', *Acta Politica*, 36 (2001), pp.117–28 and A. Lijphart, 'The Pros and Cons – but mainly Pros – of Consensus Democracy', *Acta Politica*, 36 (2001), pp.129–39.
13. It can be argued that the League of Independents (VdU) and the Freedom Party (FPÖ) also represent a pillar – the German-national one. However, this pillar has been much smaller and it did not constitute one of the two camps that had to be reconsolidated by consociational arrangements.
14. See W.H. Riker, *The Theory of Political Coalitions* (New Haven, CT: Yale University Press, 1962).
15. M. Méndez-Lago, 'Electoral Consequences of (De-)pillarization: The Cases of Austria, Belgium and the Netherlands (1945–1996)', in Luther and Deschouwer (eds.), *Party Elites in Divided Societies*, p.206.
16. J.Th.J. van den Berg and H.A.A. Molleman, *Crisis in de Nederlandse Politiek* (Alphen ann den Rijn: Samsom, 2nd edn.,1975).
17. Figures from A. Lijphart, *Patterns of Democracy* (New Haven, CT: Yale University Press, 1999).
18. M. Gallagher and P. Mitchell, 'Conclusion', in M. Gallagher and P. Mitchell (eds.), *The Politics of Electoral Systems* (Oxford: Oxford University Press, 2005), p.546.
19. W.C. Müller 'Wahlsysteme und Parteiensystem in Österreich, 1945–1995', in F. Plasser, P.A. Ulram and G. Ogris (eds.), *Wahlkampf und Wählerentscheidung. Analysen zur Nationalratswahl 1995* (Vienna: Signum, 1996), pp.233–72.
20. I. Mattson and K. Strøm, 'Parliamentary Committees', in H. Döring (ed.), *Parliaments and Majority Rule in Western Europe* (New York: St. Martin's Press, 1995), pp.249–307.
21. For a detailed description of the rule changes see B. Auracher-Jäger, *Die Mechanismen im Nationalrat* (Vienna: Verlag Österreich, 1997).
22. H. Sickinger, 'Austria', in T.D. Grant (ed.), *Lobbying, Government Relations and Campaign Finance Worldwide* (Oxford: Oceana Publications, 2005), p.23.
23. L. De Winter and M. Brans, 'Belgium: Political Professionals and the Crisis of the Party State', in J. Borchert and J. Zeiss (eds.), *The Political Class in Advanced Democracies* (Oxford: Oxford University Press, 2003), pp.45–66.
24. Döring classified government control over parliament's agenda by seven aspects (such as the authority to determine the plenary agenda, or the possibility of curtailing debate). If we sum the scores of the countries on all seven aspects to arrive at an overall scale ranging from 1

(high government control) to 28 (low government control), Austria has a total score of 19, Belgium of 22 and the Netherlands of 25. In all three countries the agenda of the plenary meeting is formally a majority decision but usually the agenda is decided by consensual agreement in the Speaker's conference of parliamentary group leaders or their representatives; the introduction of money bills is not restricted to the government in Austria and Belgium; debates before the final vote in plenary sessions can only be cut short by mutual agreement between the parliamentary parties in all three countries. See H. Döring, 'Parliamentary Agenda Control and Legislative Outcomes in Western Europe', *Legislative Studies Quarterly*, 26 (2001), pp.145–65.

25. R.B. Andeweg, 'Executive–Legislative Relations in the Netherlands: Consecutive and Coexisting Patterns', *Legislative Studies Quarterly*, 18 (1992), pp.161–82.

26. P. Gerlich, *Parlamentarische Kontrolle im politischen System* (Vienna: Springer, 1973).

27. G. Schefbeck, 'Das Parlament', in H. Dachs, P. Gerlich, H. Gottweis, H. Kramer, V. Lauber, W.C. Müller, and E. Tálos (eds.), *Politik in Österreich: Das Handbuch* (Vienna: Manz, 2006), p.158.

28. F. Fallend, 'Demokratische Kontrolle oder Inquisition?', *Österreichische Zeitschrift für Politikwissenschaft*, 29 (2000), pp.177–200.

29. G. Visscher, *Parlementaire Invloed op Wetgeving* (Den Haag: SDU, 1994), pp.261, 293, 375–76.

30. A. King, 'Modes of Executive–Legislative Relations: Great Britain, France, and Western Germany', *Legislative Studies Quarterly*, 1 (1976), pp.11–36.

31. E. Langerwerf, 'Het stemgedrag in het parlement. Onderzoek in de Kamer van Volksvertegenwoordigers voor de periode 1954–1965', *Res Publica*, 22 (1980), pp.177–88.

32. M. Verminck, 'Concensus en oppositie in het Belgisch parlement tijdens een verkiezingsjaar', *Res Publica*, 28 (1986), pp.475–87.

33. W.C. Müller and M. Jenny, '"Business as usual" mit getauschten Rollen oder Konflikt- statt Konsensdemokratie?', *Österreichische Zeitschrift für Politikwissenschaft*, 33 (2004), pp.307–24; Schefbeck, 'Das Parlament'; W.C. Müller, 'Parteiensystem: Rahmenbedingungen, Format und Mechanik des Parteienwettbewerbs', in Dachs *et al.* (eds.), *Politik in Österreich: Das Handbuch*, pp.279–304.

34. See F.C. Engelmann, 'Austria: The Pooling of Opposition', in Dahl (ed.), *Political Oppositions in Western Democracies*, pp.270–72.

35. W.C. Müller, M. Jenny, B. Steininger, M. Dolezal, W. Philipp and S. Westphal-Preisl, *Die österreichischen Abgeordneten* (Vienna: Fakultas, 2001), pp.306–18.

36. Fallend, 'Demokratische Kontrolle oder Inquisition?'

37. O. Kirchheimer, 'The Waning of Opposition in Parliamentary Regimes', *Social Research*, 24 (1957), p. 156.

38. W.C. Müller, 'Austria: Tight Coalitions and Stable Government', in W.C. Müller and K. Strøm (eds.), *Coalition Governments in Western Europe* (Oxford: Oxford University Press, 2000), pp.86–125.

39. W.C. Müller, 'Executive–Legislative Relations in Austria: 1945–1992', *Legislative Studies Quarterly*, 18 (1993), pp.467–94; W.C. Müller and F. Fallend, 'Changing Patterns of Party Competition in Austria: From Multipolar to Bipolar System', *West European Politics*, 27 (2004), pp.801–35.

40. Various studies concerned with different legislative terms first indicate very high numbers of party disciplined votes. In 1954–65, in four out of ten votes there were one or more rebels against the party line; in the 1990s this was true for only three out of ten votes. Generally, these 'rebellions' do not involve more than a single MP who abstains or cross-votes. Also, most 'rebels' abstain rather than cross the floor.

41. L. De Winter and P. Dumont, 'PPGs in Belgium: Subjects of Partitocratic Dominion', in K. Heidar and R. Koole (eds.), *Behind Closed Doors: Parliamentary Party Groups in European Democracies* (London: Routledge, 2000), pp.106–29; L. De Winter and P. Dumont, 'Do Belgian Parties Undermine the Democratic Chain of Delegation?', *West European Politics*, 29 (2006), pp.957–76.

42. L. De Winter, 'Belgium: Insider Pressure Groups in an Outsider Parliament', in P. Norton (ed.), *Parliaments and Pressure Groups in Western Europe* (London: Frank Cass, 1999), pp.88–109.

43. L. De Winter, 'Parties and Policy in Belgium', *European Journal of Political Research*, 17 (1989), pp.707–30.
44. See Luther and Deschouwer (eds.), *Party Elites in Divided Societies*.
45. M.P.C.M. Van Schendelen, 'The Netherlands: Parliamentary Parties Rival with Pressure Groups', in Norton (ed.), *Parliaments and Pressure Groups in Western Europe*, p.110.
46. M. Crepaz, 'Domestic and External Constraints on Austrian Corporatism: Challenges and Opportunities', *Acta Politica*, 37 (2002), p.171.
47. E. Tálos and C. Stromberger, 'Abkehr von der Verhandlungsdemokratie', in E. Tálos and F. Karlhofer (eds.), *Sozialpartnerschaft* (Vienna: Lit Verlag, 2005); E. Tálos (ed.), *Schwarz – Blau. Eine Bilanz des 'Neu-Regierens'* (Vienna: Lit Verlag, 2006).
48. Van Schendelen, 'The Netherlands', pp.110–23.
49. Engelmann, 'Austria: The Pooling of Opposition'; H. Daalder, 'The Netherlands: Opposition in a Segmented Society', in Dahl (ed.), *Political Oppositions in Western Democracies*, p.235.
50. R.S. Katz and P. Mair, 'Changing Models of Party Organization and Party Democracy: The Emergence of the Cartel Party', *Party Politics*, 1 (1995), pp.5–28. See, however, H. Kitschelt, 'Citizens, Politicians, and Party Cartellization: Political Representation and State Failure in Post-industrial Democracies', *European Journal of Political Research*, 37 (2000), pp.149–79.
51. O. Kirchheimer, 'The Waning of Oppositions', pp.127–56.
52. R. Koole and H. Daalder, 'The Consociational Politics Model and The Netherlands: Ambivalent Allies', *Acta Politica*, 37 (2002), p.39.
53. Lijphart, 'Typologies of Democratic Systems', p.39.
54. Dahl, 'Epilogue', p.400.
55. W.C. Müller, 'Evil or the "Engine of Democracy"? Populism and Party Competition in Austria', in Y. Mény and Y. Surel (eds.), *Populism in Western Democracies* (Houndmills: Palgrave Macmillan, 2002), pp.155–75; K. R. Luther, 'The Self-Destruction of a Right-Wing Populist Party? The Austrian Parliamentary Election of 2002', *West European Politics*, 26 (2003), pp.136–52.
56. G.A. Irwin and J.J.M. van Holsteyn, 'Never a Dull Moment: Pim Fortuyn and the Dutch Parliamentary Elections of 2002', *West European Politics*, 26 (2003), pp.41–66.
57. L. De Winter, M. Gomez-Reino and J. Buelens, 'The Extreme-right Flemish-nationalist Vlaams Blok', in L. De Winter, M. Gomez, and P. Lynch (eds.), *Autonomist Parties in Europe: Identity Politics and the Revival of the Territorial Cleavage* (Barcelona: ICPS, Vol. II, 2006), pp. 47–78.
58. See also R. Heinisch, 'Success in Opposition – Failure in Government: Explaining the Performance of Right-Wing Populist Parties in Public Office', *West European Politics*, 26 (2003), pp.91–130.

Parliamentary Opposition under (Post-)One-Party Rule: Japan

TAKASHI INOGUCHI

When T.J. Pempel edited a volume entitled *Uncommon Democracies* in 1990, not only Japan but also Italy, Sweden and Israel had a one-party dominant regime. Even Britain and West Germany were regarded as being akin to the regimes covered in the volume.[1] But since then Japan has been the only one-party dominant regime among the advanced industrial democracies, albeit with an 11-month-long out-of-power status registered in 1993–94. Table 1 shows the parliamentary power distribution as of 8 June 2006. The predominant status of the Liberal Democratic Party in the House of Representatives and its less-than-simple majority status in the House of Councillors are clear from the table.

This article gives an account of the Japanese parliamentary opposition which has been a player of a sort under a one-party dominant regime for some half a century. In what follows, first, the historical features of the Japanese political system are briefly summarised to highlight some of the structural conditions that favour a long-standing one-party dominance in a democracy. The time span of this historical summary covers centuries, starting in the late sixteenth century.[2] The article contends that the floundering of absolutism in late medieval Japan, the quasi-federal arrangements in early modern Japan,

TABLE 1
PARLIAMENTARY POWER DISTRIBUTION IN JAPAN AS OF JUNE 2006

House of Representatives		Party	House of Councillors
	292	Liberal Democratic Party	111
	113	Democratic Party of Japan + Non-affiliates	–
	–	Democratic Party of Japan+ New Green Wind	82
	31	New Komei Party	24
	9	Japan Communist Party	9
	7	Social Democratic Party + Civil League	–
	–	Social Democratic Party + Protect Constitution League	6
	6	New Nation Party + Japan Party + Non-affiliates	–
	–	New Nation Party + New Party Japan + Non-affiliates	5
	20	Non-affiliates	5
	2	Absent	–
Total	480		242

Source: Narita Norihiko, 'Koakkai (National Diet)', in *IMIDAS, Tokyo: Shueisha, 2007*, p.481.

and the nationwide inclusionary push in modernising Japan have all left their mark on the contemporary Japanese political system. Although it might seem that the historical argument is overstretched, it is very important to address, at least briefly, the nature of Japanese political development before dealing with the parliamentary opposition since 1945. Second, focusing on the post-Second World War period, the article traces the three distinctive sub-periods of Japanese democracy, (1) democracy under military occupation, (2) democracy during state developmentalism and (3) democracy in an era of globalisation. Drawing on the argument made by Ethan Scheiner, it is contended here that one-party dominance was consolidated during the second sub-period of post-war democracy in Japan. Clientelism and the centralised governmental structure were finely tuned during this period. Into the third sub-period the tide of globalisation seems to be eroding some of the key conditions of one-party dominance. Third, we examine the nature of parliamentary opposition in Japan on the basis of the historical evolution of the Japanese political system and its historical and structural settings since 1945.[3]

HISTORICAL FOUNDATIONS: FLOUNDERED ABSOLUTISM, QUASI-FEDERAL ARRANGEMENTS AND INCLUSIONARY PUSH

The three phrases in the heading above need some explanation: Floundered absolutism refers to the assassination of Nobunaga, a great warrior who put an end to the medieval period in 1582 as he was midway towards military unification of Japan; floundered absolutism means that power in Japan at the time was decentralised rather than centralised; quasi-federal arrangements mean the early modern rearrangement of the Tokugawa shogun with its monopoly of defence and foreign trade and the provision of semi-autonomy to 300-odd domains for all matters except for the critical one of anti-Tokugawa thought and action; inclusionary push means the nationwide inclusion of the population, abolishing the semi-autonomous domains and the feudal class distinction. The Tokugawa arrangement was a quasi-federal arrangement. Furthermore the Meiji Restoration in 1868 was the inclusionary centralisation by which the nationwide institution and economy were fully created. However, it is important to emphasise that the administrative institution at the highest level, the central bureaucracy, was decentralised to an excessive degree.[4] Once the four feudal class distinctions – warriors, peasants, artisans and merchants – were abolished shortly after the Meiji Restoration, the entire elite corps of warriors lost their jobs. A scramble for jobs took place and the fledgling central bureaucracy accommodated the bulk of them. Those who engineered the Meiji Restoration took the lead and hired like-minded men (who were often men from the same domain) into the central bureaucracy. What happened was that each bureaucratic agency (at least in its early years) was built on the basis of similar domain backgrounds. Hence the strong domination of the Choshu men in the Army, of the Satsuma domain in the Navy, of the Nabeshima domain in the Accounting Office, of men from the Mito, Aizuwakamatsu, and Okazaki domains in the National Police, and so on. The Imperial Constitution dispersed power at all levels under the Emperor whose authority was more symbolic than absolutist. The prime minister was little more than a *primus inter pares*, and any cabinet minister defying him easily caused the fall of the entire cabinet.[5] In this sense the Meiji Restoration inherited much from the early modern Tokugawa arrangements. With its slogan 'rich nation, strong army' the Meiji state was seemingly highly centralised on the surface and with regard to the electorate. But at the highest level of the government, it was in fact excessively decentralised with each bureaucratic agency enjoying wide-ranging autonomy and strong veto powers vis-à-vis other rival actors.[6] When the civil service examination system was introduced and meritocratic considerations came to dominate the recruitment processes, the strongly decentralised nature of the central bureaucracy became even more institutionalised.

The post-Second World War political system inherited much of these legacies. In fact, many of the individual components of the ancient regime were brought to perfection. The newly drafted constitution defined the Emperor as the symbol of the nation. The Supreme Commander of the Allied Powers, General MacArthur, delegated the entirety of his routine work to the Japanese central bureaucracy after purging some of the conspicuous wartime leaders. Also, universal suffrage was realised immediately after the start of the military occupation period. All these devices and arrangements were to be given opportunity to blossom when peace and stability dominated Japanese society.

THREE DISTINCTIVE SUB-PERIODS OF THE POST-WAR POLITICAL SYSTEM

Within our temporal focus, that is, the period between 1945 and 2007, three distinctive sub-periods can be distinguished. During each sub-period, the nature of parliamentary opposition is delineated along with several key features. Having been soundly defeated in the Second World War, Japan was occupied by Allied forces for seven years. The US (specifically General Douglas MacArthur) led the Allies, occupying and reforming Japan by indirect, rather than direct, rule. This choice was based on the perception that the forces were not dealing with the Japanese who had intrepidly resisted throughout a war they had almost no hope of winning, but rather with a Japanese people who welcomed the occupation forces warmly. Moreover, since the US government's top priority was the global confrontation with Communism, it was deemed preferable that as much of the actual governing as possible be turned over to the people of the occupied nation themselves. Few people doubt that the foundations for Japan's contemporary political system were rebuilt during the occupation years.[7] First, the groups in power who had led Japan into war were dissolved and purged. Second, most of the central bureaucrats and personnel, with the exception of war leaders and prominent bureaucrats who conspired with them, were retained nearly *in toto*. Third, the restructuring of the political parties was undertaken mostly by younger bureaucrats who rose to the top during the occupation, middle-aged politicians who were purged as war leaders or conspirators during the war and occupation, and younger politicians who emerged on the scene after the war. This restructuring paved the way for the emergence of the Liberal Democratic Party (LDP) as a centre-right party by 1955. Fourth, freedom of expression, labour unions, and a general election system emerged as part of the new framework put forth under occupation reforms, and the left wing was able to expand its power significantly as well. Fifth, Japanese citizens gradually adapted to the new framework and general elections in particular came to function as a means of conveying public opinion to politicians.

LDP ADAPTATIONS THROUGH THREE DISTINCT SUB-PERIODS

As the nature of parliamentary opposition in Japan is closely related to the structural features of a one-party dominant regime, we must briefly describe these features. The political priorities during the first sub-period addressed, the years of occupation and reconstruction formed the cornerstone of the political thinking that later came to be called the Yoshida doctrine.[8] Based on pacifism, this doctrine renounced Japanese participation in war. The Japan–US Security Treaty was designed for the continuation of the military aspects of occupation by Allied forces, leaving Japan markedly dependent on the United States in terms of security. Also devoted to economic growth, the Yoshida doctrine focused on reconstruction to boost Japan to a respected position within the international community. Initially, however, there was an extremely strong domestic opposition to the Yoshida doctrine during the occupation and thereafter, and it took a great deal of work to incorporate this doctrine into the Japanese political structure.

This was an era of intense political conflict in Japan. Immediately after the war, extreme poverty drove a large portion of the population to oppose the government. As recovery and reconstruction gradually began to take hold, the centre-right gained power with strong support from the self-employed. This happened in 1955.[9] The transition to power was instrumental for the founding of the Liberal Democratic Party of Japan the same year. The farmland reforms devised under the occupation created a large class of landowning farmers and support for the LDP increased even in outlying rural areas which had been at the heart of the massive pre-war farmers' movement. The growing support from self-employed businessmen in response to government subsidies and other frameworks also fell under this umbrella. Although it is true that the LDP was at times referred to as 'a provincial party', the vast majority of Japan was in fact provincial during the occupation. In this sub-period, policy priorities revolved primarily around economic management policy to ensure economic recovery and reconstruction through government regulation and administrative guidance designed to address various issues: guaranteeing food provisions for the people, guaranteeing energy supplies (coal for thermal power, dams for hydroelectric power, etc.), the processes for obtaining corporate capital from banks and other institutions, and obtaining the foreign currency required to achieve this.

If there was one predominant ministry during this sub-period, it was the Economic Planning Agency (known at the time as the Headquarters for Economic Stabilisation). The driving force behind this agency was the bureaucrats who had graduated from engineering departments and had experienced an economy mobilised for war during the 1930s and 1940s. The low standard of income and the high unemployment rate drove popular opposition to the government. Rising from the ashes was a matter of survival for both the nation and the individual. Based on this popular sentiment against the government, opposition parties enjoyed strong support during this period. Occupation reforms served to strengthen corporate and governmental labour unions, and opposition parties used this energy to their advantage.

Both in the electoral and the parliamentary arena, political conflict was exceptionally intense. There was, more specifically, strong opposition to the country's military relationship with the United States. At the time, factions who felt that welcoming US military bases would embroil Japan in military actions, or serve to invite war against Japan, held greater sway than those who felt it would discourage or prevent Japanese involvement in war. The party that would later become the LDP took the latter stance, while the Japan Socialist Party and the Japanese Communist Party took the former. Another aspect of political contention was the issue of whether building fundamental economic strength to promote national recovery and reconstruction should be given priority or whether greater concern should be given to improving the household finances of Japanese families and individuals. The former was put forth by a group that would later become the LDP, while the Socialist Party and the Communist Party took the latter as their platform.

During the second sub-period, the years of strong economic growth, Japan was a nation following bureaucracy-driven development. Under this model of development, bureaucrats took the lead in directing the strong momentum behind economic development in an attempt to guarantee the most effective management of the national economy.[10]

It was normal procedure for government agencies to present the general principles of policy drafted by themselves to governing parties and the business community. The fact that government agencies have at times been teased with the adage 'bureaucracy overrules politics' illustrates just how strongly Japanese development was ultimately driven by the bureaucrats in government. However, this bureaucracy-driven political structure hardly marked a completely new feature of government and administration in Japan: its roots lie in the Tokugawa period (1603–1867). It was in the early stages of the Tokugawa period that warriors were disarmed and became bureaucrats living in castle towns.[11] This marked a striking contrast to the historical developments in neighbouring Korea, where the Chosun Dynasty brought men of letters and scholars into the bureaucracy.[12]

Although with the Meiji Restoration the governing unit shifted from the feudal clan to the nation, the bureaucracy-driven regime itself remained almost intact. A parliamentary democracy was introduced in stages after the Meiji Restoration, and politicians came to occupy the political landscape in addition to bureaucrats. Japanese politicians were not necessarily part of the bureaucracy, but had a difficult time taking action without the bureaucrats on their side – as is illustrated by the fact that politicians originally emerged as a force in opposition to government, whereas bureaucrats represented the powers-that-be in the government.[13] Although the Japanese Constitution would seem to indicate that politicians hold a higher position than bureaucrats, this was not necessarily the case in constitutional practice.

It was for this reason that among LDP Diet members some were extolled as 'special interest/issue-specific legislators' who wielded considerable influence over policy due to their career histories and experience in specialised areas of party committees and Diet Committees. Though farmers and self-employed businessmen formed the basis of support for the LDP during this period, a new body of support for the party came from the 'new middle-class masses' which emerged as strong economic growth and the accompanying benefits spread throughout the entire country.[14] In the course of events, the relative importance of farmers and self-employed businessmen among LDP supporters declined steadily, which is reflected in the slight drop of the overall number of Diet seats that the party secured in general elections. However, the structural changes at the level of society did not pose too critical a problem for the LDP, as the majority of the Japanese people considered themselves to be part of the new middle-class masses.

The party's high-priority policies during this sub-period were focused on securing Japan's place among the advanced nations and on achieving a stable and competitive economic management that would enable the country to maintain this position.[15] Specifically, macro-economic management and social policy were the top priorities. While the first aspect needs no further explanation, the LDP gradually became more keenly aware that it would need to bolster its social policies if it were to keep the political and electoral support of the new middle-class masses – a realisation that was driven by the stagnation and downward trend in LDP support. As income levels rose, the majority of the population came to identify themselves as part of the new middle-class masses, and the elderly accounted for only 5–7 per cent of the population.

Given the rise in income levels coupled with a decline in the ratio of workers organised in labour unions, one would expect the opposition parties to lose political and electoral support. However, with extreme fluctuations in the overall strength of government and opposition parties, support for the opposition parties in fact rose considerably during this period. The extreme fluctuation in the rate of support can be attributed to the fact that the opposition parties were able at times to attract a significant portion of the massive block of the new middle-classes. While the opposition parties have moved closer to the political trajectory of the governing parties, it is also true that too much similarity between multiple parties can cause conflicts. It is equally true that the constant appeal by opposition parties for greater emphasis on social policies basically prompted the governing parties to prioritise social policies, and opposition parties' advocacy of pacifism has caused the governing parties to give greater weight in their policies to strengthening ties with other nations than the United States. Though support for the opposition parties traditionally came from the social strata among the new middle classes that value pacifism and equality, this support declined in more than a few mass production/mass consumption industries that acquired foreign currency as market liberalisation steadily advanced. Pacifism can lead to protectionism, and this tendency diluted the influence of this variety of principled stance. It is, however, the nature of politics that governing parties at times lose to opposition parties. There is no shortage of scandals involving bribes, corruption, and slips of the tongue, and it is these scandals that allow the opposition parties to make significant progress in terms of electoral gains.

The third sub-period to be examined is that of globalisation, which spans roughly from 1985 through to the present. It was in 1985 that the Plaza Accord was signed by the G5 nations. The Plaza Accord was a revolutionary agreement that normalised purchases of one currency in another currency. Before this, goods and service trading had been the norm, with very little currency trading taking place. In the one-year period from 1985 to 1986, however, currency trading was 50 to 100 times higher than goods and service trading, and has remained at this level ever since. Dramatically promoting financial integration on a global scale, the Plaza Accord symbolises the galloping stride of globalisation.[16]

Globalisation ignores national borders, it divides national economies, and it facilitates the merger of the highly competitive. The less competitive gradually slide to lower and lower income levels. This increasing intensity of division and reintegration is what defines the period of globalisation. In its broadest sense, globalisation is constantly occurring. With revolutionary progress in computer technology and goods transported daily by air, the momentum behind this phenomenon gained further strength at the end of the twentieth century.

In an era of globalisation, where does the LDP find its base of support? The Japanese citizens who have supported the LDP during this sub-period were those who sympathised with the resolve of the leaders to take an optimistic and aggressive approach to forging new roads in the face of the future uncertainties presented by globalisation.[17] They have been won over by the enthusiasm and courage of the leaders and their willingness to take risks. The majority of the population has a vague sense that, despite the fact that government deregulation and market liberalisation symbolised by postal privatisation may seriously affect their own lives, Japan will face a difficult future without these changes. This public sentiment has been based on Prime Minister Koizumi's unparalleled enthusiasm and courage in taking on these risks himself, and was further reinforced by the Prime Minister's skill in concisely expressing carefully thought-out ideas during the election campaign. In this sense, the body of support for the LDP comes more from those individuals with a strong belief that Japan should now venture optimistically into the vast uncertainty of the future, rather than from a group of people characterised by similar sociological attributes.

High priority policies have shifted from macroeconomic management to those designed to alter economic standards and regulations as Japan faces the challenges presented by the irreversible advancement of globalisation. Equally important are policies that address financial relief for the less competitive in society who are left behind in the rough seas of globalisation, as well as programmes to help these people maintain their standard of living without losing hope for the future. In many respects, Japan has yet to establish a welfare safety net, and even in some areas where there would appear to be such a safety net we are beginning to see signs of stress. The social policies (the pension system, social welfare, nursing care, healthcare and the like) put in place during the years of strong economic growth, when young people made up a significant proportion of the country's population, are causing economic strain due to the considerable changes in demographics and the decline of economic growth. The lack of gender equality is striking, and any change must defy social mores and prejudices. It is clear that, first and foremost, revolutionary change in corporate culture is necessary.

Globalisation, however, has brought to the fore a number of issues that had not previously been considered to pose significant problems. Competing in an environment of globalisation without addressing these issues is becoming increasingly difficult. For this reason, with the exception of deregulation and cutting national government expenditure, we are seeing less policy emphasis on the Ministry of Land, Infrastructure and Transport, the Ministry of Health, Labour and Welfare, the Ministry of Education, Culture, Sports, Science and Technology, the Ministry of Internal Affairs and Communications and other ministries that have traditionally been allocated large portions of the national budget. Naturally, the issues taken up by individual extraordinary ministers within the Cabinet may at times bring certain policies to the fore. This has been the case with the move to postal privatisation endorsed by the Minister of State for Economic and Fiscal Policy and the prominence of the position of Minister of State for Gender Equity and Social Affairs. Only ministers of state can make a particular ministry or agency predominant. At the larger ministries and agencies, bureaucrats offer strong resistance to political manoeuvring, and government agency culture is not conducive to prompt decision-making or swift action. With policy allocation being a matter of long-established routine, it is difficult to marshal the will within agencies to redesign policy. This is another reason why the prime minister and cabinet ministers are taking increasingly prominent roles in driving government policy. The Cabinet and the Prime Minister's office are now more directly in charge than bureaucrats for an increasing number of matters. This process has been prominently referred to as 'presidentialisation'.[18]

There can be no doubt that the cabinet and the prime minister have been the dominant government agencies during the globalisation sub-period.

Although there are significant systemic differences between presidential and prime ministerial systems, globalisation serves to position prime ministers as presidents in countries that have no such elected official. In countries with presidents that merely play a symbolic role, the prime minister may effectively act like a president. In cases of prime ministers playing no more than a symbolic role, ministerial secretaries, campaign strategists, or political consultants work behind the scenes on issues related to globalisation. Against a backdrop of critical public opinion, the slightest statement by a politician is carefully weighed and measured against anticipated negative public reaction. In this particular environment, even the employment of specialists carefully crafting these political statements cannot guarantee success.

During this sub-period of globalisation, where do the opposition parties find their bases of support? The recent transition in the Lower House electoral system from medium-sized to smaller electoral districts marked a significant element of reform that changed the structural parameters under which both governing and opposition parties vie for a single seat in a single electoral district. No less significantly, with government spending strained to the limit, the status quo of granting large-scale public works expenditures and subsidies in the form of local transfers from the central government to local governments, or budgetary subsidies to implement large-scale social policy as an agent of the central government, is no longer viable. In order to obtain public works expenditures or subsidies, in the form of matching funds, local governments must secure budgets equal to or greater than the expenditure disbursed by the central government. Pork barrel spending and other funding schemes will no longer come from the central government, at least not on a regular basis. Voters are no longer enticed by the promises of Diet members to bring money back from the central government (see Table 2).[19]

What is it then that gains a politician the support of voters? Today, much depends on the political message sent out to the electorate. Ozawa Ichiro's slogan in the Chiba by-election, for example, was 'From the line of vision of the people'. To illustrate his point, he spoke on the campaign trail standing on a pile of crates and rode his bicycle around his district to speak directly with the people. He did not emulate Koizumi's much-lauded boldness, skilful rhetoric, or his method of giving speeches to large groups of onlookers from the top of a campaign truck. In fact, Ozawa had a great sense of competition with Koizumi. He pursued a campaign strategy based on face-to-face meetings with each of the organizations in the district. Not long ago, such 'street-side campaigning' was the forte of the LDP, while exaggerated rhetoric was what the opposition parties were known for. Despite the explicit confrontation on political issues, with little chance of opposition parties taking the actual reins of government, these parties were content to stay with grandeur and overstatement, resigning themselves to a permanent position outside

power. Today, however, the situation has changed. The primary support for
the sweeping LDP policy vision comes from critical voters and those who
are anxious about an uncertain future; to them the party appeals with its rhetoric and an image of courage and energy. The reason for choosing this strategy
over detailed explanations of policy on the campaign trail is that the public
finds it difficult to comprehend concrete policies in the face of inevitable cut-
backs in government spending, increasingly strong signs that the tax rate will
rise, and intensifying international competition.[20] By contrast, the opposition
parties have forgone the strategic exaggeration that parties resigned to being
permanently in opposition have conventionally adopted. Taking advantage
of the fact that they are not in charge of government policy today, they
have taken up a strategy of setting themselves slightly apart from the realm
of day-to-day policy, emphasising instead the human touch: shaking hands
and speaking with as many voters as possible throughout their districts,

TABLE 2

FEATURES OF THE LDP-DOMINATED POLITICAL SYSTEM IN JAPAN IN THREE
HISTORICAL SUB-PERIODS

Military Occupation	
LDP (predecessor) support base	Self-employed farmers, self-employed businessmen
Priority policies	Employment, energy, financing, obtaining foreign currency, industrial infrastructure
Predominant government ministry	Economic Planning Agency
Public sentiment and concerns	Survival
Reasons for supporting opposition parties	Platform for elimination of poverty, removal of military bases
State Developmentalism	
LDP support base	New middle-class masses
Priority policies	Macroeconomic policies, social policies
Predominant government ministries	Ministry of International Trade and Industry, Ministry of Finance, Ministry of Health and Welfare Desire for economic rebuilding
Public sentiment and concerns	Platform for peace and equality
Reason for supporting opposition parties	
Globalisation	
LDP support base	Voters who appreciate optimism in the face of stresses from globalisation
Priority policies	Value of currency, science and technology, gender, population
Predominant government ministries	Prime Minister and his Cabinet
Public sentiment and concerns	Desire for risk-sharing and optimistic approach to future
Reason for supporting opposition parties	Platform for community-based system with a more human touch

Source: Rien T. Segers, *A New Japan for the Twenty-First Century: An Inside Overview of Current Fundamental Changes.* London: Routledge, 2008.

listening to their troubles, providing a sympathetic ear, and creating the impression that they are the ones who really represent people and respond to the voice of the people.

PARLIAMENTARY OPPOSITION IN THREE DISTINCTIVE SUB-PERIODS

Having described the historical background and the structural features of the current one-party dominant regime in Japan, we have now come to the point where the parliamentary opposition in Japan can be characterised. The nature, composition, issues and electoral bases of the parliamentary opposition vary considerably between the different sub-periods. Let us compare and contrast them.

The key actors in each period are Miyamoto Kenji, a communist leader, Eda Saburo, a socialist leader who became the leader of structural reform of capitalism *à la* Togliatti in Italy, and Ozawa Ichiro, a leader of the Democratic Party of Japan, a defector from the Liberal Democratic Party (see Table 3). Miyamoto was vehemently anti-American and opposed the Japan–United States Security Treaty. The Communist Party was backed by trade unions and supported broadly by pacifist-leaning men on the street. The parliamentary opposition in the first sub-period often took to the streets against the low wage levels, the Security Treaty, and the government's moves towards revising the constitution. The Communists were replaced by the United Socialists soon after the military occupation ended. Once independence was achieved and poverty eradication progressed steadily, the electoral support for Communists diminished.

The second sub-period was characterised by state developmentalism and high growth of the economy. Exposed to excessively negative consequences of the high economic growth in the second sub-period, the parliamentary opposition opposed state developmentalism and argued for more equal distribution of income, alleviating environmental aggravation, and reducing

TABLE 3
FEATURES OF THE OPPOSITION IN JAPAN UNDER THE LDP-DOMINATED
POLITICAL SYSTEM IN THREE HISTORICAL SUB-PERIODS

	Military rule **1945–52**	**State developmentalism** **1952–85**	**Globalisation** **1985–today**
Key actors	Miyamoto Kenji	Eda Saburo	Ozawa Ichiro
Nature	anti-Americanism	anti-state developmentalism	anti-market liberalisation
Composition	Communists Socialists	Socialists Buddhist Sect	Omnibus
Issues	alliance	hazards of growth	hazards of globalisation
Electoral bases	workers, wage earners	new middle-class mass urban	disintegrated new middle mass non-metropolitan

working hours. But, again, once the fruits of high economic growth reached virtually each and every corner of Japanese society, the Socialists and the politically active Buddhists were 'tamed' into the system. The electoral bases of the parliamentary opposition coalesced with what was called the new middle-class masses. The intermittent scandals and mishaps of the government and the governing party occasionally handed the parliamentary opposition centre stage. But their strength was not normally sustained for a prolonged period of time, and much less were they able to capture power.

The third sub-period is one during which the tide of globalisation is steadily permeating Japanese society and some of its effects resulted in protest from those negatively affected. Government deregulation in such areas as the postal service, and market liberalisation in such areas as agriculture and financial service, undermines the electoral bases of the governing party. Only when the government succeeds in striking a chord among the electorate, as in the general election called for by Prime Minister Koizumi who turned the issue of postal privatisation into an issue of confidence in himself, can the governing party win an election overwhelmingly. In contrast to the second sub-period, the electorate is not composed primarily of economic blocs, such as unionised workers, the agricultural sector, the steel sector, the construction sector, self-employed merchants and so on. The electorate of the third sub-period has been marked by multi-dimensional atomisation. The contrast becomes clear when one compares the electoral strength of sectoral interest groups and associations like the postal service, medical doctors, and war veteran families in statistics indicating the number of votes association-backed candidates receive.[21]

LEGISLATIVE OPPOSITION

Although the parliamentary opposition in Japan is constrained by the dominance of central bureaucracy in the pre-legislative process, the dominance of the Liberal Democratic Party in the National Diet, and the yearning of people for continuity and stability, the opposition still finds some room for manoeuvre and may influence legislative politics. In fact, under one-party dominance the opposition displays its characteristics most clearly in the legislative process.

Apart from the exceptionally close cooperation between the governing party and the numerous bureaucratic agencies on the legislative agenda and schedule, four major features of Japanese legislative politics may be noted: (1) bureaucratic dominance which means that most legislative bills put forward are cabinet-sponsored bills which have been drafted by bureaucratic agencies;[22] (2) the intense scrutiny of bills within the governing party, which marks a rather informal and non-transparent process; (3) the salience of two parliamentary committees, the committee of National Diet affairs and the committee of Rules and Administration, which deal with the nitty-gritty of parliamentary logrolling and other compromises and confrontation, and whose internal processes are marked by informality and limited transparency; (4) plenary and committee sessions of the National Diet are not centre stages of legislative politics, instead the large majority of issues are settled informally either within the governing party or within the committees of National Diet affairs and Rules and Administration before bills are passed on to the policy area-related committees of the National Diet;[23] and (5) bills sponsored by parliamentary members are few in number and often ill-fated unless they are linked with cabinet-sponsored bills.[24]

In the framework of legislative politics in Japan, the opposition has a few devices at their disposal that may be used to influence the legislative process and its outcomes. (1) The Japanese polity operates a bicameral system in which the House of Representatives is the more powerful chamber in legislative politics. Even if the House of Councillors votes down a bill, the House of Representatives can override its veto in a second round of voting. This notwithstanding, the House of Councillors is an important player in Japanese legislative politics. Withheld support for a bill may inflict major damage to the government's legislative agenda, as bills may be lost, if not for good, at least for the current legislative session. The parliamentary process in the Diet is based on the principle of legislative discontinuity, that is, draft bills which have not been voted upon within a given parliamentary session are abandoned and must start from scratch in the following session (except in those cases where draft bills are voted on with some added agendas for discussion). This system gives some space to the opposition as well as to dissenters within the governing party as prolonging or even blocking the committee and plenary sessions concerned would obviously delay the government's legislative schedule and potentially jeopardise its legislative priorities.

Since the House of Councillors is mostly elected on the basis of a PR system which tends to give some advantages to the opposition parties, the latter tend to be better represented in the House of Councillors than in the House of Representatives whose members are primarily elected on the basis of an Anglo-American-style plurality system. In Japan's one-party dominant system, the major governing party tends to retain a majority in the House of Representatives.[25] In the House of Councillors, the primarily PR-based selection of members has tended to create a power configuration in which the governing parties have rarely held a clear-cut majority.

Legislative proceedings under the pre-war Imperial Constitution focused on the parliamentary plenary session. It was modelled after the British system. The first reading of a draft bill was conducted in the plenary session. The second reading took place in a special committee set up for each bill. It was here where the opposition had space and time to oppose or amend the (mostly cabinet-sponsored) bills under consideration. The third reading, to be followed by the final vote, was conducted in the plenary session. Using the American system as a role model, the post-war constitution strengthened the parliamentary committees. However, whereas the American model has been marked by a combination of powerful legislative committees and a constitutional separation-of-powers structure in which the bulk of legislation does not directly involve the executive, and power within the legislative branches tends to be dispersed, the Japanese system is still a genuinely parliamentary regime with a fusion-of-power structure that is based on the governing parties' parliamentary majority.

In the committees, this role involves putting down cabinet-sponsored bills. Often the opposition is very constructive to the legislative process, in that it helps to clarify agenda setting for a bill as well as monitoring the administrative process associated with the implementation of a given bill. Also, in the plenary the opposition's role does not exactly involve aggressively challenging the government. With the fairly strict party discipline imposed on the parliamentarians' voting, the passage or non-passage of bills is highly predictable.[26]

The typology of legislatures proposed by F.E. Loake, as applied by Sone Yasunori and Iwai Tomoaki,[27] is helpful for a better understanding of the Japanese legislative opposition. Loake's key concepts are responsiveness and effectiveness. Responsiveness refers to the legislature's key task of forming the collective preference of the electorate's deputies called parliamentarians. Its key role is to debate and its prototype is Great Britain. Through parliamentary debates, policy agendas are made clearer, and also the implementation of government policies are being monitored. By effectiveness Loake means ensuring swift and efficient policy decisions. The legislature's key role is to legislate and its prime example is considered to be the United States.

Overall, the Japanese legislature looks more like that of Great Britain. Yet the major difference between the legislatures of Japan and Great Britain is that the cabinet and the governing party retain their respective autonomy in Japan whereas in Britain the cabinet and the governing party are one and the same (at least compared to the situation in Japan). The Japanese cabinet is tied very closely to the central bureaucracy that, for its part, has retained a high degree of autonomy. The governing party plays the role of articulating societal interests and aggregating them in harmony with government policy as much as possible through the governing party's committees, the Policy Affairs council and the General Affairs council. The coordinating role is formally played by the secretary general of the governing party and the chief cabinet secretary of the government. In such a system the role of the opposition is bound to be limited. Opposition parties essentially focus on challenging cabinet-sponsored bills in the plenary and committee sessions in ways that would undermine the government's popularity and maximise their own electoral fortunes. In doing so, opposition parties have to try to take advantage of the fairly brief period of the ordinary session held for 150 days a year. Given the normally overcrowded legislative needs, prolonging committee sessions, and especially the budget committee session, is the strategy most easily resorted to by the opposition.

There have been several recent changes at the level of legislative politics that seem worth noting. To begin with, the electoral support structure of both the governing and opposition parties is no longer based primarily on certain economic and social sectors but has become much more complex.[28] Electorates have many faces whereby they identify themselves. They are atomised and have multiple loyalties. Similarly, the political agendas of parliamentarians have become much more complex. Members of Parliament have multiple interests and beliefs to defend and advance in the legislative process. Those parliamentarians who specialise in guarding or advancing the interests of one policy area are referred to as 'legislative tribes'. Construction, agriculture, transport, health and welfare, education, science and technology, and finance are among those policy areas that have formed the basis of legislative tribe building. The governing party set the principle of each parliamentarian affiliated with one policy committee of the governing party, which facilitated the growth of legislative tribes with a specialised policy expertise.[29] However globalisation permeates; parliamentarians increasingly want to belong to a number of policy committees and, responding to growing pressure, the governing party has allowed them to hold multiple memberships.

Another important changing feature of legislative politics in contemporary Japan relates to the issue of party discipline in parliamentary voting, and the informal mechanism installed to achieve high levels of party discipline. The governing party has held very strictly to the principle of party discipline in parliamentary voting. To achieve the highest possible party cohesion in parliamentary voting, the informal stages of the legislative process within the governing party (to be managed by its General Affairs Council) have been designed to produce a broad consensus, or in fact unanimity, on any bill considered. But this principle was broken in May 2005 when the LDP held a vote on the postal privatisation bill, and some dissenting voices were suppressed in a call for the overall positive effects of the measure. It looks as if the key principle of achieving consensus in the General Affairs Council of the governing party has been broken since.[30] This is one symptom of the globalisation age when national consensus has become much more difficult to achieve since the forces of globalisation fragment the previously well-integrated national economy and its various sectors.

As to the opposition parties, the legislative tribes within the opposition camp have largely ceased to exist. Those who single-mindedly focused on the protection of Article 9 of the constitution stipulating no use of force and the full protection of union rights have become increasingly feeble. Also, the party discipline in parliamentary voting among the opposition parties has weakened. Where party discipline is imposed strictly, it only increases the likelihood that dissenters will consider the exit option. On the whole, legislative opposition in Japan has been relatively moderate. During the second sub-period, the largest opposition party, the Japan Socialist Party, registered some 70 per cent of voting, together with the Liberal Democratic Party, for cabinet-sponsored bills. During the third period, the largest opposition party, the Democratic Party of Japan registered an even much higher rate of voting for cabinet-sponsored bills.[31]

CONCLUSIONS

Several conclusions emerge from the analysis above. Conclusion one is that parliamentary opposition in Japan has been somewhat structurally weak, which is to some considerable extent a direct result of the government's strength. The major governing party has been able to benefit from the strong ties with the central bureaucracy. Although curiously decentralised at the pinnacle of the government, the central bureaucracy exercises enormous power in legislation and implementation of policy. Furthermore, the governing party is a party of politicians mostly from districts. Their clientelism brings a folksy touch to the electorates and constitutes its power base.

Conclusion two is that parliamentary opposition in Japan has nevertheless been able to exercise some influence on the legislative process and outcomes of parliamentary legislation, which is to some extent due to the basic institutional features of the legislature. Key components include the relatively short parliamentary sessions and the principle of parliamentary discontinuity, both of which may possibly jeopardise the legislative priorities of the government whose legislative schedule is usually tight and sensitive to any sort of delaying tactics or parliamentary obstruction. Aside from the parliamentary opposition, the role of extra-parliamentary opposition cannot be underestimated. If it touches a resonant chord in the mass media, the opposition has occasionally been strengthened to a considerable degree.[32]

Finally, it would seem worthwhile to consider, if very briefly, the future of the parliamentary opposition. Despite all the institutional and structural weaknesses of parliamentary opposition, two developments seem to give some hope for the future of parliamentary opposition in Japan: the growing influence of the media, and the gradually felt impact of electoral reforms (implemented in 1984 and in 1994). The mass media, in particular television, have been increasingly powerful in conveying the style, message and atmosphere of politicians. Whereas the prime minister is at the core of the media's interest, parliament has not been excluded from media attention. The major parliamentary sessions are often televised live. In addition, the strict prohibition of the Internet for electoral campaigning, as stipulated in the current electoral campaign law, might be relaxed in the future. As the tide of globalisation permeates each and every part of Japanese society, with electorates being increasingly atomised, media influence is bound to grow further. The question is who will be able to capture the audience through calculated and well-crafted style and message.

The other major driving force of (possible) change is the consolidation of the mixed electoral system which was completed in 1994. The Anglo-American small district system and the Continental European proportional representation system are combined in Japan (and in most East and Southeast Asian democracies for that matter).[33] With the accumulation of several general elections, after some 10 to 15 years of trial and error, many believe that the time has come for the opposition to capture power.[34] The increasing blurring of electorates in terms of socioeconomic affiliations is likely to effect a large swing, if such a swing is still moderated by the very mixed nature of the two different electoral systems.

NOTES

1. T.J. Pempel (ed.), *Uncommon Democracies* (Ithaca, NY: Cornell University Press, 1990). On Japan, see T. Inoguchi, 'The Political Economy of Conservative Resurgence under Recession: Public Policies and Political Support in Japan, 1977–1983', in T.J. Pempel, *Uncommon Democracies*, pp.189–225.

2. T. Inoguchi, *Japanese Politics: An Introduction* (Melbourne: TransPacificPress, 2005); T. Inoguchi, 'Tanegashima Tokitaka kara Plaza Goui made' [From Lord Tokitaka of Tanegashima to the Plaza Accord of 1985], *Gakushikaiho: koenkai tokushu*, November 1997.

3. E. Scheiner, *Democracy without Competition* (Cambridge: Cambridge University Press, 2006). Portions of section three derive primarily from T. Inoguchi, 'Japanese Politics: Towards a New Interpretation', in R. Segers (Ed) *A New Japan for the Twenty-First Century: An Inside Overview of Current Fundamental Changes* (London: Routledge, 2008).

4. This point has been overlooked – mostly by western accounts of modern Japanese history – largely because the early modern period is often left out of these accounts of modern Japanese history whether they start in 1868 or in 1945.

5. Army ministers often toppled the cabinet primarily because the Army's demand for an increased budget was not fully accommodated by the cabinet.

6. 'Shoueki atte, kokueki nashi' or 'what we have is agency interests, not national interests' is the saying to denote this feature.

7. M. Iokibe, *Beikoku no Nihon senryo seisaku* [United States Occupation Policy in Japan] (Tokyo: Chuo Koronsha, 1985).

8. For the historical evolution of the Japanese foreign policy line since 1945, placing the Yoshida doctrine in perspective, see T. Inoguchi and P. Bacon, 'Japan's Emerging Role as a Global Ordinary Power', *International Relations of the Asia-Pacific*, 6 (2006), pp.1–21.

9. M. Junnosuke, *Nihon Seijishi* [Japanese Political History], 4 vols. (Tokyo: University of Tokyo Press, 1988).

10. C. Johnson, *MITI and the Japanese Miracle* (Stanford, CA: Stanford University Press, 1982).
11. E. Ikegami, *The Taming of the Samurai* (Cambridge, MA: Harvard University Press, 1995).
12. S. Sato, 'Response to the West: Korean and Japanese Patterns', in A.M. Craig (ed.), *Japan: A Comparative View* (Princeton, NJ: Princeton University Press, 1979), pp.105–29.
13. Y. Shimizu, *Seito to kanryo no kindai* [The Search for Modernity Competed between Two Political Parties and Bureaucracy] (Tokyo: Fujiwara shoten, 2007).
14. M. Yasusuke, *Shin chukan taishu* [The New Middle Mass] (Tokyo: Chuokoronsha, 1984).
15. T. Inoguchi and D. Okimoto (eds.), *The Political Economy of Japan. Vol. 2: The Changing International Context* (Stanford, CA: Stanford University Press, 1988).
16. R. O'Brien, *Financial Globalization: The End of Geography* (London: Pinter Publishers, 1992).
17. D. Acemoglu and J. Robinson, *Economic Origins of Dictatorship and Democracy* (Princeton, NJ: Princeton University Press, 2006).
18. E. Krauss and B. Nyblade, '"Presidentialization" in Japan? The Prime Minister, Media and Elections in Japan', *British Journal of Political Science*, 35 (2005), pp.357–68. For an account of the players in the Koizumi administration, see I. Iijima, *Koizumi kantei hiroku* [A Secret History of Prime Minister Koizumi's Office] (Tokyo: Nihonkeizai Shimposha, 2006); H. Takenaka, *kozo kaikaku no shinjitsu* [Truth about Structural Reform] (Tokyo: Nihonkeizai Shimposha, 2006).
19. T. Inoguchi and T. Iwai, *Zoku giin no kenkyu* [A Study of Legislative Tribes] (Tokyo: Nihon keizai shimbunsha, 1987); T. Inoguchi and T. Iwai, 'The Growth of Zoku: Legislative Tribes in Japan', paper presented at the Annual Meeting of the Association of Asian Studies, 1984.
20. I. Kabashima, T. Takeshita, and Y. Seriyama, *Media to Seiji* [Mass Media and Politics] (Tokyo: Yuhikaku, 2007).
21. See 'Kanryo yori jimae koho' [LDP Candidates Better Recruited from Those Sectors Concerned than Those Bureaucratic Agencies], *Asahi shimbun*, 15 Nov. 2006, p.4.

	Candidates Pushed Back by Associations in the House of Councillors Proportional Representation Scheme		
Sectoral Interest Associations	2001	2004	Bureaucratic Origins of Candidates
construction	278,521	253,738	X
war veterans	295,613	101,651	
medical doctors	227,042	250,426	
war veterans' families	264,888	171,945	
land improvement	207,867	167,350	X
pharmaceutical	156,380	96,463	X
dental/medical doctors	104,581	–	
dental engineers	–	82,146	
nurses	174,517	152,685	
transport	94,332	196,499	X
local governments	156,656	105,737	X
facilities for the aged	–	199,510	
agriculture and fisheries	166,070	118,540	
food	–	51,664	X
fishermen	–	–	

22. While cabinet-sponsored bills accounted for 60 per cent of bills introduced in the 64th ordinary session of the National Diet (20 Jan.–18 June 2006), cabinet-sponsored bills constituted 85 per cent of bills passed in the same session.
23. In 2005, the number of days of both the ordinary and extraordinary sessions of the National Diet was 242 days. But the amount of time for the plenary sessions of both houses combined is 103 hours and 21 minutes! Most time was spent for committees. Furthermore, much more

substantial and substantive time was spent at the committees of the governing party which parallel to those committees in both houses of the National Diet.

24. M. Nakajima, *Rippogaku* [Legislative Studies] (Kyoto: Horitsu bunkasha, 2004). The figures for bills put forward and raised are taken from N. Narita, 'Koakkai (National Diet)', in IMIDAS (Tokyo: Shueisha, 2007), p.486; the figures for the amount of time spent for the plenary sessions of both Houses are taken from N. Narita, p.487.
25. S. Reed, *Japanese Electoral Policies* (London: Routledge Curzon, 2003).
26. M. Nakajima, *Rippogaku*. For the Japanese legislature, see also A. Miyoshi, 'The Diet in Japan', *Journal of Legislative Studies*, 4 (1998), pp.83–102; M. Masuyama and B. Nyblade, 'Is the Japanese Diet Consensual?', *Journal of Legislative Studies*, 11 (2004), pp.250–62. For the American and British legislatures and their changing features, see C.C. Campbell and R.H. Davidson, 'US Congressional Committees: Changing Legislature Work-shops', *Journal of Legislative Studies*, 4 (1998), pp. 124–42; J.E. Owens, 'From Committee Government to Party Government: Arranging Opportunities for Amendment Sponsors in the US House of Representatives: 1945–98', *Journal of Legislative Studies*, 5 (1999), pp.75–103; P. Norton, 'Nascent Institutionalization: Committees in the British Government', *Journal of Legislative Studies*, 4 (1998), pp.143–62. The combination of the parliamentary form of government with strong parliamentary committees as found in Japan, is also typical of such parliamentary democracies as Scandinavia, Germany or Italy.
27. Y. Sone and T. Iwai, 'Seisaku katei ni okeru gikai no yakuwari' [The Role of the Legislative in the Policy Process], *Nempo Seiji Gaku* [Annals of Political Science], 35 (1987).
28. 'Kanryo yori jimae koho', [LDP Candidates Better Recruited from Those Sectors Concerned than Those Bureaucratic Agencies], *Asahi Shimbun*, 16 Nov. 2006, p.4.
29. Inoguchi and Iwai, *Zoku giin no kenkyu*.
30. H. Takenaka, *Shusho shihai* [Prime Minister's Control] (Tokyo: Chuokoron shinsha, 2006).
31. Author's interview with T. Ikenaga, Professor of Political Science at Nihon University and an expert on legislative politics, Tokyo, 24 Jan. 2007.
32. E.S. Krauss, 'The Mass Media and Japanese Politics: Effects and Consequences', in S.J. Pharr and E.S. Krauss (eds.), *Media and Politics in Japan* (Honolulu, University of Hawaii Press, 1996), p.360; I. Kabashima, T. Takeshita and Y. Seriyama, *Media to Seiji*; see also the special issue of the *Japanese Journal of Political Science*, 8/1 (2007), on mass media and politics, edited by I. Kabashima and S. Popkin.
33. A. Hicken and Y. Kasuya, 'A Guide to the Constitutional Structures and Electoral Systems of East, South, and Southeast Asia', *Electoral Studies*, 22 (2003), pp.121–51.
34. S. Reed and M. Thies, 'The Consequences of Electoral Reform in Japan', in M. Soberg and M.P. Wattenberg (eds.), *Mixed-Member Electoral Systems: The Best of Both Worlds?* (Oxford: Oxford University Press, 2001), pp.380–403.

Parliamentary Opposition in Post-Communist Democracies: Power of the Powerless

PETR KOPECKÝ and MARIA SPIROVA

The formal powers of the parliamentary opposition in the post-communist world and the ways in which oppositions have used these powers to influence the political process have not been subject to much systematic comparative examination. There are several reasons for this. Firstly, much of the transition and consolidation literature that dominated accounts of institutional developments in the early post-communist years was marked by an analytical bias towards governmental effectiveness and executive stability. Without a modicum of executive stability, the post-communist democracies were deemed to fail in the face of the simultaneous challenges of state reform and the introduction of market economy. Consequently, rather than being concerned with the powers of the parliamentary opposition, much of the literature focused on government powers and longevity, and the factors underlying the differing performance of post-communist countries in this respect.

The second reason for the relative lack of attention to the role of parliamentary opposition has to do with the exceptional elusiveness of the subject. The widespread instability of parties and governments has made it difficult even to identify who is in opposition at any given time. The changing institutional framework has hindered a clear-cut assessment of the opposition's institutional opportunity structure, while the complex nature of the political process has made any evaluation of the role of the opposition in constitutional practice a challenging task.

This article aims to fill the void in the literature on parliamentary opposition, and that on political institutional relationships more generally. The first section reviews the existing literature on parliamentary opposition in post-communist Europe. The article then moves on to develop an analytical framework within which the empirical discussion is set. The empirical sections discuss the modes of executive–legislative interactions, the consequences of these modes for the position of the opposition, the formal powers of the opposition in Eastern Europe, and finally, the link between party stability and the ability of the opposition to influence the policy-making process. These sections focus on the political systems of three countries of the region: Hungary, the Czech Republic and Bulgaria.

OPPOSITION IN POST-COMMUNIST EASTERN EUROPE

The study of the opposition in the post-communist world, has, in many ways, reflected the development of the opposition movements themselves. The voluminous literature on democratic transition and consolidation has examined the role different extra-parliamentary opposition forces played in the early stages of the transition to democracy.[1] Indeed, the collapse of communism was often seen as the victory of civil society over authoritarian regimes, despite the fact that, with the exception of Poland, opposition movements in Eastern Europe were neither very large, nor particularly powerful prior to the demise of the communist regimes. Nevertheless, the opposition groups that sprang into existence just before or during the communist regime collapse played an important role in the various transition scenarios that unfolded throughout the region at the end of 1989. The Round Table Talks were the formal institutional arenas through which the opposition wielded its influence; it was there that important decisions such as the timing of the first multiparty elections and the type of electoral system to be used were made. The opposition took an active part in these negotiations,[2] and so, in fact, the transition appeared to be the time of the opposition.

The 'repositioning' of the opposition, its transformation from an outsider challenging the political order into an insider actively participating in parliamentary and executive decisions that followed the period of mass mobilisation in 1989 has been reflected in the academic literature. On the one hand, numerous studies have focused on the formation, role and strength of *extra-parliamentary opposition*, commonly referred to as civil society. Given the popularity of the concept among both Eastern European dissidents and western policy-makers, civil society has continued to attract huge attention in the academic community, despite the rather daunting empirical experiences with and future perspectives for organised associational life in the post-communist region. Indeed, whether one looks at studies of individual civil society groups,[3] or studies on citizen participation in these groups,[4] the picture that emerges is one of civil society weakness or decline.[5] This is especially true in countries such as Bulgaria where there were only a handful of dissident groups before 1989 and where civil society was particularly late in developing after 1989.

True, the development of the non-governmental sector has been quite rapid in the region. Civil society, including the media and independent think-thanks, also contributed to the downfall of authoritarian incumbents like Meciar in Slovakia (1998), as well as to the victory of the opposition during the 'rose' and 'orange' revolutions in Georgia (2003) and Ukraine (2004–5). But it is also true that many non-governmental organisations (NGOs) in the region remain elite-dominated and dependent on the state for resources. Importantly, success of civic initiatives in influencing policy usually depends on cooperation between the extra-parliamentary and the parliamentary opposition. And although there have been 'success cases', such as in Bulgaria when extra-parliamentary opposition and the main opposition party at the time, the Union of Democratic Forces (SDS), joined forces with the labour unions and student organisations to stage widespread protests that helped bring about the collapse of the Bulgarian Socialist Party (BSP) government and new elections,[6] most of such efforts have been seen as an attempt by parties to co-opt and politicise the civil society rather than achieve any meaningful cooperation on an equal footing. In other words, the post-communist period is commonly seen as the area of relatively weak extra-parliamentary opposition.

On the other hand, studies focusing on the powers and roles of the repositioned *parliamentary opposition* in the post-communist political process have remained comparatively sparse. There is some literature that analyses, and often explicitly acknowledges, the demobilisation of anti-communist groups and the inclusion of leading protagonists of the transition era, such as Vaclav Havel or Lech Walesa, into the new political order as key aspects of the democratic consolidation process.[7] However, there is no work comparable to Helms' systematic categorisation and analysis of the powers of the opposition in advanced democracies.[8] In the Eastern European context, the subject as such has only been touched upon through the study of executive–legislative relations,[9] comparative or case studies of parliaments,[10] and governmental stability.[11] Although all these works focus on separate issues, they provide some references to the powers of parliaments to control the executive and thus, indirectly, to the powers of the opposition.

What emerges from this literature is that parliamentary oppositions in Eastern Europe find themselves in a political setting characterised by institutional fluidity, relatively weak parliaments (and parliamentary committees in particular), dominant executives, and unstable parties. Although there is some disagreement between scholars over recent developments – for example, Kopecký contends that executives have been strengthened since the early 1990s, while Baylis maintains the opposite – most authors identify weakly institutionalised and fluid political parties as key factors determining other institutional features.

If we were to judge the strength of the opposition by the performance of governments, the relative executive instability in Eastern Europe might lead us to conclude that the parliamentary opposition has a strong position in the political system of these new democracies (see Table 1). But in fact, it is the instability of political parties – both government and opposition – that explains the short lives of many Eastern European cabinets.[12] By contrast, assuming uniformly fluid and unstable parties and party systems might prevent us from discerning differently set up institutional arrangements that might allow different powers to the parliamentary opposition. Harfst, for example, using an index of parliamentary powers vis-à-vis the executive, distinguishes among less and more powerful parliaments of Eastern Europe, categorising the Russian Duma as the least powerful and the Slovenian Parliament as the most powerful. However, he finds no evidence for a strong correlation between the powers of Eastern European parliaments (and thus the opposition) and the degree of government stability.[13] Thus a more detailed examination of the actual powers of the parliamentary opposition in the post-communist world and the extent to which these powers have been used in the political process is clearly needed.

FRAMEWORK FOR ANALYSIS

Before assessing the actual powers of the opposition in Eastern Europe, we first try to identify the parliamentary opposition. However, rather than describing in detail different configurations of parties and groups of MPs that have formed the opposition in these countries, we try to identify and locate the source of parliamentary opposition in institutional terms. In order to do so, we use a modified version of King's typology of different modes of

TABLE 1
GOVERNMENTS AND OPPOSITION IN BULGARIA, HUNGARY AND THE CZECH
REPUBLIC

Government Period and Prime Minister	Parties in Government and their Seat Share in Parliament	Parties in Opposition[1]
	Bulgaria	
1990 Lukanov (BSP)	BSP 211 (53%)	SDS 144 (36%) DPS 23 (5.75%) BZNS 16 (4%)
1990–91 Popov (IND)	Caretaker	
1991–92 Dimitrov (SDS)	SDS 110 (46%) DPS 24 (10%)	BSP 106 (44%)
1992–94 Berov (IND)	DPS[2] 24 (10%) BSP 106 (44%)	SDS 110 (46%)
1994 Indjova (IND)	Caretaker	
1995–97 Videnov (BSP)	BSP 125 (52%)	SDS 69 (28%), BZNS-DP 18 (7.5%), DPS 15 (6.3%) BBB 13 (5.4%)
1997 Sofianski (SDS)	Caretaker	
1997–2001 Kostov (ODS)	ODS 137 (57%)	BSP 58 (24%) ONS 19 (8%) EvroLef 14 (5.8%) BBB (5%)
2001–5 Sakskoburggotski (NDSV)	NDSV 120 (50%) DPS 21 (8.75%)	ODS 51 (21.25%) BSP 48 (20%)
2005–7 Stanishev (BSP)	BSP 82 (34%) NDSV 53 (22%) DPS 34 (14%)	Ataka 21 (8.75%) ODS 20 (8.3%) DSB 17 (7%) BNS 13 (5.4%)
	Hungary	
1990–93 Antall (MDF)	MDF 165 (43%) FKgP 44 (11%) KDNP 21 (5%)	SZDSZ 92 (24%) MSZP 33 (9%) FIDESZ 21 (5%), ASZ 1, Independents 6
1993–94 Boross (MDF)	MDF 165 (43%) FKgP 44 (11%) KDNP 21 (5%)	SZDSZ 92 (24%), MSZP 33 (9%) FIDESZ 21 (5%), ASZ 1, Independents 6,
1994–98 Horn (MSZP)	MSZP 209 (54%) SZDSZ 70 (18%)	MDF 38 (10%) FKgP 26 (7%) KDNP 22 (6%) FIDESZ 20 (5%) ASZ 1
1998-2002 Orban (FIDESZ)	FIDESZ 163(42%) FKgP 48 (12%) MDF (4%)	MSZP 134 (35%) SZDSZ 24 (6%) MIEP 14 (4%) Independents 1
2002–4 Medgyessy (MSZP)	MSZP 178 (46%) SZDSZ 19 (5%)	FIDESZ-MDF 188 (49%)
2004–6 Gyurcsany	MSZP 178 (46%) SZDSZ 19 (5%)	FIDESZ-MDF 188 (49%)
2006–7 Gyurcsany II	MSZP 187 (48%) SZDSZ 18 (5%)	FIDESZ 164 (46%) MDF 11 (2%)
	Czech Republic	
1992–1996 Klaus, Vaclav (ODS)	ODS-KDS 66 + 10 (38%) KDU-CSL 15 (7.5%) ODA 14 (7%)	LB 35 (17.5%) CSSD 16 (8%) LSU 16 (8%) SPR-RSC 14 (7%) HSD-SMS 14 (7%)
1996–97 Klaus, Vaclav (ODS)	ODS 68 (34%) KDU-CSL 18 (9%) ODA 13 (6.5%)	CSSD 61 (30.5%) KSCM 22 (11%) SPR-RSC 18 (9%)

(Continued)

TABLE 1
CONTINUED

Government Period and Prime Minister	Parties in Government and their Seat Share in Parliament	Parties in Opposition[1]
1997–98 Tosovsky, Josef (KDU-CSL)	ODS 68(34%) KDU-CSL 18 (9%) ODA 13 (6.5%)	CSSD 61 (30.5%) KSCM 22 (11%) SPR-RSC 18 (9%)
1998–2002 Zeman, Milos (CSSD)	CSSD 74 (37%)	ODS 63 (31.5%) KSCM 24 (12%) KDU-CSL 20 (10%) US 19 (9.5%)
2002–4 Spidla, Vladimir (CSSD)	CSSD 70 (35%) KDU-CSL 21 (10.5%) US 10 (5%)	ODS 58 (29%) KSCM 41 (20.5%)
2004–5 Gross, Stanislav (CSSD)	CSSD 70 (35%) KDU-CSL 21 (10.5%) US 10 (5%)	ODS 58 (29%) KSCM 41 (20.5%)
2005–6 Paroubek, Jiri (CSSD)	CSSD 70 (35%) KDU-CSL 21 (10.5%) US 10 (5%)	ODS 58 (29%) KSCM 41 (20.5%)
2007– Topolanek, Mirek (ODS)	ODS 81 (40%) KDU-CSL 13 (6%) SZ 6 (3%)	CSSD 74 (37%) KSCM 26 (13%)

[1]Found at: http://www2.essex.ac.uk/elect/database/indexCountry.asp?country=BULGARIA &opt=elc.
[2]The DPS supported the SDS Cabinet in Parliament but did not participate in the actual government.

Bulgarian Parties
BBB – Bulgarian Business Block; BNS – Bulgarian People's Union; BSP – Bulgarian Socialist Party; BZNS – Bulgarian Agrarian National Union; DP – Democratic Party; DPS – Movement for Rights and Freedoms; DSB – Democrats for a Strong Bulgaria; EvroLeft – Bulgarian Euroleft; NDSV – National Movement Simeon the Second; ODS – United Democratic Forces, alliance of SDS, BZNS-DP and others; ONS – Union for National Salvation, alliance of DPS and smaller parties; SDS – Union of Democratic Forces.

Hungarian Parties
MDF
FIDESZ – Federation of Young Democrats; FKGP – United Smallholders Party; KDNP – Christian Democratic Party; MDF – Hungarian Democratic Forum; MIEP – Hungarian Justice and Life Party; MSZMP – Hungarian Socialist Workers Party; MSZP – Hungarian Socialist Party; SZDSZ – Alliance of Free Democrats.

Czech Parties
CSSD – Czech Social Democratic Party; HSD-SMS – Movement for Self-Governing Democracy-Society for Moravia and Silesia; KDS – Christian Democratic Party; KDU-CSL – Coalition of Christian Democratic Union-Czech People's Party; KSCM – Communist Party of Bohemia and Moravia; LB – Left Bloc; LSU – Movement for Self-Governing Democracy-Society for Moravia and Silesia; ODA – Civic Democratic Alliance; ODS – Civic Democratic Party; SPR-RSC – Rally for the Republic-Republican Party of Czechoslovakia; US – Freedom Union.

executive–legislative relations. King distinguished five modes of interaction between governments and parliaments: the non-party, intra-party, inter-party, opposition, and cross-party modes, arguing that:

in fact it is usually highly misleading to speak of 'executive–legislative' *tout court* and that, if we wish to understand the phenomena subsumed under this general heading, we need to identify and consider separately a number of distinct political relationships. We need, to put it another way, 'to 'think behind' the Montesquieu formula.[14]

This disaggregate approach to the complexity of interactions between parliaments and governments is exactly what made King's framework so attractive for country-specific studies,[15] as well as for cross-national analysis of executive–legislative relations in Western Europe.[16] Particularly in Andeweg and Nijzink's comparative study, King's original typology was critically evaluated and modified into a typology with three modes of interaction between ministers and MPs. The same redefined typology will be used in the following analysis. The typology consists of three modes of executive–legislative relations, which are fostered by different institutional frameworks. Important to note in the context of this article, each of these modes of executive–legislative relations also gives rise to a different type of opposition.

Firstly, there is an *inter-party mode*, in which ministers and MPs from one party interact with ministers and MPs (or, if it is an opposition party, only MPs) from another party. Within this mode, two sub-modes can be distinguished: an intra-coalition mode in which ministers and MPs of one governing party interact with ministers and MPs of another governing party; and an opposition mode in which ministers and MPs belonging to the governing majority interact with opposition MPs. In the inter-party mode, parliament is regarded as an arena for party political struggles. The MPs and ministers are loyal partisans, competing with others from different parties. Consequently, under this mode it is political parties that are the key source of opposition in the relationships between parliament and government.

Secondly, there is a *cross-party mode*, in which cross-party coalitions of ministers and MPs interact with each other. These interactions are based on social and other interests, which not only cut across institutional boundaries, as in the inter-party mode, but also ignore party boundaries. In this mode parliament can best be considered a marketplace for the competitive trading of social interests. Consequently, if a cross-party mode prevails in a given system of executive–legislative relations, the key source of parliamentary opposition is not political parties, but rather different groups of MPs who find themselves united by commonly shared interests: sectoral, regional, ethnic or professional.

Thirdly, there is a *non-party mode*, in which ministers and parliamentarians interact with each other as members of two different institutions. This type of interaction is associated with the lack of political parties in the parliament, or with parties being nothing more than very loosely organised groups of MPs. It also most clearly corresponds to Montesquieu's two-body image, criticised by King as an inadequate description of the complexity of executive–legislative relations.[17] Here, the principal sources of parliamentary opposition are neither parties nor interest groups of MPs, but rather individual MPs who see themselves primarily as agents and representatives of a distinct institution, the Parliament, opposing the representatives of another distinct institution, the Government.

Each of these modes represents a different pattern of executive–legislative relations and a different pattern of opposition. It is important to note that the modes are not mutually exclusive and can co-exist in the daily reality of executive–legislative relations. Indeed, if one relates these modes to distinct behavioural patterns of individual MPs,[18] it is likely that they will not only co-exist, but at least occasionally be in conflict with each other. For example, an MP is usually a member and representative of his or her own political party but, at the same time, he or she is also a member and representative of a specialised parliamentary committee. The peaceful co-existence of modes is ensured as long as the views of the specialist are adopted by the parliamentary party. However, it may also happen that, on certain issues, an MP will have to reconcile his or her view as a policy specialist with a very different position of his or her political party. In this case, different modes of interactions between parliament and government may generate conflict. Our focus in this article is not so much on when, how and to what extent different modes co-exist; rather, we seek to ascertain whether one pattern has replaced another pattern in the course of post-communist developments.

Indeed, the cursory overview of the literature on political opposition in post-communist Europe presented above does yield a certain hypothesis in this respect. To the extent it is true that the immediate period following the breakdown of communism was characterised, above all, by the weakness of political parties, it is obvious that it was the cross-party and non-party mode of interactions that dominated parliament–government relations in that era. As one observer of the former Czechoslovak Federal Assembly (1989–92) remarked, the Assembly had 'more in common with the American Congress than with any European parliament',[19] largely because of the organisational weakness of political parties and an individualistic style of politics among many of the then new MPs. This situation might have changed since, however, and we may now expect the inter-party mode to have become more important, if not dominant in the interactions between ministers and MPs in at least some post-communist countries. If parties have become better organised and dominant, as is being suggested by several recent accounts,[20] we should find empirical evidence for the emergence of situations in which 'MPs and ministers see themselves as partisans, loyal to their party and its programme, engaged in a democratic competition with ministers and MPs from other parties, and accountable to those party bodies that hold the power over their re-nomination'.[21]

In order to probe these expectations, as well as to explore potential cross-national differences, the following empirical analysis will focus on the Czech

Republic, Hungary and Bulgaria. The former two are those post-communist countries that arguably are home to the most stable parties and party systems of the region, while Bulgaria is a country with a party system characterised by a higher level of fluidity and instability. At the same time, all three countries display a very similar institutional design: they are parliamentary systems of government, in which the cabinet depends on the support of (the majority in) the parliament, and where presidents as heads of the state perform only ceremonial functions.[22]

There is one final caveat. The typology of different modes of executive–legislative relations helps us to identify on a more precise and systematic level who is the parliamentary opposition in institutional terms. However, it tells us relatively little about what exactly the powers of the opposition are. For example, we may find the inter-party mode dominating executive–legislative relations in all the three countries in our sample. This would mean that it is the parties that are the primary source of opposition in that system. Yet, those parties, and especially the opposition parties (opposition in the usual sense of the word), may possess very different institutional devices to check and scrutinise the government and its supporting parties: in one system the parties may have to overcome a constructive vote of no-confidence in order to bring the government down; in another country a simple vote of no-confidence will suffice. The typology of different modes of executive–legislative relations does not explicitly pay attention to these important institutional differences. We shall do so in the final empirical part of this article by examining the institutional settings in which the parliamentary opposition in the three countries operates and the extent to which it has made use of these institutional devices. To put things in context, however, Table 1 lists all the cabinets in Bulgaria, Hungary and the Czech Republic, their political support in parliament, and their opposition.

MODES OF LEGISLATIVE–EXECUTIVE INTERACTIONS IN POST-COMMUNIST EUROPE

Several indicators have been used for assessing the dominant mode of interaction between parliaments and governments. Following King and Andeweg,[23] we look into the recruitment patterns of cabinet ministers, the (non-)existence of coalition agreements, the level of party discipline and stability in the legislature, the powers of parliamentary committees and the frequency of conflicts between cabinets and parliaments.

Inter-party Mode

One of the main indicators of the inter-party mode is the way cabinet ministers are recruited. The higher the number of ministers being recruited from parliament, the larger the fusion between the two branches of government, and hence the stronger the inter-party mode. In Hungary, the Czech Republic and Bulgaria cabinet members are usually recruited from the parliamentary groups of the governing parties.

In Bulgaria, only three (17 per cent) of the current 18 ministers have not (previously) been members of parliament. The high rate of MPs in the cabinet has not been a constant phenomenon, though. Of the five cabinets between 1991 and 2005, three (those of 1997–2001, 1995–97 and 1991–92) were recruited predominantly from parliament but two (1992–94 and 2001–5) were not. In 1997, Prime Minister Kostov explicitly pointed out that he preferred to choose good politicians rather than experts as members of his cabinet, and recruited most of his ministers from parliament. Similar trends characterised the recruitment of ministers in the 1995 and 1991 cabinets.

By contrast, in 2001 the National Movement Simeon the Second (NDSV) campaigned with an explicit promise to bring non-partisan experts into the government and only four of the 16 ministers (25 per cent) were drawn from the parliament. Prime Minister Saxcoburgotksi himself was never a member of parliament. In 1992 Prime Minister Berov, who also had no legislative experience, looked outside parliament for members of his cabinet.[24]

In Hungary, four cabinet members (22 per cent) out of 18 have come from outside the legislature. The 2002 and 1994 cabinets were also drawn predominantly from parliament.[25] Similar to Bulgaria, however, this trend has not been exclusive. Fifty per cent of the 1998 cabinet led by the Federation of Young Democrats (FIDESZ) leader Orban were non-parliamentarians and, in general, the government did not include exclusively professional politicians.[26]

In the Czech Republic, the only legal limit to a complete fusion between government and parliament is a constitutional provision that bars MPs (and senators) who are members of the cabinet from the positions of Chair and Vice Chair of the Chamber of Deputies and the Senate, as well as from the membership of parliamentary committees and other commissions. In practice, cabinet members have generally come from the parliamentary party groups of the governing parties. In 1996, all ministers were recruited from the ranks of the parliament, while the somewhat higher figures of non-parliamentary ministers in the 1992 cabinet had more to do with nomination procedures than with any principled commitment to selecting cabinet members from outside parliament.[27] Similarly, the short-lived caretaker government (January–June 1998) under Prime Minister Tosovsky not only included several ministers recruited from outside the parliament, but also five ministers without party affiliation. However, the recruitment from outside parliament proved an exception rather than the rule in all Czech Social Democratic Party (CSSD)-led cabinets (1998–2006). Indeed, the Civil Democratic Party

(ODS)-led cabinet under Prime Minister Topolanek formed in 2007 includes only two ministers (out of 18) who do not simultaneously hold either a deputy or a senatorial seat in the parliament.

In sum, Hungary and Bulgaria have seen some variation in the way members of cabinet have been selected. The more dominant trend, however, has been to recruit ministers from the ranks of parliament, pointing to the dominance of the inter-party mode of executive–legislative relations. This trend is most obvious in the case of the Czech Republic.

In addition to the patterns of cabinet recruitment, the nature of the government formation process is also useful in discerning the dominant mode of executive–legislative relations. The presence of detailed coalition agreements points to the importance of the political party in general, and of the inter-party mode in particular, in the system of executive–legislative relations. This is because coalition agreements typically define the terms of cooperation between government parties and lay out a programme for policy areas which is binding for all parties involved.

In Bulgaria, coalition agreements have only become the norm since 2001, as most of the cabinets of the 1990s were treated as single-party ones.[28] The programme of the Kostov cabinet, however, became a central document during the four years of its tenure and the cabinet repeatedly updated and referred back to it as a way of checking their achievements. In 2001 and 2005 an elaborate coalition agreement between the governing parties was drawn up. In addition, a coalition council – a body comprising the chairmen of the three parties in government – was established in 2005. Since then, the council has acquired a powerful position in the policy-making process, although its functions are not formalised in any legislation.

Hungary has known coalition agreements since 1994, when the Hungarian Socialist Party-Alliance of Free Democrats (MSZP-SZDSZ) governing coalition agreed on an elaborate 144-page coalition agreement that specified the policy objectives and coalition principles of the newly formed government.[29] Since then coalition agreements have been signed on the formation of every government – there was a three-party coalition government in 1998, and a two-party one in 2002 and 2006.

In the Czech Republic, coalition agreements have been the norm since 1992. The first Klaus cabinet (1992–96) was the first to operate on the basis of a written agreement about policy objectives, distribution of portfolios and basic rules of communication that proved to be an 'important point of reference in all coalition negotiations'.[30] Cabinets established since 1992 have followed this practice without exception. Even the CSSD minority single-party government led by Milos Zeman (1998–2002) signed an agreement, the (in)famous 'Opposition Agreement', with the major opposition party (ODS) in which the latter offered the social democrats tacit support in parliament. What is particularly noteworthy in this context is not so much the existence of coalition agreements as such, but rather the fact that they have become more detailed over the years. Thus, while early coalition agreements were largely confined to basic rules of cooperation and the distribution of government and other posts, more recent agreements, including that of Topolanek's cabinet (2007), also contain detailed policy agreements and government performance targets. In that sense, the inter-party mode has become strongly institutionalised in the Czech Republic.

Party discipline is another indicator used for assessing the mode of executive–legislative relations.[31] Party cohesion in roll-call voting has been traditionally high in Hungary.[32] In addition, the rate of party defections has decreased substantially since the 1990 term. Then, 24 per cent of MPs changed their party affiliation, while 12 per cent did so in the 1994 parliament; only six per cent defected in the 1998 legislature and less than five per cent had defected by late 2005 from the 2002 Parliament.[33] And even these defections have been the result of party splits rather than individual MPs leaving their respective parties.[34]

In the Czech Republic, party discipline has also increased over the years. While party cohesion as measured by roll call voting might not have been as high as in some West European countries,[35] voting patterns clearly divide opposition and governing parties.[36] Party defection rates have also decreased substantially since the more turbulent parliamentary terms of the early 1990s, but after 2000 there was hardly any party switching and no founding of new parliamentary groups.[37] However, the formation of Topolanek's 2007 cabinet was made possible only because of the defection of two social democratic MPs, who tipped the 100–100 coalition–opposition balance in favour of the governing parties during the investiture vote. Afterwards, both MPs left the CSSD parliamentary party group but remained in parliament as independents.

In Bulgaria, the level of party discipline has been more varied. Unfortunately, no roll call data are available. Judging from the rate of party defections, parliamentary groups tended to be quite unstable at the beginning of the democratic period. In the 1991–94 Parliament, for example, *all* parties experienced a defection rate of about 20 per cent of their members.[38] During the 2001–5 term, defection rates were much more varied. Two parties had defection rates of just four per cent each, while another saw 17 per cent of its members defect, and still another split up into three separate parliamentary factions. So, while the general level of party defections seems to have increased (to about a quarter of all MPs), individual parties differ substantially on this count. In addition, the high defection rate in 2001–5 was mostly the result of a single party split rather than individual defections. Parties that maintained unity experienced very few individual defections.

Cross-party Mode

To ascertain whether we are observing elements of the second mode of inter-actions, the cross-party mode, we look into the structure of the parliamentary committees and analyse their powers to influence the decision-making process. A strong position of the committee vis-à-vis the cabinet and the parliamentary majority would indicate the importance of sectoral or special interests rather than party interest in the work of legislatures and executives.

The current Bulgarian legislature has 24 committees; their number has consistently been around 20. In four of the six legislatures since 1990, the committees have mirrored the government ministries.[39] This trend has been consistent since 1997: currently only five of the 24 committees do not correspond to a ministerial jurisdiction. Just as the committee structure increasingly resembles the executive one, committees also 'lost part of their role as institutions of pluralistic politics and became more focused on fulfilment of party policies and government proposals'.[40] Parliamentary committees have been dominated by the parliamentary groups and since committee seats are allocated proportionally, the work in the committees has effectively reinforced the split between governmental and non-governmental parties.

The number of committees in the Hungarian Parliament has increased consistently, from 14 in the 1990 term to 23 in the 2002 term. As in Bulgaria, committees in Hungary follow the jurisdictions of the ministries; their structure has been changed to reflect the emergence of new ministries and issues.[41] Originally not very well structured and only weakly institutionalised, the committees became more active actors and major arenas of legislative initiative in the 1994–98 Parliament.[42] However, since 1998 committees have become highly dominated by the majority parliamentary parties and the government.[43] Seats in the committees are distributed proportionally to parliamentary seats.

Committees in the Czech Republic have been less numerous than their counterparts in Hungary and Bulgaria. Their numbers increased only marginally during the 1992–96 and the 2002–6 terms; only two standing committees were added to the original 12.[44] In addition, the structure of the committees does not perfectly reflect the distribution of jurisdictions among the ministries. There have always been fewer committees than ministries and, in contrast to developments in Hungary and Bulgaria, the structure of the committee system has not evolved in accordance with changes to the departmental structure. This is explained by tradition, the small size of the Czech Chamber of Deputies (200), and the unwillingness of the parliamentary institutions to accommodate the ever-changing departmental structure of governments.[45] According to Mansfeldová and her collaborators, this also seems to be indicative of the stronger role of the Czech committees vis-à-vis the cabinet and the parliamentary groups in comparison to the situation in Hungary and Bulgaria. Although

committee seats are similarly allocated proportionally, thus effectively providing the majority party with a majority in each of the committees, the Czech
committees seem to enjoy quite some autonomy. The 'committees have a
great deal of independence' and the 'government doesn't have the right to
make decisions on anything within the CDCR or to interfere in the legislative
agenda of the Chamber of Deputies or its committees'.[46]

This is undoubtedly true and judging from a number of amendments to
government legislation emanating from committees, the cross-party mode
enjoys some prominence in executive–legislative relations in the Czech
Republic. However, there are also several factors that potentially weaken
the committees. Firstly, since the mid-1990s, bills are referred to committees
only after having passed the first reading on the floor. Although committees
can still propose amendments, and even reject a bill altogether, they have
lost some of the discretion over bills they enjoyed prior to this change of
the formal legislative procedure. Second, MPs can be members of two
permanent standing committees and, in practice, very often are. The introduction
of double membership was the result of the difficulties coalition parties experienced between 1992 and 1996 with maintaining majorities in all committees
given both the incompatibility of cabinet posts with committee membership
(see above), and the small size of some governing parties. While these problems no longer trouble the parliamentary party groups, the double membership has somewhat mitigated the effect of specialisation and hence impedes
the prospect for the cross-party mode to become dominant.

Non-party Mode

To ascertain whether executive–legislative relations in the post-communist
countries are characterised by the non-party mode of interactions we look
into how often parliaments have rejected government bills, the proportion
of bills initiated by parliamentary backbenchers and the role of investigative
commissions. In the non-party mode, members of parliament and members
of the cabinet interact as members of two institutions posed against each
other. Opposition to the government thus comes not necessarily from the
parties that are out of office, but from the parliament as a whole.

In Bulgaria, parliament has rarely rejected bills introduced by the government. In the 2001–5 Parliament, only three (0.5 per cent) out of 651 bills
introduced by the cabinet were rejected, while 532 (81.7 per cent) were
accepted and the rest were still in discussion. Similarly, the Hungarian
Parliament has enacted most of the bills proposed by the cabinet consistently
since 1990. The approval rate of government bills during 1994–2006 has been
at a stable average level of 91 per cent of all governmental proposals.[47] The
Czech Parliament rarely acted to reject governmental legislative proposals
between 1992 and 1996, and if it did it confined its activities to bills that

directly affected parliament as an institution.[48] The initially high success rate of governmental bills has decreased somewhat since and at 75 per cent it reached the lowest point during the minority cabinet between 1998 and 2002. However, it again reached 90 per cent during the 2002–6 term.[49]

Another indicator of non-party interaction between parliament and the executive relates to the legislative activity of individual MPs. Unfortunately, the Bulgarian parliamentary statutes do not allow for a distinction between bills initiated by individual MPs and bills initiated by parliamentary groups; they all appear as bills initiated by MPs belonging to a group. Overall, 45 per cent of *all* bills were initiated by the parliamentary groups but of these, 56 per cent were initiated by the governing parties. It is also worth noting that of the bills securing parliamentary approval only 3.3 per cent were initiated by the opposition parties, 16 per cent by the governing parties and the rest by the cabinet.[50] In Hungary, the number of proposed and, especially, enacted individual member bills has declined steadily over the years. If in the first term of the Hungarian Parliament (1990–94) 30 per cent of all enacted bills had been initiated by individual members, this was true for only nine per cent of all bills enacted in the 1998–2002 period and even these bills were often initiated by members of the governing parties in an effort to support the government.[51] In the Czech Republic, the number of both proposed and enacted member bills has been declining over time as well: in the 1992–96 term 42 per cent of proposed and 25 per cent of passed bills were initiated by MPs; by contrast, in the 2002–6 term the figures were only 31 per cent and 15 per cent respectively.[52] Overall, the legislative process in the Czech Republic, as in Bulgaria and Hungary, is increasingly dominated by the executive.

The ability of members of parliament to set up investigative commissions is the last indicator of the strength of the non-party mode of legislative–executive relations discussed here. In all three countries of our sample, investigative commissions can be set up on the suggestion of one-fifth of the MPs.[53] During 2001–5, the Bulgarian Parliament established six investigation commissions specifically designed to investigate different acts of the cabinet.[54] The previous two parliaments had only set up five and three investigation commissions, respectively.[55] In Hungary, similarly, seven investigation commissions were set up during 1994–98.[56] During 1998–2002 the parliament made less extensive use of these powers, but during 2002–6, 20 commissions were set up, of which at least six were aimed specifically at examining actions of the current government and government members.[57] These included the high-profile commissions set up in 2003 to investigate the political past of the members of the government after revelations that the current prime minister had worked for the Secret Service during the days of the old regime.

In the Czech Republic, between 1992 and 1996, only one investigative commission was established, on a multi-party basis, in order to examine the involvement of the former state security police in anti-regime demonstrations in 1989. A number of opposition proposals to set up other such commissions were dismissed by the governing majority. However, the number of investigative commissions has increased since: there were three commissions each in the 1996–98 and 1998–2002 parliaments and no fewer than five during the 2002–6 term.[58] Most of these commissions were created to investigate highly questionable privatisations and other forms of economic mismanagement, usually of the previous governments. These commissions were also mostly composed of an equal number of government and opposition MPs, with the exception of the 1998–2002 terms (during the reign of Zeman's minority cabinet), when government MPs were outnumbered by the opposition. However, the work of these commissions never caused any ministerial or governmental resignations.

THE MODES OF EXECUTIVE–LEGISLATIVE RELATIONS: CONSEQUENCES FOR THE OPPOSITION

This brief overview of several indicators of executive–legislative interactions in Bulgaria, Hungary, and the Czech Republic complements others that also highlight the dominance of the inter-party mode of interactions between the legislatures and executives in the post-communist world.[59] Cabinet members are drawn from the ranks of parliamentarians, coalition agreements and party manifestos have been important reference documents for the bulk of the cabinets, party discipline within the legislature is usually strong, and investiture votes are mandatory.

While the role of committees in legislative decision-making in the post-communist countries has varied slightly, indicating the co-existence of the cross-party mode with the inter-party mode, there has been a modest involvement of individuals and organisations from outside parliament in the work of committees in any of the three countries. For the most part, committee work is dominated by the parliamentary groups. Thus, even in a setting that would appear to be first to further the evolution of a cross-party mode of interaction, the inter-party mode prevails.

The relative dominance of the inter-party mode in post-communist Eastern Europe indicates that opposition to governments tends to come largely from the ranks of the parliamentary groups of those parties that are not in government. We rarely see indications of cross-sectoral or individually based opposition. What does this entail for the powers of the opposition? Others have argued that in the inter-party mode, '[b]y definition, the opposition is a minority and therefore powerless except for the rare occasions when a wedge can be driven between the governing parties'.[60] This is also true for the post-communist world: the opposition has a serious impact on the government only if, and to what extent, it manages to disrupt the party dynamics of the governing parties. Their ability to do so depends on two main factors: the formal powers of the opposition as defined by the institutional setting and the stability of the parties in government *and* in opposition.

FORMAL POWERS OF THE PARLIAMENTARY OPPOSITION

As in other democracies, the parliamentary opposition in the post-communist countries can challenge the work of the government through different channels. Among them are: political control of the cabinet through votes of (no-)confidence and question hours, influence on the content of government bills through participation in the legislative process, and ex post control of governmental policies by challenging laws before the constitutional court or initiating referenda. A brief overview of the formal powers and their use will reveal the similarities and differences in these institutional arrangements in the three countries under consideration.

Direct Control over the Cabinet

The most sophisticated variant of a vote of no-confidence is that to be found in Hungary. Shaped after the German prototype created in 1949, the Hungarian no-confidence vote is a 'constructive' one. A vote against a current prime minister may be initiated by one-fifth of the MPs, but any such move requires prior agreement on an alternative candidate to replace the incumbent prime minister directly. The vote against the PM is considered a vote against the government, and, if successful, a vote of investiture for the PM-designate.[61] The main reason for the adoption of this procedure was, of course, a reasonable level of government stability. While by 2007 such stability has been achieved, 'its cost has been the effective nullification of prime-ministerial responsibility', which rendered the opposition largely 'powerless'.[62]

In fact, the constructive vote of no-confidence has never as yet been used. However, the threat of using it has been real on at least one occasion. In August 2004, coalition disagreements between the MSZP and SZDSZ emerged. They added to the internal party problems within the MSZP evolving around the personality of Prime Minister Medgyessy, and ultimately created the first opportunity for a successful vote of no-confidence. However, rather than facing the vote, Medgyessy eventually resigned.[63]

In Bulgaria, a vote of no-confidence can be initiated by one-fifth of the members of parliament and requires the support of an absolute majority of MPs to be successful; however, if such a move fails, no new vote can be initiated within the next six months.[64] The Bulgarian opposition has made extensive use of this instrument, albeit unsuccessfully. Since 1997, no fewer than 12 votes of no-confidence have been launched: four times against

Prime Minister Kostov, six times against Prime Minister Sakskoburggotski, and twice against Prime Minister Stanishev.[65] However, the only occasion on which a vote had any significant effect was in early 2005, when the governing party, the NDSV, was experiencing significant internal cohesion problems. A group of younger MPs not represented in the NDSV and government leadership expressed strong discontent with their party and ultimately formed a separate faction in parliament. In their attempt to achieve policy concessions from the NDSV, the new faction united with the opposition to call for a vote of no-confidence, leading to the first occasion when the vote seemed destined to succeed. In a last minute decision, however, the NDSV agreed to the personnel changes in the cabinet demanded by the splinter faction, thereby ensuring their continued parliamentary support. Thus, to the great chagrin of the opposition, the vote proved unsuccessful again. However, this incident demonstrates what the opposition might achieve when the governing parties are experiencing internal problems.

In the Czech Republic, a vote of no-confidence is also not a constructive one, but nevertheless slightly more difficult to initiate than in Bulgaria. Fifty MPs (a quarter of the total number of MPs) are required for initiating a vote of no-confidence. As in Bulgaria, the support of an absolute majority of deputies is necessary to make it effective.[66] To date, no government has been forced to resign by a successful vote of no-confidence. Indeed, probably in anticipation of failure, the opposition has largely shied away from using its constitutional prerogative to put the government on line and initiated only two no-confidence votes between 1992 and mid-2007.

Legislative Influence

As in most other countries, passing legislation requires a simple majority of the MPs present in all three countries under inspection. Therefore, the power of the opposition to veto legislation is usually limited to constitutional amendments, for which there are special majority requirements. In Bulgaria, Hungary and the Czech Republic constitutional amendments require a qualified majority of two-thirds of all MPs, providing the opposition parties with an opportunity to block any such measures. However, as most constitutional amendments have been necessitated by the EU integration process, which was an overarching goal of all three countries, the opposition has made sparse use of this institutional device.

There have been some exceptions, though: in Hungary, the opposition was able to prevent a constitutional amendment initiated by the cabinet in 1999. The Fidesz-Hungarian Civic Party (FIDESZ-MPP) cabinet sought to introduce 'references to the Hungarian Crown' in the preamble of the constitution. Facing public controversy and resistance from the parliamentary opposition no constitutional amendment was introduced.[67] A major constitutional amendment of 2002, providing for the changes of Hungarian law made necessary by the country entering the EU, also strongly reflected the preferences of the opposition. Responding to criticism voiced by the FIDESZ, 'the government agreed to drop from the final draft three provisions ... [that] concern ministerial decrees, refugees, and the transfer of powers to international organizations'.[68]

In Bulgaria, the opposition has tried to influence constitutional policy on several occasions, but has never been powerful enough to achieve any results. In 1991, part of the opposition boycotted the vote on the adoption of the constitution, but a sufficiently large number of their members supported it, so that its adoption was not endangered. Similarly, part of the opposition opposed the third and fourth amendments of the Constitution in 2005 and 2006 respectively, but virtually without any effect.

In addition to vetoing, opposition parties in parliament can influence legislation by introducing their own bills or cooperate in committees to introduce 'co-sponsored' bills. During the 2001–5 term of the Bulgarian parliament, the opposition parties introduced about 19 per cent of all legislation, but with an approval rate of just about ten per cent their contribution to the overall legislative output of parliament has been rather limited.[69] In Hungary, from 1990 to 2006, the opposition introduced about 23 per cent of all legislation. However, while in the first parliamentary period about nine per cent of all opposition proposals were adopted, this rate dropped to about one per cent in the 1998–2002 parliament and picked up only slightly to reach 3.4 per cent in the 2002–6 one. Thus, overall, 1.7 per cent of all legislation adopted since 1990 has been initiated by the opposition.[70]

Furthermore, as the dominance of the inter-party mode suggests, the work of the standing committees is dominated heavily by the parliamentary parties. In all three countries committee seats are allocated proportionally to the size of the parliamentary groups. As a result, the majority party/coalition is usually in a position to dominate committee activity in all three parliaments. There has been some variation over time in the practice of distributing the chairs of committees between parties, however. The control of a committee's chairmanship has consequences for the agenda of the committee, and thus its legislative activity. In Bulgaria, from 1991 until 2001, or in three of the five parliaments since 1991, the opposition has either been denied or refused to accept any chair positions.[71] In the 2001 parliament, in tune with the NDSV's attempt to govern in a consensual way, four (19 per cent) of the 21 chairs were in opposition hands with the ODS and the BSP chairing two committees each. In the 2005 parliament, four (16 per cent) out of 24 committees are chaired by opposition parties divided equally among the four parties in opposition.[72]

In Hungary, during the 1990s, chair positions have also traditionally been in the hands of the government, although 'some were given to the opposition'.[73] However, by the 2006 parliament, things seemed to have changed. Of the 19 committees established, the opposition controlled eight (44 per cent), with FIDESZ being in charge of six and the Christian Democratic Party (KDNP) and Hungarian Democratic Forum (MDF) in charge of one each. In the Czech Republic, the opposition did not control a single parliamentary committee between 1992 and 1996. Since then, however, things have changed. After lengthy discussions it was agreed that not only committee membership, but also committee chairs be distributed on a (more) proportional basis. As a result, three out of 12, and five out of 14 committees were chaired by opposition MPs in the 1996–98 and 2002–6 terms respectively. However, the real 'opposition' parliament emerged between 1998 and 2002, during the rule of Zeman's minority cabinet, when opposition MPs chaired a majority of parliamentary committees (eight out of 13). Similarly, following the tight elections in 2006 and the resulting division of opposition and coalition MPs into two blocks of 100, the opposition secured eight out of 17 committee chairs.[74]

The Constitutional Courts

In addition to governmental scrutiny and legislative influence, the parliamentary oppositions in post-communist Europe can influence policies and politics through the Constitutional Courts. In Bulgaria and the Czech Republic, one-fifth (48 and 41, respectively) of the members of parliament can invoke the Constitutional Court to consider the constitutionality of a law or other act. By contrast, in Hungary anybody, including any number of MPs, can do so. These provisions allow the opposition in the three countries to take any law or decision of the government to the highest judicial authority.

The Bulgarian Constitutional Court has been invoked numerous times by opposition MPs and, on at least one occasion, its decision was crucial for the party in government. In 1996, opposition MPs invoked the Constitutional Court to establish whether the BSP presidential candidate, Pirinski, was eligible, given the constitutional provisions that only Bulgarian citizens by birth can run for the office of president.[75] The Constitutional Court's interpretation of the provision declared Pirinski ineligible for the post. Despite 'a torrent of vicious attacks ... against the Court'[76] Pirinski was denied registration by the Electoral Commission. As this happened only months before the elections, the BSP, having accepted the Court's decision, proved unable to recover from the blow. With a relatively unknown alternative candidate from the BSP, the opposition had few problems getting their candidate, Stoyanov, elected as President of the Republic.

In the Czech Republic, the 'court option' has been used frequently by opposition MPs in their battle against government bills. In addition to the lower chamber, (the opposition in) the Senate has also been active in petitioning the Court. Arguably the most notorious case of government defeat occurred in 2001, when the Court struck down all but one provision that would have significantly changed the electoral law to the lower chamber towards a more disproportional system.[77] Although the petition was officially presented by the then President Havel, it was signed also by opposition MPs and Senators. In Hungary, the Constitutional Court has also been used by the opposition as a final arena for challenging government bills. One of the more notorious cases was the conflict over the Media Law in 1999. At first sight, the conflict was over personnel changes initiated by the ruling FIDESZ in bodies supervising the national media, but the bigger issue concerned the question of political control of state-owned media. In this case, the Constitutional Court delivered an 'ambiguous ruling', which was interpreted as a victory on both sides.[78]

While the opposition in the post-communist countries can easily use the Constitutional Court to challenge governmental policies, these actions are confined to issues relating to constitutional provisions. Thus, the powers of the opposition remain fairly limited in this respect. However, the relatively high frequency with which the constitutional courts of all three countries have been petitioned (successfully), as well as the fact that all three constitutions and their related Bills of Freedoms and Rights provide a relatively wide ground for judicial disputes, suggests that challenging bills before the constitutional courts may in fact be considered one of the most powerful and effective weapons of the parliamentary opposition, especially during periods marked by a solid and stable governing majority.

Referenda

Finally, in two of the three countries under study the parliamentary opposition has the power to challenge governmental policies, or to initiate new ones through referenda. In Hungary one-third of all elected MPs are needed to call for a referendum; in Bulgaria only one-quarter of all MPs need to agree to do so. However, in both countries the parliament needs formally to initiate a referendum, which has made opposition-backed referenda highly unlikely.[79] In the Czech Republic there are virtually no provisions for national referenda on general issues, though in 1998 a one-time referendum was held on the accession of the country to the EU.

In neither Hungary nor Bulgaria has the opposition been able to use this formal power to challenge policies to date. In Bulgaria, in fact, no national referendum has been held since 1989. Legislation providing for direct democracy only came into being in 1996 and is quite restrictive as it does not allow citizens to initiate referenda.[80] On several occasions, the opposition has raised the issue of calling a referendum, and on at least one occasion it initiated a parliamentary vote on it but it was struck down by the parliamentary majority.

In Hungary, five referenda have been held since 1989 but none of these has been initiated by the parliamentary opposition as such; they have been either cabinet-backed or initiated by extra-parliamentary organisations. However, as of June 2007 the main opposition party, FIDESZ appeared set to initiate a referendum on several issues relating to the government's healthcare, education and agriculture policies.[81]

CONCLUSION: PARTY STABILITY AND THE OPPOSITION

The previous discussion offers several conclusions about the parliamentary opposition in post-communist Eastern Europe. First of all, executive–legislative relations in all three countries of that region appear to be increasingly characterised by the inter-party mode of interactions. The main divisions that define the interactions between parliaments and governments are party ones: belonging to the governing party or not appears to be the key determinant of MPs' behaviour. Thus, because of both institutional parameters and political circumstances, political parties are the key source of opposition in what are essentially regular parliamentary systems of government. We contend that this would seem likely to hold true for other such systems of government in the post-communist countries not covered in our survey, such as Estonia, Slovenia, Slovakia and Poland. In contrast, other dynamics are likely to occur in systems with a different formal design and executive–legislative relations dominated by powerful presidencies – Russia and Ukraine are clear examples.[82]

Moreover, as the dominance of the inter-party mode suggests, the parties in opposition can achieve little as long as party discipline remains strong and the governing party or coalition cohesive. Only if this is not the case can the opposition make effective use of its formal powers to influence the law-making and law-implementation process. Overall, we observe relatively little variation in the formal powers of the opposition in Eastern Europe. Hungary stands out in our sample of countries in that the opposition has to overcome a constructive vote of no-confidence to bring the government down. To be sure, in none of the three countries covered here were governments forced to resign because of a successful vote of no-confidence. However, in both Bulgaria and the Czech Republic the opposition has at least been able to call for it, which helped to increase their visibility in day-to-day politics. Also, the opposition's impact on government bills has been rather weak, while the somewhat more effective use of their right to challenge laws before the constitutional court has remained quite limited in scope.

Quite importantly, however, for the opposition to be able to use its powers effectively it also needs to be united itself. Thus, the most opposition-friendly situation is one in which the governing party or coalition is unstable while the opposition parties are stable and united. As Table 1 indicates, however, the opposition in both Bulgaria and (to a lesser extent) the Czech Republic has become increasingly fragmented over the years. Hungary, by contrast, has seen a general decline in the number of parties, including the number of opposition parties. Given the additional variation – both across and within systems – of the level of party ideological cohesion, development and organisational strength, it is not surprising that the role of the opposition has been rather limited.

The few occasions on which the opposition has had a significant impact in the parliamentary arena – the 1997–98 period in the Czech Republic, and the 2004 government resignation in Hungary, merit special mention – related to periods in which the government was unstable while the parties constituting the 'opposition' were united and cohesive. As Hungary has consistently seen strong parties, the influence of the opposition there appears to be the most significant of the three countries studied. Similarly, the Czech opposition has become more powerful since 1996, though not necessarily due to increased cohesiveness, but rather because government majorities have become more and more fragile and governments less ideologically cohesive. In terms of the strength of the opposition, the Czech Republic thus lies somewhere between Hungary and Bulgaria. Bulgaria has indeed seen periods of *either* stable governmental majorities *or* unstable governments but equally unstable and disjointed oppositions. As a result, the opposition's overall impact has probably remained most limited there.

NOTES

1. J. Linz and A. Stepan, *Problems of Democratic Transition and Consolidation* (Baltimore, MD: John Hopkins University Press, 1996), and M. Waller, *The End of the Communist Power Monopoly* (Manchester and New York: Manchester University Press, 1993).
2. J.M. Colomer, 'Strategies and Outcomes in Eastern Europe', *Journal of Democracy*, 6 (1995), pp.74–85; J. Elster (ed.), *Roundtable Talks and the Breakdown of Communism* (Chicago, IL: University of Chicago Press, 1996); E. Matynia, 'Furnishing Democracy at the End of the Century: The Polish Round Table and Others', *European Politics and Societies*, 15 (2001), pp.454–71; A.P. Melone, 'Bulgaria's National Round-Table Talks and the Politics of Accommodation', *International Political Science Review* 15 (July 1994), pp.245–68.
3. See, for example, S. Baker and P. Jehlicka (eds.), 'Dilemmas of Transition: The Environment, Democracy and Economic Reform in ECE', *Environmental Politics* (special issue), 7 (1998); S. Crowley and D. Ost (eds.), *Workers After Workers' States: Labor and Politics in Postcommunist Eastern Europe* (Lanham, MD: Rowman & Littlefield, 2001); S. LaFont, 'One Step Forward, Two Steps Back: Women in the Post-Communist States', *Communist and Post-Communist Studies*, 34 (2001), pp.203–20.
4. M.M. Howard, *The Weakness of Civil Society in Post-communist Europe* (Cambridge: Cambridge University Press, 2002).
5. For an alternative view see P. Kopecký and C. Mudde (eds.), *Uncivil Society? Contentious Politics in Post-communist Europe* (London: Routledge, 2003).
6. E. Kalinova and I. Baeva, *Bulgarskite Prehodi 1944–1999* [The Bulgarian Transitions 1944–1999] (Sofia: Tilia, 2000), p.188.

7. P.G. Lewis, 'The Repositioning of Opposition in East-Central Europe', *Government and Opposition*, 32 (1997), pp.614–30; A. Stepan, 'Democratic Opposition and Democratization Theory', *Government and Opposition*, 32 (1997), pp.656–73; J. Barber, 'Opposition in Russia', *Government and Opposition*, 32 (1997), pp.598–613.

8. L. Helms, 'Five Ways of Institutionalizing Political Opposition: Lessons from the Advanced Democracies', *Government and Opposition*, 39 (2004), pp.22–54.

9. P. Kopecký, 'Power to the Executive! The Changing Executive–Legislative Relations in Eastern Europe', *Journal of Legislative Studies*, 10 (2004), pp.142–54; T.A. Baylis, 'Presidents versus Prime Ministers: Shaping Executive Authority in Eastern Europe', *World Politics*, 48 (1996), pp.297–323; T.A. Baylis, 'Embattled Executives: Prime Minister-ial Weakness in East Central Europe', *Communist and Post-Communist Studies*, 40 (2007), pp.81–106.

10. P. Kopecký, *Parliaments in the Czech and Slovak Republics. Party Competition and Parliamentary Institutionalization* (Aldershot: Ashgate, 2002); P. Norton and D.M. Olson (eds.), *Post-Communist and Post-Soviet Parliaments: The Initial Decade*, special issue of *The Journal of Legislative Studies*, 13/1 (2007); D.M. Olson and P. Norton (eds.), *The New Parliaments of Central and Eastern Europe* (London and Portland, OR: Frank Cass Publishers, 1996); D.M. Olson, 'Institutionalization of Parliamentary Committees: the Experience of Post-communist Democracies', Paper presented at the ECPR Congress Workshop #16, Turin, 22–27 March 2002; D.M. Olson and W.E. Crowther (eds.), *Committees in Post-Communist Democratic Parliaments: Comparative Institutionalization* (Columbus, OH: Ohio State University Press, 2003), pp.21–43.

11. J. Blondel and F. Müller-Rommel, *Cabinets in Eastern Europe* (New York: Palgrave, 2001); P. Harfst, 'Government Stability in Central and Eastern Europe: The Impact of Parliaments and Parties', Paper presented at the ECPR Joint Session of Workshops, Copenhagen, 14–19 April 2000.

12. Parties in post-communist systems tend to fall within three general categories: the successors of the old communist parties and their satellites (the socialist BSP in Bulgaria and MSZP in Hungary, and the communist KSCM and Christian democratic KDU-CSL in the Czech Republic), the parties that formed (from) the original opposition movements (the conservative MDF and FIDESZ and the liberal SZDSZ in Hungary, conservative SDS, centrist BZNS and the ethnic MRF in Bulgaria, and liberal/conservative ODS and ODA, and social-democratic CSSD in the Czech Republic) and the new parties that have emerged since then. The new parties are most prominent in Bulgaria where the liberal and populist NDSV dominated politics between 2001 and 2005. The presence of anti-system parties has been rather limited: examples include MIEP in Hungary during 1994–2002 and Ataka in Bulgaria since 2005. For a more detailed discussion of parties in the post-communist world see P.G. Lewis, *Political Parties in Post-communist Eastern Europe* (London and New York: Routledge, 2000); P.G. Lewis, *Party Development and Democratic Change in Post-Communist Europe: The First Decade* (London: Frank Cass, 2001); M. Spirova, *Political Parties in Post-communist Societies: Formation, Persistence and Change* (Basingstoke: Palgrave, 2007).

13. Harfst, 'Government Stability in Central and Eastern Europe'.

14. A. King, 'Modes of Executive–Legislative Relations: Great Britain, France and West Germany', *Legislative Studies Quarterly*, 1 (1976), p.11.

15. R.B. Andeweg, 'Executive–Legislative Relations in the Netherlands: Consecutive and Coexisting Patterns', *Legislative Studies Quarterly*, 17 (1992), pp.161–82; T. Saalfeld, 'The West German Bundestag after 40 Years: The Role of Parliament in "Party Democracy"', in P. Norton (ed.), *Parliaments in Western Europe* (London: Frank Cass, 1990), pp.68–89.

16. R.B. Andeweg and L. Nijzink, 'Beyond the Two Body Image: Relations between Ministers and MPs', in H. Döring (ed.), *Parliaments and Majority Rule in Western Europe* (Frankfurt: Campus Verlag, 1995), pp.152–78.

17. King, 'Modes of Executive–Legislative Relations'.

18. See Andeweg and Nijzink, 'Beyond the Two Body Image'.

19. D.M. Olson, 'The New Parliaments of New Democracies: The Experience of the Federal Assembly of the Czech and Slovak Federal Republic', in A. Agh (ed.), *The Emergence of East Central European Parliaments: The First Steps* (Budapest: Hungarian Centre of Democracy Studies Foundation, 1994), p.45.
20. Spirova, *Political Parties in Post-communist Societies*; J. Toole, 'Government Formation and Party System Stabilization in East Central Europe', *Party Politics*, 6 (2000), pp.441–63.
21. Andeweg, 'Executive–Legislative Relations in the Netherlands', p.163.
22. In all three countries, presidents act as heads of state with quite circumscribed constitutional powers, including powers to nominate the prime minister, dissolve parliament, suspend veto on legislation, some legislative initiatives, and certain powers in foreign relations. The indirectly elected Hungarian parliament has retained a relatively unimportant role in Hungarian politics, while the directly elected Bulgarian one and the indirectly elected Czech parliament have attempted to go beyond their formal powers and on several occasions this has proved crucial for the making and breaking of governments. This happened twice with President Zhelev in Bulgaria (1992 and 1997) and once with President Havel in the Czech Republic (1997). However, these were the only occasions when an incumbent government was not able to maintain cohesion. Therefore, while we leave presidents out of our empirical analysis, the experience with presidential influence in the political process in all three countries clearly underscores the point we make later about the link between the stability of government parties and the *de facto* power of the parliamentary opposition.
23. King, 'Modes of Executive–Legislative Relations'; Andeweg, 'Executive–Legislative Relations in the Netherlands'.
24. Kalinova and Baeva, *Bulgarskite Prehodi*, p.177.
25. G. Ilonszki and S. Kurtan, 'Hungary', *European Journal of Political Research*, 28 (1995), pp.359–68.
26. EJPS, 32 (1999).
27. Following the disintegration of Czechoslovakia, many ministerial posts were eventually given to MPs from the then dissolving Federal Assembly because this is where parties normally nominated their heavyweights. See Kopecký, *Parliaments in the Czech and Slovak Republics*, pp.104–5.
28. The governments of the 1990s are usually considered to have been single-party majority governments. However, at least three of them – the Berov government in 1992, Videnov in 1995 and Kostov in 1997 – were either supported by more than one parliamentary party (Berov), or the 'majority' party itself was an alliance of several parties. The Videnov cabinet included members of two smaller parties that had been part of the BSP electoral alliance and the Kostov cabinet included ministers from three individual parties that had made up the ODS alliance. However, no coalition agreements were signed. And, at least in the case of the Berov cabinet, this facilitated the downfall of the cabinet.
29. G. Ilonszki and S. Kurtan, 'Hungary', *European Journal of Political Research*, 28 (1995), p.364.
30. Kopecký, *Parliaments in the Czech and Slovak Republics*, p.109.
31. Andeweg, 'Executive–Legislative Relations in the Netherlands', p.167.
32. K. Montgomery, 'Electoral Effects on Party Behavior and Development', *Party Politics*, 5 (1999) pp.507–23.
33. Percentages calculated using data (p.50) in G. Ilonszki, 'From Minimal to Subordinate: A Final Verdict? The Hungarian Parliament, 1990–2002', *Journal of Legislative Studies*, 13/1 (2007), pp.38–58.
34. Ilonszki, 'From Minimal to Subordinate', pp.38–58.
35. L. Linek and P. Rakušanová, 'Why Czech Parliamentary Party Groups Vote Less Unitedly: The Role of Frequent Voting and Bog Majorities in Passing Bills', *Czech Sociological Review*, 41 (2005), pp.401–23.
36. Kopecký, *Parliaments in the Czech and Slovak Republics*, pp.100–101.
37. L. Linek and Z. Mansfeldová, 'The Parliament of the Czech Republic, 1993–2004', *The Journal of Legislative Studies*, 13/1 (2007), pp.12–37.

38. G. Karasimenov, 'The Legislature in Post-Communist Bulgaria', in Olson and Norton (eds.), *The New Parliaments of Central and Eastern Europe*, p.57.
39. G. Karasimenov, 'Bulgaria: Parliamentary Committees – Institutionalization and Effectiveness', in Olson and Crowther (eds.), *Committees in Post-Communist Democratic Parliaments*, pp.93–117.
40. Karasimenov, 'Bulgaria: Parliamentary Committees', p.101.
41. Ilonszki, 'From Minimal to Subordinate', pp.47–8.
42. G. Ilonszki, 'A Functional Clarification of Parliamentary Committees in Hungary, 1990–98', in Olson and Crowther (eds.), *Committees in Post-Communist Democratic Parliaments*, pp.21–43.
43. Ilonszki, 'From Minimal to Subordinate', p.49.
44. Linek and Mansfeldova, 'The Parliament of the Czech Republic, 1993–2004', p.24. However, the 2006 parliament created 17 committees.
45. Z. Mansfeldová, J. Syllová, P. Rakušanová and P. Kolář, 'Committees of the Chamber of Deputies of the Czech Republic', in Olson and Crowther (eds.), *Committees in Post-Communist Democratic Parliaments*, pp.69–89.
46. Mansfeldová *et al.*, 'Committees of the Chamber of Deputies of the Czech Republic', p.89.
47. Ilonzki, 'From Minimal to Subordinate', p.52; data for 2002–6 provided by the Information Centre of the Hungarian Parliament.
48. Kopecký, *Parliaments in the Czech and Slovak Republics*, p.132.
49. Linek and Mansfeldova, 'The Parliament of the Czech Republic, 1993–2004', p.33.
50. Figures calculated by the authors with data from *Bulgarian Parliament Legislation Database*, available at www.parliament.bg/?page=app&lng=bg&aid=4.
51. Ilonzki, 'From Minimal to Subordinate', p.51.
52. Linek and Mansfeldová, 'The Parliament of the Czech Republic, 1993–2004', p.33. Data refer only to the period 2002–4.
53. Bulgarian Constitution, Art. 31.
54. Figures calculated from *Bulgarian Parliament Archives: 39th Parliament*, available at www.parliament.bg/?page=archive&lng=bg
55. Karasimenov, 'Bulgaria: Parliamentary Committees'.
56. Ilonzki, 'From Minimal to Subordinate', p.53.
57. Ilonzki, 'From Minimal to Subordinate', p.53; figures for 2002–6 calculated by the authors with data from the Information Centre of the Hungarian Parliament.
58. Figures from www.psp.cz.
59. J.W. Schiemann, 'Hungary: The Emergence of Chancellor Democracy', *Journal of Legislative Studies*, 10 (2004), pp.128–41; Kopecký, *Parliaments in the Czech and Slovak Republics*, pp.96–144, Ilonszki, 'From Minimal to Subordinate', pp.38–58.
60. Schiemann, 'Hungary: The Emergence of Chancellor Democracy', pp.128–41; Kopecký, *Parliaments in the Czech and Slovak Republics*, pp.96–144; Ilonszki, 'From Minimal to Subordinate', pp.38–58.
61. Hungarian Constitution, Art. 39/A.
62. G. Schöpflin, 'Hungary: Country without Consequences', *OpenDemocracy*, 22 Sept. 2006, http://193.41.101.59/debates/article.jsp?id=3&debateId=33&articleId=3926.
63. G. Ilonszki and S. Kurtan, 'Hungary', *European Journal of Political Research*, 44 (2005), p.1033.
64. Bulgarian Constitution, Art. 89.
65. Rates calculated by the authors with data from *Kapital Weekly Archives*.
66. Czech Constitution, Art. 72.
67. G. Ilonszki and S. Kurtan, 'Hungary', *European Journal of Political Research*, 38 (2000), p.407.
68. 'Hungary', *The World of Parliaments Quarterly Review*, Issue 9 (2003), available at www.ipu.org/news-e/9-7.htm.
69. Figures calculated by the authors with data from *Bulgarian Parliament Archives: 39th Parliament*, available at www.parliament.bg/?page=archive&lng=bg.

70. Figures calculated by the authors with data provided by the Information Centre of the Hungarian Parliament.
71. Karasimenov, 'Bulgaria: Parliamentary Committees'.
72. Rates for the 2001 and 2005 Parliament calculated by the authors with data from *Bulgarian Parliament Archives: 39th Parliament* and *Bulgarian Parliament: 40th Parliament*, available at www.parliament.bg/?page=ns&lng=bg.
73. Ilonzki, 'From Minimal to Subordinate', p.47.
74. Figures calculated by the authors on the basis of information from www.psp.cz.
75. Pirinski had been born in the USA and became a naturalised Bulgarian citizen.
76. V. Ganev, 'The Bulgarian Constitutional Court 1991–1997: A Success Story in Context', *Europe-Asia Studies*, 4 (2003), p.602.
77. See P. Kopecký, 'Czech Republic: Entrenching Proportional Representation', in J.M. Colomer (ed.), *Handbook of Electoral System Choice* (Basingstoke: Palgrave, 2004), pp.347–58.
78. 'Constitutional Watch', *East European Constitutional Review*, 9 (2000).
79. The situation in Hungary is more favourable to the opposition. Since referenda backed by citizens are not only allowed but also binding irrespective of how parliament feels on the issue, the opposition can use this road to initiate national referenda. However, on several occasions the majority has successfully challenged the legality of opposition-backed referenda, thereby preventing them (*East European Constitutional Review Constitutional Watch*, 7/1, 1998.)
80. Balkan Assist, *Pryakata Demokraciya: Pregled na Istoiyatata i Praktikite* [Direct Democracy: Review of its History and Practice] (Sofia: Balkan Assist, 2005).
81. B. Koranyi, 'Hungary's top court backs opposition referendum', www.reuters.com/article/health-SP/idUSL0581268220070605.
82. For a treatment of some of these cases see P. Norton and D.M. Olson (eds.), 'Post-Communist and Post-Soviet Parliaments: The Initial Decade', special issue of the *Journal of Legislative Studies* 13/1 (2007).

Parliamentary Opposition in Non-Parliamentary Regimes: Latin America

SCOTT MORGENSTERN, JUAN JAVIER NEGRI
and ANÍBAL PÉREZ-LIÑÁN

What is the best way to analyse the role of the opposition in Latin America? In parliamentary systems, policy debates turn on government–opposition relations. In the United States, the debate is typically about executive–legislative relations. In this article we argue that both vernaculars are relevant to Latin American politics.

The opposition is clearly defined for parliamentary politics as the parties not included in the executive cabinet. In the United States discussions revolve around executive–legislative relations because the independence of the branches makes defining the ins and outs more complicated. If the president is a member of the same party as the majority of both houses of Congress, then the opposition is simply the minority party. If, however, the president and the majority of members of one house of Congress are from different parties, then government and opposition lines are blurred, because policies can only be approved with the agreement of the president's party and some moderate legislators willing to 'cross the aisle'. In most Latin American countries the issue is even more complicated, because presidential systems are frequently conjoined with multipartism. As such, the definition and more importantly the role of the opposition in Latin America blends some ingredients from both the US and European models.

Many Latin American systems borrow a notion of coalitional government from the Europeans, despite early research that predicted the inability of presidential systems to form coalitions. As their own parties lack majority control of the legislature, and multiple parties hold important numbers of seats, some Latin American presidents have offered cabinet seats to opposition parties in an attempt to build European-style legislative support. This has led to some successes, but without the glue of confidence votes to hold the system together they have not always worked to cement legislative support.

A second possibility for the Latin American presidents is to run minority governments. Kaare Strom[1] found that about one-third of European parliaments are minority governments, and we find that 52 per cent of Latin American single-party governments are minority governments and that 51 per cent of Latin American presidents lack legislative majorities, even when offering cabinet posts to some legislative parties.[2] As in European-style minority governments, these presidents must rely on informal coalitions to pass their legislation (though some also try to evade the legislature altogether).

While the multipartism yields comparisons with European minority governments, presidential constitutions also yield a relation between the government and opposition that resembles the United States under times of divided government. At these times the Latin American presidents must bargain with legislatures that are frequently prone to reject executive proposals, thus forcing the president to compromise, buy support with policy or pork, or attempt to evade the legislative process.

While a model of government–opposition for Latin America would have to blend key components from Europe and the United States, the Latin Americans also have their own special ingredients. In particular, the institutional context is such that the legislatures do not generally play as significant a role in the policy process as in the United States. They are sometimes very influential – even to the point of removing the executive from office – but their role in policy-making is often more limited than that of the US Congress. As such, the opposition in Latin America (if defined as parties not in the executive's coalition) is even more marginalised than in the United States. The second difference is that the Latin American legislatures' fractionalisation can mean that no party controls a majority of the legislature. In these cases, there is not *an* opposition, but *multiple* oppositions. This creates new and greater collective action problems than in the US case, with implications not only for executive–legislative relations, but also for legislative organisation.

The goal of this paper is to explore these definitions and roles in several ways. In the first part of the paper we explore the size and shape of the opposition in Latin American governments. We provide information about the fractionalisation of the Latin American legislatures with an eye towards the degree of presidential support. We also explore coalition politics, arguing that while some presidents try to build cabinet-style coalitions, others rely on informal arrangements for their legislative support. In the second part of the paper we discuss the apparent trade-off between presidential powers and the power of the opposition. Against common assumptions in the literature, we argue that the strength of the president and the opposition are not inversely related. The reason is that strong party organisations may empower both camps, while weak parties may hinder the operational capacity of the two branches of government. Thus, it is better to conceptualise govern-ment–opposition relations as a positive-sum game anchored in the party system rather than as a zero-sum game anchored in inter-branch disputes.

In the third part of the paper we analyse the role of the Latin American opposition and its impact on the political system. We consider this issue from several vantage points. From an opposition–government perspective, we use legislative surveys to map the roles played by opposition legislators in the policy-making process. The data suggest that, even though the opposi-tion participates in the elaboration of laws, legislators tend to define their distinctive role as oversight rather than policy-making. From an executive–legislative relations perspective, we explore the degree to which those legis-lators exercise oversight in its most extreme form – by removing the president from office. Our analysis of 123 South American cabinets between 1958 and 1995 indicates that coalition politics in Latin America historically reduced the risk of military interventions against the president. At the same time, the analysis of more recent presidential downfalls in Latin America between 1980 and 2004 indicates that the opposition in Latin America has the capacity to oversee the executive and impeach the president (or force his or her resig-nation) when necessary, although this power is often misused for partisan reasons or invoked in an opportunistic manner when the president is unpopular.

DEFINING THE OPPOSITION IN LATIN AMERICA

Traditional research on Latin American executive–legislative relations has focused on the difficult relation between the branches. In contrast to parlia-mentary regimes, where the executive is formed by and is responsible to the assembly, the independent election of presidents means that only one party can win the grand prize. Still, this model presumes that there is an opposition that can stymie the president. Generally, the opposition is not carefully defined in these models, but Mainwaring argued that the executive–legislative conflict would be compounded by multipartism, because this would increase the likelihood that the president would lack a working majority in the assembly.[3] The model suggests, therefore, that the separation of powers would inevitably generate irresolvable conflict between the branches thus threatening stability and democracy.[4] This model of executive–legislative relations does highlight an important challenge to presidentialism as institutional challenges have played important roles in recent constitutional crises (for example, Ecuador) and more distant breakdowns of democracy (Chile). Still, by and large a more prosaic form of politics generally ensues, with the two branches bargaining over policies and reaching compromises on many bills. This sort of successful politicking results from an important aspect of presidentialism that has been too often ignored in studies: coalitions.

Until recently, scholarship has ignored the possibility that coalitions could help overcome the 'difficult combination' of multipartism and presidentialism, perhaps because presidential systems lack some of the mechanisms that help cement parliamentary coalitions together (namely the appointment of the cabinet by the parliament, and confidence votes). Several recent works, however, have documented the great frequency with which presidents form supportive coalitions.[5] Deheza finds that 69 of 123 (56 per cent) cabinets formed in nine South American countries between 1958 and 1995 were coalition governments. Further, of the 66 cases where the president had majority support, in only 22 cases did that support rest on a single party.[6] Similarly, Cheibub, Przeworki and Saiegh[7] found that more than one-half of presidents who face a minority of their co-partisans in the legislature also form coalitions.

As a result of the prevalence of coalitions, we define the opposition in presidential systems as the group of legislators who do not belong to the president's party or to any party which has membership in the president's cabinet. This is, of course, a simplifying definition, that assumes that members of the president's party or members of parties in the president's cabinet are more likely to be supportive than other legislators. This is not always true, but it does allow for a precise categorisation that can shift over time as different parties enter or leave the cabinet.

In order to assess the relative size and the leverage of the congressional opposition in Latin America, we collected information for six indicators in 18 countries (Argentina, Bolivia, Brazil, Chile, Colombia, Costa Rica, Dominican Republic, Ecuador, El Salvador, Guatemala, Honduras, Mexico, Nicaragua, Panama, Paraguay, Peru, Uruguay and Venezuela) between 1978 (or the installation of democracy) and 2004. We use the following indicators in our analysis:

1. The size of the president's party. This variable measures the share of seats controlled by the president's party in Congress (as a proportion; computed separately for the lower house and for the Senate). In the case of Uruguay, we measured the size of the president's 'fraction' in Congress – a better

indicator of the core legislative support for the chief executive – whenever information was available.[8] Unfortunately, information for factional align-ments was not available for Uruguay after 1995, or for countries with similar situations such as Colombia. In those cases, the variable simply reflected the size of the ruling party.

2. The size of the government's coalition. We defined the government's coalition in Congress as the president's party *plus* any other party or faction aligned with the executive. We compiled information on this subject from multiple sources.[9] In general, these sources defined govern-ment coalitions based on the distribution of cabinet positions, although the definition in the case of Beck *et al.* is less clear.[10] Information on coalitions is often imperfect, yet it allowed us to identify additional sources of support for the executive.

3. The size of the opposition. The size of the opposition in Congress was defined as the share of sets not controlled by the president's coalition.

4. Partisan cohesion. We computed a simple measure of cohesion among opposition parties by taking the ratio between the largest opposition party (in the House or the Senate) and the total proportion of seats con-trolled by the opposition in the respective chamber. Opposition cohesion, therefore, is assumed to decline as the number of parties in the opposition grows.

5. Effective number of parties. As a standard measure of party system frag-mentation, we also computed the effective number of parties in the House and the Senate. The effective number of parties is defined as $1/(\Sigma p_i^2)$, where p is the proportion of seats controlled by the i-th party.[11] The index thus captures the number of parties in the chamber, weighted by their respective size.

6. The durability of coalitions. Because presidents have fixed terms in office, in presidential systems the dissolution of a ruling coalition cannot be equated to the end of the government. We used the data collected by Grace Ivana Deheza for nine South American countries between 1958 and 1995, and identified whether the end of coalitions resulted from a cabinet reshuffle, or from the end of an administration (because a newly elected president took office, because the president resigned, or because there was a military coup).[12]

Patterns of Opposition

Table 1 presents the average size of the president's party and the congressional opposition in 18 Latin American countries between 1978 and 2004. In the typical country, during a typical year, the opposition controlled 46 per cent

TABLE 1
AVERAGE SIZE AND UNITY OF THE OPPOSITION IN LATIN AMERICA (1978–2004)

Country	President's party		Opposition[a]		Unity[b]	
	House	Senate	House	Senate	House	Senate
Colombia	0.39	0.39	0.30	0.33	0.53	0.59
Brazil	0.14	0.15	0.34	0.24	0.34	0.45
Bolivia	0.31	0.45	0.39	0.28	0.51	0.77
Nicaragua	0.54		0.39		0.69	
Chile	0.26	0.22	0.42	0.56	0.56	0.41
Mexico	0.55	0.76	0.43	0.23	0.54	0.83
Panama	0.27		0.44		0.64	
Guatemala	0.38		0.45		0.59	
Paraguay	0.55	0.52	0.45	0.48	0.77	0.70
Peru	0.50	0.42[c]	0.46	0.52[c]	0.52	0.54[c]
Latin America	0.39	0.43	0.46	0.40	0.62	0.68
Argentina	0.48	0.51	0.48	0.46	0.64	0.65
Honduras	0.49		0.48		0.92	
El Salvador	0.42		0.49		0.65	
Venezuela	0.39	0.40[d]	0.50	0.49[d]	0.59	0.76[d]
Costa Rica	0.49		0.51		0.79	
Uruguay	0.30	0.24	0.53	0.49	0.70	0.72
Dominican Republic	0.43	0.55	0.55	0.45	0.78	0.86
Ecuador	0.15		0.62		0.35	

Notes: [a]Opposition is defined as the share of seats not controlled by the president's party or the president's coalition; [b]Largest opposition party/Total seats for the opposition; [c]Prior to 1992; [d]Prior to 1999.

of the House and 40 per cent of the Senate. More than five percentage points above this average were the oppositions in Uruguay, the Dominican Republic, and Ecuador. More than five percentage points below this average were the oppositions in Colombia, Brazil, Bolivia and Nicaragua. A large opposition did not necessarily mean a cohesive one: in Ecuador, where the opposition typically controlled more than 60 per cent of the seats in the unicameral Congress, the largest opposition party barely comprised 35 per cent of this bloc (that is, 22 per cent of the total seats).

Country averages mask significant dispersion across administrations, as suggested by Figure 1. The boxplots show the degree of variation in the size of the opposition faced by 108 administrations in the lower house during this period. The frame of each box indicates the upper and lower quartiles for each country – above the box lie one-quarter of the administrations facing the largest opposition contingents; below the box lie the 25 per cent of the presidents facing the weakest oppositions. The horizontal line dividing the box indicates the median case for each country. (Vertical lines stretch to

FIGURE 1

BOXPLOTS: SIZE OF THE OPPOSITION IN LOWER HOUSE TO 108 LATIN AMERICAN
ADMINISTRATIONS, 1978–2004

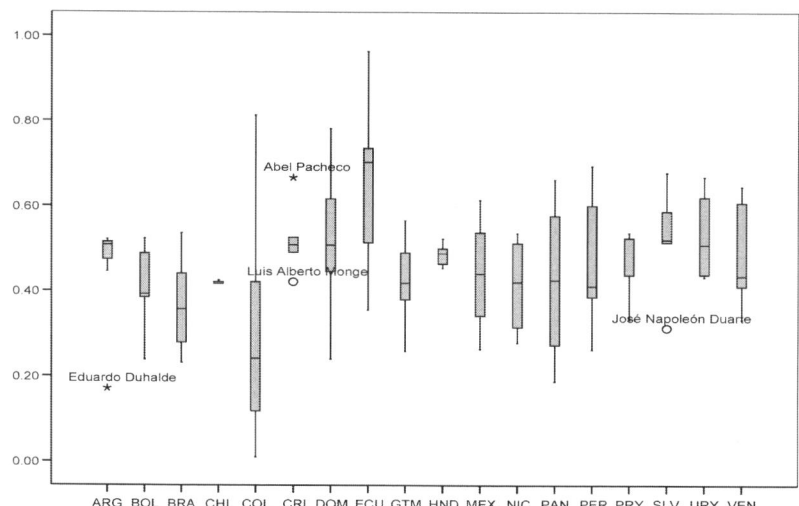

mark the extreme values within a range equivalent to one and a half times the
inter-quartile range; outliers outside this range are individually identified.)
Dispersion is relatively small in Argentina, Chile, Costa Rica (with some
exceptions), and Honduras, while the size of the opposition may be hard to
anticipate in Colombia, Ecuador, Panama, or Peru. The figure confirms the
typically weak position of presidents in Ecuador, who lack strong parties
and often rely on 'ghost' coalitions in Congress.[13] By contrast, figures
showing a weak opposition (and a large dispersion) in Colombia reflect not
only concrete historical conditions (presidents were often able to rely on relatively large parties plus additional allies in Congress) but also important
measurement problems (it is difficult to identify the dissident factions
within the president's party in Colombia and to code the alignment of the
many micro-parties created in the 1990s). As a result, Colombian figures
should be interpreted carefully.

The size of the opposition bloc, combined with the degree of partisan unity,
determines four distinctive patterns of opposition. The first one, represented by
the upper-left corner in Figure 2, indicates a pattern of *resistance* in which the
opposition is small but remains united. This pattern constitutes about 39 per
cent of the administrations in the sample. (Since the data points reflect
averages for the whole administration, they may mask congressional realign-
ments, as in the case of Nicaragua's Violeta Chamorro who lost support among

FIGURE 2
FOUR PATTERNS OF OPPOSITION IN LATIN AMERICA (108 ADMINISTRATIONS;
1978–2004)

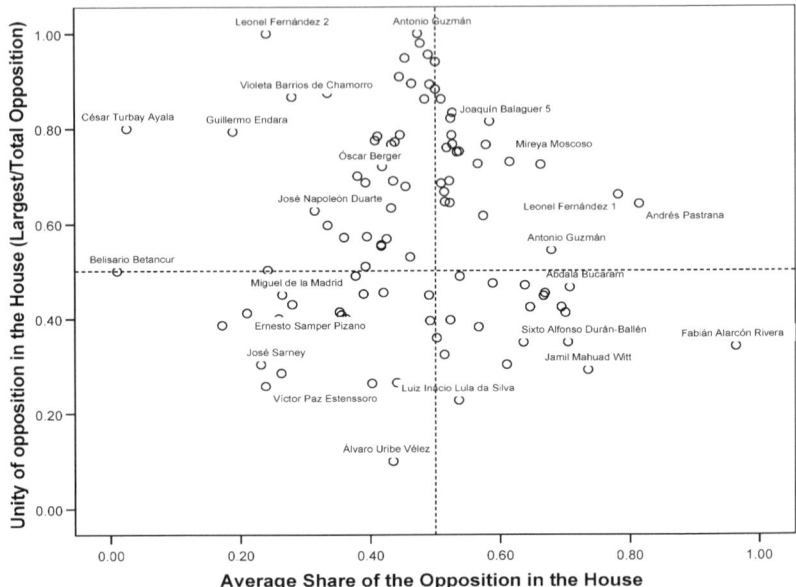

the Unión Nacional Opositora (UNO).) The second pattern, reflected in the upper-right quadrant, indicates a typical situation of *divided government* – in which a united opposition controls at least one of the legislative chambers. If we focus on the lower house, about 21 per cent of the cases fall in this category. The third pattern, in the lower-left corner, corresponds to a potentially *feeble opposition*, a small and divided contingent with little capacity to veto the policies of the president and his allies (about 20 per cent of the administrations). The fourth pattern, by contrast, is one of potential *disarray*: albeit large, the opposition may be weak because it is highly divided, and the president may be able to offer selective incentives to particular parties or individual legislators to create ad-hoc coalitions. This pattern, corresponding to some 20 per cent of the cases, has been distinctive of the Ecuadorian setting.

Coalition Stability

Because we have defined the opposition as a residual category (that is, the members of Congress not in the president's coalition), the size of the opposition may vary over time according to the ability of the president to hold his or her coalition together. The above section gives a snapshot of the size of the opposition at a particular point in time – the average year for each administration. Governing coalitions, however, are not always stable. Using Deheza's[14] data on cabinets in South America between 1958 and 1994, Table 2 compares the duration of cabinets according to their legislative support. We have classified cabinets as single-party (minority or majority) or coalition governments (minority, minimal-winning, and oversized). The table shows that, at least during the period 1958–95, single-party governments were more stable than coalition governments and majority-supported governments were more stable than minority governments. We computed the average duration for all cabinets (N = 123) and for non-terminal cabinets (those that ended during the life of a presidential administration and not because the

TABLE 2

AVERAGE DURATION OF CABINETS IN SOUTH AMERICA BY TYPE OF GOVERN-
MENT, 1958–95

Type	Duration (months)		Longest cases	Shortest cases
	All cases	Non-Terminal*		
Single minority party government	26.4	20.6	Venezuela: 1969–74, 1979–84	Bolivia 1985; Peru 1967–68; Uruguay 1972; Venezuela 1964, 1992–93
Single majority party government	28.5	29.3	Venezuela 1984–89, 1974–79; Peru 1985–90	Argentina 1973, 1973–74; Bolivia 1964, 1969 Uruguay 1967
Minority coalition	14.4	14.3	Peru 1963–67; Chile 1958–61	Bolivia 1982–83, 1984 (2), 1984–85; Brazil 1992 Chile 1972–73 Ecuador 1981 82
Minimal winning coalition	21.8	19.3	Bolivia 1989–93; Peru 1980–84; Chile 1990–94	Brazil 1960–61, 1963, 1963–64; Ecuador 1961–62, 1962–63
Oversized coalition	25.4	23.9	Colombia 1974–86; Venezuela 1960–64; Brazil 1987–90	Brazil 1961, 1963, 1985,

Note: *Non-terminal cabinets are cabinets that end during an administration, and not as a result of the end of the administration.

president finished his or her term, N = 71). The results are not substantially different: minority coalitions are particularly unstable, averaging only 14 months of life. If, however, presidents are able to build an oversized coalition, they raise the life expectancy of the government by almost 80 per cent.

Figure 3 illustrates the patterns identified in Table 2 from a different perspective. The graph shows the survival function for cabinets with different types of legislative support. The lines indicate the proportion of cabinets surviving until a certain point in time (based on life-tables constructed at six-month intervals). More than half of the minority coalition governments last less than a year. In contrast, majority coalitions (minimal winning and oversized are treated as a single sub-population) behave similarly to single-party governments: half of them survive for more than a year, and over 40 per cent survive longer than 18 months. About a quarter of single-party and majority coalition governments survive for three and a half years. Figure 3

FIGURE 3
SURVIVAL FUNCTION FOR SOUTH AMERICAN CABINETS, 1958–95

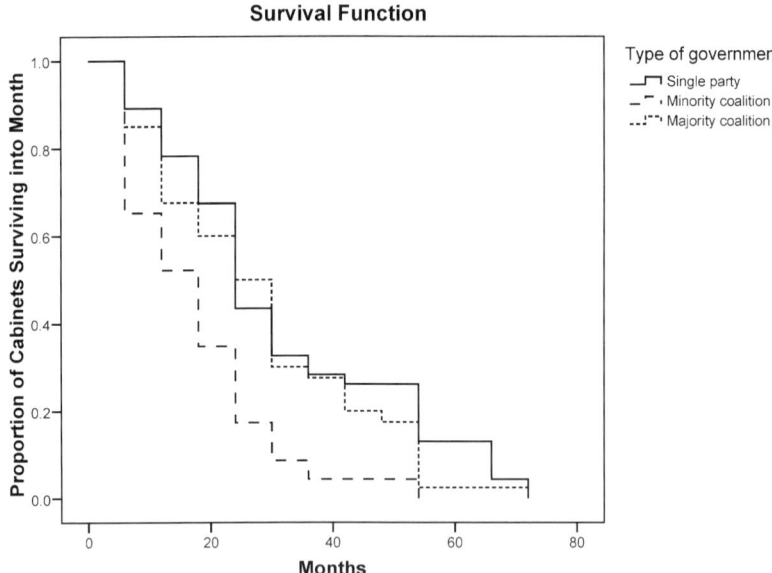

Note: Sample includes 123 cabinets included in Deheza's database. Terminal cabinets (cabinets terminated by the end of the administration) were treated as 'censored' cases in the life tables in order to avoid inflating the number of coalition dissolutions. Single-party cabinets were considered 'terminated'when the status of the party in Congress changed (i.e., the ruling party won a majority of the seats or became a minority party in the mid-term election) or if another party was incorporated into the cabinet.

Source: Based on G.I. Deheza, 'Gobiernos de coalición en el sistema presidencial: America del Sur' (Doctoral dissertation, European University Institute, 1997).

suggests that a large, viable, opposition tends to encourage a faster dissolution of the government coalition.

Having defined the opposition and evaluated its size, we now turn to an investigation of the out-parties' political influence. Multiple variables affect this influence. Here we focus on the interaction of the shape, size, and durability of coalitions with the presidents' 'partisan' and 'legislative' powers. Partisan powers are those tools that allow the executive to control the behaviour of legislators based on their partisan affiliation while legislative powers are generally constitutional prerogatives that determine the degree of influence of the president in directing the flow of legislation. As we explain below, this combination of variables determines the role of the opposition in the budget and policy process, the stability of governing coalitions, and presidential resignations.

Partisan Powers

Students of presidentialism have emphasised that a fragmented party system weakens the 'partisan powers' of the president.[15] The implication, then, is that fragmentation empowers the opposition. There is not necessarily, however, a direct link between a president's partisan powers and the power of disparate legislative parties in their efforts to counter the executive. An important empirical question, then, is what is the effect of the party system on the size and cohesion of the opposition?

Figure 4 displays a matrix of scatterplots (the graphical equivalent of a correlation matrix) for our main indicators (the effective number of parties, the size of the president's party, the size of the opposition, and opposition's partisan unity). Each data point represents the lower (or only) legislative chamber in one Latin American country in one particular year between 1978 and 2004 (N = 395). The diagonal represents the plot of each variable against itself, and therefore is blank. (Graphics located above the diagonal mirror the ones located below the diagonal).

Consider the graph presented at the top of the first column (second row of first column), where cases fill the south-west half of the plot. This lower-triangular distribution indicates that a highly fragmented party system is sufficient to prevent the presence of a large presidential party in the lower house. In a system with few parties, the president may or may not have a majority party in Congress, but a large number of parties dividing the legislative seats guarantee that the president will lack a partisan majority. However, it does not follow from this fact that a fragmented party system will secure control of Congress by the opposition. The 'cloud' displayed in the plot located in row three of the first

FIGURE 4
BIVARIATE PLOTS FOR EFFECTIVE NUMBER OF PARTIES, SIZE OF THE
PRESIDENT'S PARTY, SIZE OF THE OPPOSITION, AND OPPOSITION'S PARTISAN
UNITY IN SOUTH AMERICA (LOWER CHAMBERS, 1978–2004)

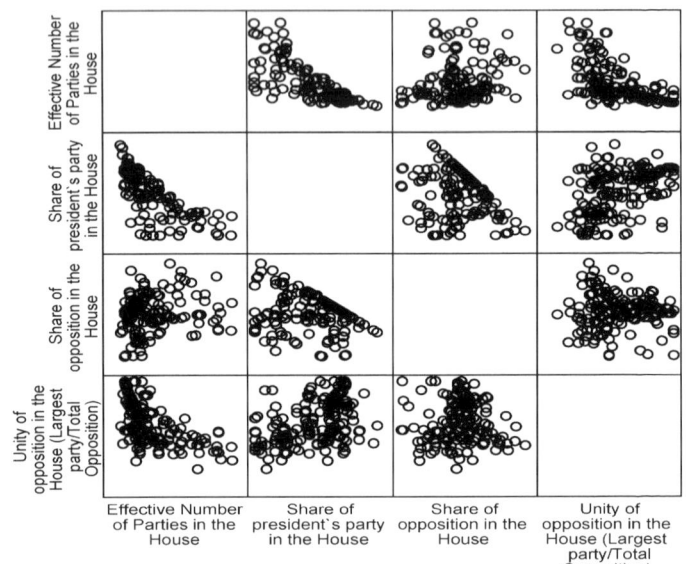

column illustrates the situation for the lower house. Although the effective number of parties is positively correlated with the size of the opposition, the correlation is surprisingly low ($r = .15$, $p < .01$) because presidents with minority parties (representing 263 country-years in our sample) were able to build majority coalitions in the House in 41 per cent of the years. The plot located at the bottom of the first column indicates, at the same time, that a fragmented party system weakens the opposition by preventing partisan unity. The lower-triangular distribution again suggests that a fragmented party system is sufficient to impede partisan unity among the opposition (or, conversely, that a small number of parties is necessary to achieve unity). Thus, extreme multipartism affects the 'partisan powers' of both the president and the opposition. But because the executive branch has more resources at its disposal, the president often has a clear advantage over the leaders of the opposition in order to build legislative coalitions.

Legislative Powers

In an effort to compare the legislative powers of the presidents, Shugart and Carey created an index that combines six items into a single aggregate measure.[16] The components are: (1) whether the president has a package veto over legislation (and the size of legislative majority necessary to override the veto); (2) whether the president has an item veto over legislation (and, again, the size of legislative majority necessary to override the veto); (3) whether the president has constitutional decree authority (and how constrained it is); (4) whether the president is granted exclusive rights to introduce some types of legislation; (5) the degree of presidential control over the budgetary process; and (6) the ability of the president to initiate referendums. Each item is coded using a scale that ranges between 0 and 4 points (where 4 indicates greater constitutional powers for the executive branch), and the six items are aggregated simply by adding their scores.[17] Simple addition of ordinal scores is problematic, but the scale does provide a useful approximation of presidential powers, especially towards the extremes. Theoretically the scale can vary between 0 and 24 points, but empirically Shugart and Carey identified values ranging between 0 and 12, and our own coding of Latin American constitutions in force between 1978 and 2004 produced a range from 2 (for El Salvador's 1983 constitution) to 11 (for the constitutions adopted in Brazil in 1988; in Ecuador after the 1984 amendment and in 1998; and in Venezuela in 1999).[18]

Figure 5 plots the 108 administrations according to the president's constitutional power (in the horizontal axis) and the size of the opposition (in the vertical axis). Administrations were classified according to the patterns of opposition previously introduced in Figure 2: the opposition was considered potentially 'feeble' if it only controlled a minority of the seats in the House and it was divided (that is, no party controlled a majority of the seats within the opposition bloc); it was considered 'in disarray' if it controlled a majority of the seats but it was divided; it was coded as 'resisting' the government if it controlled a minority of the seats but it was united (that is, one party held a majority of the seats in the opposition bloc), and it was coded as a case of 'divided government' if it had a legislative majority *and* it was united.

The limited quality of the data on government coalitions, combined with the fact that data points in the figure indicate yearly averages for each administration, suggest that the location of specific presidents should be interpreted with caution. For instance, although Brazilian President Fernando Collor de Mello (1990–92) initially relied on a centre-right coalition that formally represented about 60 per cent of the seats in the Chamber of Deputies, Collor's reluctance to negotiate with the legislators, combined with his liberal use of the presidential powers granted by the Constitution, eventually eroded his legislative base.[19] By the time he was impeached on corruption charges in late 1992, only 12 per cent of the deputies supported the president.

Despite these caveats, the figure suggests a distinctive pattern linking the constitutional powers of the president with the nature of the opposition.

FIGURE 5

SIZE AND TYPE OF OPPOSITION, BY PRESIDENT'S LEGISLATIVE POWERS LATIN AMERICA (1978–2004)

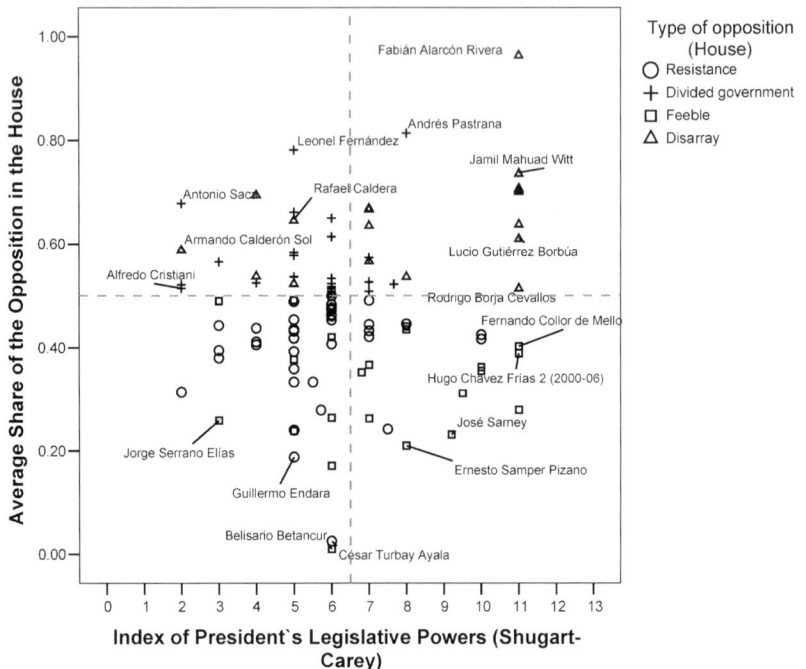

Source: Horizontal axis was computed according to: M.S. Shugart and J.M. Carey, Presidents and Assemblies. Constitutional Design and Electoral Dynamics (Cambridge: Cambridge University Press, 1992).

Presidents with relatively weak constitutional powers typically face a *resisting* opposition or a situation of *divided government*. In contrast, presidents with strong legislative powers typically confront an opposition that is potentially *feeble* or in *disarray*. In other terms, constitutionally weak presidents usually confront united opponents, while constitutionally strong presidents often face divided adversaries. How can we explain this pattern? One possible interpretation is that constitutional powers allow the executive branch to divide and conquer the opposition forces in Congress. Another, and possibly more important explanation is that the very same party systems that lead to the creation of strong presidential constitutions also account for the fragmentation of opposition forces. According to Matthew Shugart, countries with few, powerful parties tend to produce constitutions with relatively weak presidents, while countries with many weak parties tend to empower the executive branch.[20] By empowering the president, constitutional designers in countries with weak and fragmented parties free opposition legislators from direct responsibility in national policy issues, but also limit the spending powers of those legislators in order to prevent excessive spending.

POLITICAL IMPACT OF THE OPPOSITION IN PRESIDENTIAL REGIMES

As described above, the opposition in most Latin American governments is generally characterised by divisions in its own ranks, thus limiting its ability to define and pursue a common policy. This weak position is compounded by multiple factors. First, as we also detailed above, most Latin American legislatures are hampered by constitutions that do not balance the executive and legislative powers; instead many Latin American presidents are endowed with special prerogatives over the budget and other policy areas, the ability to influence the legislative agenda, the line item veto, and other powers. Second, the Latin American legislatures lack important resources that limit their political roles. Few of these legislators have access to a large professional or technical staff or agencies such as the Congressional Budget Office in the United States. Further, because re-election rates are low, the legislators themselves generally lack expertise on policy or the political process. Finally, the legislators are often tied to parties in ways that limit their individual incentive actively to engage in the business of legislation.

The result of these limitations leads to two levels of opposition influence. On the first level the opposition has only a limited involvement in the policy process. On the second, however, the opposition has actively and successfully pressured for the removal of problematic or unpopular presidents. We describe these two levels in the next two sections.

The Opposition and Policy Making

A first indicator of the opposition's influence in the policy process comes from the legislators' own views. Over the past decade the University of Salamanca has surveyed Latin American legislators on a wide range of issues.[21] One of the key items in Salamanca's survey of parliamentary elites reads: 'Thinking of your work as a deputy, how important would you rate your parliamentary activity – a lot, a significant amount, little, or none – in regard to the following roles?' Among the legislative roles analysed are: (1) Elaborating laws; (2) Elaborating the budget; and (3) Controlling the government.[22] We analyse responses from questionnaires utilised between 1998 and 2001.

Figure 6 focuses on the legislators' responses to the question about their role in 'elaborating legislation'. The data yield two important findings. First, in several countries only one-half – and in Chile less than 40 per cent – of legislators see themselves as playing an important role in developing legislation. Second, the figure shows only limited differences between the

FIGURE 6
PERCENTAGE OF SOUTH AMERICAN LEGISLATORS CLAIMING TO HAVE A LARGE
OR MINIMAL ROLE IN ELABORATING LAWS*

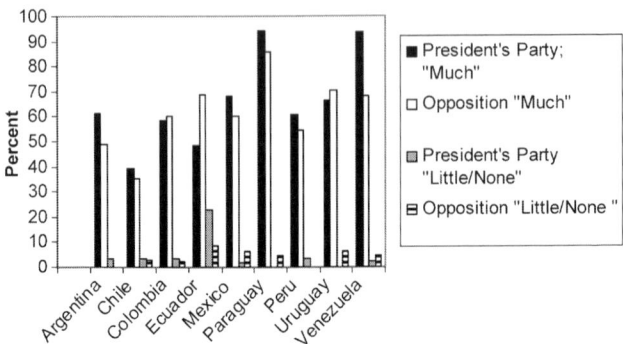

Note: Dates for Surveys: Argentina May–June 1998; Chile April–July 1998; Colombia July–Aug. 1998;
Ecuador Aug.–Sept. 1998; Aug.–Sept. 1998; Mexico March–April 1998; Peru Aug.–Oct. 2001;
Uruguay Oct.–Nov. 2000; Venezuela Oct.–Nov. 2000.
President's Party: Argentina PJ; Chile PDC; Colombia PC; Ecuador DP; Mexico PRI; Paraguay ANR
(Colorados); Peru Perú Posible; Uruguay PC; Venezuela MVR.
Opposition: Argentina UCR + Frepaso; Chile UDI + RN; Colombia (1) PL; Ecuador PRE + PSC;
Mexico PRD + PAN; Peru APRA (PAP); Paraguay PLRA; Uruguay FA + PN + EP Venezuela AD +
Copei
Excluded from the analysis are legislators from organisations that supported the Executive and thus do
not qualify as either the president's party or the opposition (parties of the Concertación in Chile, and
MAS in Venezuela).
Source: *University of Salamanca's Survey of Parliamentary Elites.

in- and out-parties in most countries. In Chile, for example, 39 per cent of the
members of the president's party answered that they played a significant role
in developing legislation and almost the same percentage answered similarly
for the two main opposition parties. There were somewhat larger differences
in Ecuador and Venezuela; interestingly, in the former, more members of the
opposition said they had a larger role in the development of legislation while
the opposite was true in Venezuela in spite of criticism that their president,
Hugo Chavez, wields excessive power.

Next, Figure 7 considers the legislators' responses with regard to their role
in developing the budget. Here again we see important differences among and
within countries. Except for the outliers of Ecuador (where only 6.3 per cent of
the opposition said they had a large role in the budgetary process) and Paraguay (where 94.4 per cent of government legislators claimed to play a big
role in the budget), the range in response to this question lies between 27.6
per cent of legislators of the Chilean president's party saying that they
played an important role in elaborating the budget to 66.7 per cent of the president's party in Uruguay. The opposition claimed a similar or only slightly
larger role in most cases (with Peru as an exception), though they claimed

FIGURE 7
PERCENTAGE OF SOUTH AMERICAN LEGISLATORS ANSWERING THAT THEY
HAVE A LARGE OR MINIMAL ROLE IN ELABORATING THE BUDGET

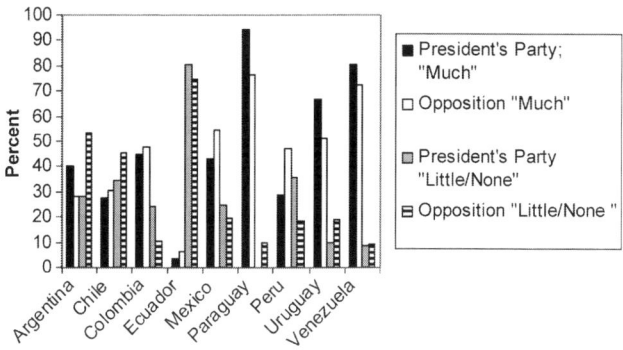

Note: See Figure 6 for further information.

significantly less involvement in Argentina (12 per cent) and Uruguay (15 per cent).

The second two bars for each country report the percentage of presidential party and opposition legislators that report having only a minimal role with respect to the budget. Here there are several significant differences between the ins and outs. In particular, a significantly greater percentage of out-party legislators in Argentina, Chile, Mexico, Paraguay and Uruguay made this claim, while in Colombia and Peru more in-party legislators answered that elaborating the budget was an unimportant part of their job. Again there is an impressive range in this response to the question, with almost no legislators responding in this way in some countries, while half or more legislators suggested that the legislature plays a minimal role with regard to the budget in others.

A final indicator of the differences among governing and opposition parties comes in the legislators' responses to questions about their branch's role in oversight. Specifically the legislators were asked how important their role was in relation to 'controlling government activity'. Here we do find some significant differences both among countries and among parties in the different countries (Figure 8). In several cases there are large differences between the presidents' party's legislators and those of the opposition; in Argentina almost 20 per cent more of the opposition answered in this manner, in Chile the differences were over 30 points, and approached 40 points in Ecuador. Contrary to expectations, however, more legislators from the president's party in Peru and Venezuela (barely) saw controlling the government as a highly important role than did the opposition party legislators in those countries. In most countries few answered that oversight was

FIGURE 8
SOUTH AMERICAN LEGISLATORS' VIEWS REGARDING THEIR ROLE WITH
RESPECT TO GOVERNMENT OVERSIGHT

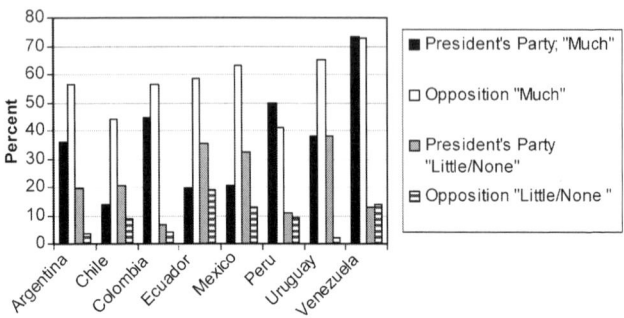

Note: See Figure 6 for further information.

unimportant, but a significant percentage of legislators from the president's party did not see this as important in Ecuador and Uruguay. Especially in Uruguay the president's party responses are dramatically different from those of the other parties.

Figures 6 to 8 suggest two main conclusions. First, the ways in which legislators define their own roles vary across countries more than between government and opposition within each country. This opens important questions for further research. Legislative roles may be shaped by institutional designs or by historical legacies operating at the national level. It is also possible that the observed variance across countries is partially a result of when surveys took place (for instance, some countries may have been in the midst of the budget debate when legislators were interviewed). Second, to the extent that opposition legislators identify a distinctive role for themselves, they claim the right to oversee the executive branch. Closer to their colleagues in parliamentary regimes (and in contrast to their counterparts in the United States), Latin American opposition legislators do not take direct responsibility for the policy-making process, but they may be willing to use their powers to check the executive branch. We discuss the implications of this role for horizontal accountability in the following section.

Although opposition legislators may not assume responsibility (or, alternatively, claim credit) for major policies, this should not be interpreted as proof that the opposition is systematically excluded from the policy-making process. In addition to the survey responses, we also investigated the propensity for different parties to vote with the majority on different bills. Morgenstern investigated 'policy coalitions' in Argentina, Brazil, Chile and Uruguay using roll-call votes and found that the opposition parties were frequently voting with the majority on controversial decisions (controversial voters are those where at least ten per cent of the legislature voted against the majority).[23] Table 3 highlights some of these results for the lower house.

These data focus on the main opposition party in each of these four countries, not parties that form part of the president's coalition. Even those parties, the table shows, are not consistently excluded from the policy process. In Argentina the Peronists held a near majority during Menem's initial years in the Casa Rosada, yet the opposition who had followed the discredited policies of his predecessor, Raúl Alfonsín, still sided with the majority on more than one-third of the votes. In Brazil the opposition is in an even weaker position, given the multiparty nature of the system. Further, during the period under investigation, the PT was considered the fringe left, and it held only about ten per cent of the legislative seats. In spite of these limitations, the PT sided with the legislative majority on 38.1 per cent of the controversial votes in 1995–98, though this proportion fell by more than one-half for 1995–98. In Chile the centre-left coalition (the Concertación) has controlled a majority of the seats in the lower house since the return to democracy in 1990. The two rightist parties, however, cannot claim that the left has excluded them from policy decisions, as they have been on the winning side of about one-half of the (controversial) legislative votes. Finally, in Uruguay the Frente Amplio found itself voting with the legislative majority on over 80 per cent of these votes. This figure must be considered carefully, however, as these votes were in favour of overturning presidential vetoes. The Frente Amplio, then, was siding against the president in each of these decisions.

TABLE 3

PERCENTAGE OF CONTROVERSIAL CONGRESSIONAL VOTES IN WHICH SOUTH AMERICAN OPPOSITION PARTIES VOTED IN THE MAJORITY

Country	Years	Opposition party or coalition	Controversial votes in which party voted with the majority (%)
Argentina	1989–91	UCR	35.0
Brazil	1991–95	PT	38.1
Brazil	1995–98	PT	16.2
Chile	1997–99	RN	47.8
Chile	1997–99	UDI	53.0
Uruguay*	1985–89	FA	82.4
Uruguay*	1990–94	FA	86.7

Note:*veto overrides.

Source: S. Morgenstern, Patterns of Legislative Politics: Roll-Call Voting in Latin America and the United States (Cambridge: Cambridge University Press, 2004).

The Opposition and Political Stability

As we have emphasised, many Latin American presidents who lack a majority party in the legislature are able to build coalitions. These coalitions, however, are not always stable. Figure 3 showed that minority coalitions are particularly likely to disintegrate in the short run. In the European context, this is generally discussed in terms of government stability (that is, changes in the cabinet's composition), but in Latin America the concern has been with regime stability. In parliamentary systems, a large and cohesive opposition may dismiss the cabinet through a vote of no confidence and form a new government. In presidential systems, in contrast, a large and cohesive opposition is not supposed to affect the stability of the government because the terms in office (for the legislators as well as for the chief executive) are constitutionally fixed. Throughout the 1990s, however, the influential debate about the 'perils of presidentialism' emphasised the propensity of presidential regimes to face military interventions when minority presidents were unable to build stable coalitions and inter-branch conflict compromised the democratic process. Frustration with gridlock, it was argued, would encourage military intervention.[24] In this section we discuss the role of the opposition in shaping regime instability during the second half of the twentieth century as well as its role in cases of government instability in more recent years.

Regime instability, 1958–95. In order to examine how majority status and coalitional arrangements affected regime breakdown during the second half of the twentieth century, we classified the 123 cabinets included in Deheza's study according to the form in which they ended. Fourteen of them were terminated by a military coup, while the remaining 109 ended in some other way (the coalition dissolved, a new president took office, and so on).[25]

In Table 4 we present data on the frequency of military coups for different types of governments. Coalition governments in the Southern Cone were less exposed to military intervention than single-party governments. Indeed, coalition-making, more than majority status, seems to account for the lower rate of coups. Single majority party rule ended in a coup 18.2 per cent of the time, while single minority party governments faced military coups 15.4 per cent of the time. In contrast, only 3.6 per cent of the oversized coalitions and 4.2 per cent of minority coalitions ended with the fall of the regime. Taken as a group, 16.7 per cent of single-party governments faced military coups, compared to 5.8 per cent of coalition governments. The difference in risk is statistically significant at the 0.05 level.[26] Interim governments may be the most likely to end in military coups (one-third of them led to the breakdown of democracy) but the small number of cases prevents any comparison of risk across categories. The results presented in Table 4 suggest that styles of

TABLE 4
TERMINATION OF SOUTH AMERICAN CABINETS BY MILITARY COUPS, 1958–98

| Type of cabinet | Form of termination | | Total |
	Coup	No Coup	
Single party			
Minority	4	22	26
%	15.4	84.6	100.0
Majority	4	18	22
%	18.2	81.8	100.0
Coalitions			
Minority	1	23	24
%	4.2	95.8	100.0
Minimal winning	2	15	17
%	11.8	88.2	100.0
Oversized	1	27	28
%	3.6	96.4	100.0
Interim	2	4	6
%	33.3	66.7	100.0
Total	14	109	123
%	11.4	88.6	100.0

Note: Coups terminating cabinets took place in Argentina (1962, 1966, 1976); Bolivia (1964, 1969, 1979, 1980); Brazil (1964); Chile (1973); Ecuador (1961, 1963); Peru (1962, 1968); and Uruguay (1973).
Sources: Based on G.I. Deheza, *Gobiernos de coalición en el sistema presidencial: America del Sur* (Doctoral dissertation, European University Institute, 1997), and P.H. Smith, *Democracy in Latin America: Political Change in Comparative Perspective* (Oxford: Oxford University Press, 2005).

government, more than executive–legislative deadlock per se, constituted the source of democratic breakdowns in Latin America in the past. When politicians adopted a majoritarian view of democracy the risk of breakdown was significantly greater than when they were willing to negotiate a consensus with the opposition via coalitions.

Government instability, 1980–2004. Since a wave of democratisation transformed the Latin American landscape in the 1980s, the military have for the most part withdrawn from politics.[27] However, even though in recent years democratic *regimes* have not broken down, democratically elected *governments* have collapsed on several occasions. Table 5 reports on the way in which 87 Latin American presidents left office between 1980 and 2004. We have classified the pattern of exit according to the type of opposition (as presented in Figure 2). A vast majority of presidents (70) completed their terms and a few others (3) died in office or retired due to health problems. But a relatively large number, 14 elected heads of state (17 per cent of those without health issues), were forced to leave office before their terms were completed. This happened in four different ways:

TABLE 5

LATIN AMERICAN PRESIDENTS' PATTERNS OF EXIT FROM OFFICE, 1980–2004

Type of opposition	Normal exit		Termination (early exit)				Total
	Finished term	Illness or death	Negotiated early exit	Resigned	Impeached or declared incapacitated	Ousted by military	
Resistance	26	2	0	0	1	0	29
Divided government	19	0	2	2	1	0	24
Feeble	16	1	2	1	1	1	22
Disarray	9	0	0	1	1	1	12
Total	70	3	4	4	4	2	87

(1) *As a negotiated exit*. Four presidents – Hernán Siles Zuazo (Bolivia, 1985), Raul Alfonsín (Argentina, 1989), Joaquín Balaguer (the Dominican Republic, 1996), and Eduardo Duhalde (Argentina, 2003) – negotiated with the opposition an early exit from power as a way to defuse governability crises. Siles and Alfonsín accelerated the transfer of power to the next government in the midst of hyperinflation, Balaguer agreed to call for anticipated elections in 1996 as a result of severe accusations of fraud in the 1994 contest, and Duhalde called for elections to avoid civic unrest following a repressive incident in which the police killed two demonstrators during the Argentine economic debacle of 2001–3.

(2) *As a unilateral resignation*. Four other presidents – Alberto Fujimori (Peru, 2000), Fernando de la Rúa (Argentina, 2001), Adolfo Rodriguez Saá (Argentina, 2001), and Gonzalo Sánchez de Lozada (Bolivia, 2003) – resigned when they realised that they were in an untenable position due to the eruption of mass protests against their administrations and increasing political isolation. Prompted by corruption scandals and accusations of abuse of power and electoral fraud, Fujimori left the country and submitted his resignation from Japan. An infuriated Congress declared the president 'morally incapacitated' after he had resigned. In turn, de la Rúa, Rodriguez Saá, and Sánchez de Lozada (as well as some of their replacements) abandoned their offices when they realised that popular mobilisation was hard to control and that former political allies were no longer willing to support their administrations.

(3) *Following an impeachment or declaration of incapacity*. Presidents Fernando Collor de Mello (Brazil, 1992), Carlos Andrés Pérez (Venezuela, 1993), Abdalá Bucaram (Ecuador, 1997), and Raúl Cubas Grau (Paraguay, 1999) were directly accused by Congress and impeached or declared unfit to govern the country.

(4) *Following military interventions*. The last two cases correspond to instances in which military action forced the president to abandon the office. Confronting a hostile Congress, Guatemalan President Jorge Serrano attempted a self-coup in 1993, but refusal of the middle ranks to support his move led Serrano to resign. Congress then met and appointed the human rights ombudsman as interim president to complete the term. In 2000, a coalition of indigenous demonstrators and young military officers ousted Ecuadorian President Jamil Mahuad. The *junta* was unable to take over, but Congress legalised the exit of Mahuad and swore the vice-president in.

What was the role of the opposition in the fall of those administrations? This question is relevant for two reasons. On the one hand, a strong legislative opposition may be able to hold the president accountable, impeaching the head of the executive branch if there is evidence of corruption or abuse of power. On the other hand, a strong legislative opposition may misuse its oversight powers or ally with other actors (military or civilian) outside the legislature to destabilise the government.

Three historical traits were common to all 14 crises. First, in none of them was the military able (or willing) to impose a dictatorship. This fact marks a break with the past, indicating a significant difference in the stability of democracy achieved in Latin America over the last two-and-a-half decades and the situation in earlier historical periods. Second, in all episodes popular protests were an important factor that weakened the position of the president and facilitated his downfall. Third, in all instances the opposition played an important role, either by negotiating a peaceful solution, removing the president from office by legal means, or securing a constitutional transfer of power after the president had resigned.

However, Table 5 indicates that the size and cohesion of the opposition is not enough to explain the recent demise of elected presidents. Presidents have been removed from office when the opposition was large and when it was small, when the opposition was united and when it was divided. Although our measures of the size and cohesion of the opposition are not sensitive enough to reflect short-term changes (an important factor because coalitions may easily dissolve in the midst of scandal or of protests against the government), the table suggests that – not surprisingly – other factors should also be taken into consideration.

In order to assess the relevance of the congressional opposition in those crises, we collected information on 467 presidents in office during particular years (for instance Alberto Fujimori in Peru in 1994) for 18 Latin American countries between 1980 and 2004.[28] The dependent variable (early exit) was coded as a dummy indicating whether the president was removed from office (or forced to resign) in any given year. Thus, the number of events is 14 out of 467 administration-years. For each country year, we collected additional information on five issues:

(1) *The size of the opposition relative to the majorities required to remove the president.* Using our estimates of the size of the opposition presented in previous pages and the relevant articles of each country's constitution, we created three dummy variables indicating whether: (i) the opposition had enough votes in Congress to impeach the president (that is, to initiate the accusation in the respective chamber); (ii) the opposition had enough votes in Congress to remove the president from office once the accusation was initiated; and (iii) the opposition had enough votes to declare the president physically or mentally incapacitated if the constitution allowed

Congress to do so. Although the three variables reflect similar institutional conditions, they are not highly correlated because the size of the opposition in each chamber and the supermajorities required for each decision vary (correlations range between 0.36 and 0.52).

(2) *The unity of the opposition.* We also included in the analysis our indicator of the opposition's cohesion in the lower house. This measure varies between zero and one, and it reflects the size of the largest opposition party divided by the total proportion of seats controlled by the opposition.

(3) *Presidential powers.* This variable reflects presidential powers in legislative affairs, according to the Shugart-Carey index (as explained above, points are assigned for package veto, item veto, constitutional decree authority, exclusive rights to introduce legislation, control over the budgetary process, and ability to initiate referendums). Scores range (in our sample) between 2 and 11, with a mean of 6.3.

(4) *Scandals.* We coded the presence of media scandals using *Latin American Weekly Report* (LAWR) as our historical source. Scandals were measured using a dummy with a value of 1 for years when LAWR reported that exposés about corruption or abuse of power had involved the president personally.

(5) *Protests.* We also used LAWR to collect information on popular protests against the president. This dichotomous variable was coded as 1 when the newsletter reported that popular protests had taken place to demand the resignation of the president, 0 otherwise.

Table 6 presents the results of a rare-event logistic analysis including those predictors. The first three models include the opposition variables separately, without significant results. The fourth model includes the three variables at once, and also controls for the partisan unity of the opposition. This model suggests that one of the critical factors shaping the outcome of a presidential crisis is whether the opposition has enough votes to remove the president from office through impeachment. It is less relevant whether the opposition can initiate the accusations (because the threat is not credible unless the decisive vote can be controlled by the opposition) or initiate a declaration of incapacity (this constitutional power is available to Congress in only nine countries, and it is often difficult to invoke). Paradoxically, a united opposition *reduces* the risk for the president. This is consistent with some of the previous findings in this paper, which indicate that a united opposition tends to co-exist with larger presidential cohorts in Congress and facilitates negotiations across blocs.

The last model includes the opposition variables plus the indicators of legislative powers, scandals and protest. Popular protest emerges as a strong predictor of presidential removals, but the opposition variable remains

TABLE 6

MODELS OF LATIN AMERICAN PRESIDENTIAL REMOVALS FROM OFFICE,
1980–2004

Opposition had the constitutional power and the votes to:	6.1	6.2	6.3	6.4	6.5
(1) Impeach (accuse)	−0.068			−0.382	−0.719
	(0.697)			(0.666)	(0.392)
(2) Impeach & remove		1.041		1.988*	2.061*
		(0.567)		(0.687)	(0.654)
(3) Declare unfit			−0.108	−1.318	−0.833
			(0.927)	(0.811)	(0.653)
Unity of opposition				−1.941*	−0.665
(House)				(0.852)	(1.494)
Legislative powers					−0.068
					(0.127)
Scandal					0.729
					(0.796)
Protest vs. president					3.724*
					(0.696)
Intercept	−3.390*	−3.572*	−3.386*	−2.200*	−3.724*
	(0.375)	(0.332)	(0.352)	(0.483)	(1.353)

Note: Entries are rare-event logistic coefficients (standard errors clustered by country).
Dependent variable is early exit. N = 467 (administration-years); *p < 0.05; two tailed.

significant. This finding suggests that extra-parliamentary mobilisation and parliamentary opposition acting together constitute a serious threat for the president.

How relevant is the role of congressional elites when compared to popular protests? Based on the last model, Table 7 presents the expected probability of a presidential downfall under different conditions. The column labelled 'P(Exit)' indicates that, in a situation with no protests and a weak opposition (defined for the sake of the simulation as an opposition able to accuse the president or declare the president incapacitated, but not to remove him or her from office on impeachment charges), the probability of a presidential removal is virtually nil. If protest is activated, but the opposition remains weak, the probability of a downfall is about 16 per cent. If, in contrast, the opposition is strong but there is no popular call for the president's resignation, the probability of a removal remains low (about three per cent). However, when both popular protest and a strong opposition are present, the probability of an anticipated exit from office increases to almost 60 per cent. Thus, although mass mobilisation appeared to be the most important factor shaping the outcome of recent political crises, it is clear that parliamentary opposition has played an important role in their definition. This result

TABLE 7
IMPACT OF CONGRESSIONAL OPPOSITION AND POPULAR PROTEST IN THE
DEMISE OF LATIN AMERICAN PRESIDENTS

Protest	Opposition	P(Exit)	Lower 95%	Upper 95%
No	Weak	0.00	0.00	0.03
Yes	Weak	0.16	0.03	0.51
No	Strong	0.03	0.00	0.21
Yes	Strong	0.58	0.16	0.92

Note: Stochastic simulation of expected probabilities was computed using *relogitq*, based on Model 6.5. P(Exit) indicates the expected probability of a presidential removal (median of the simulated posterior density); upper and lower bounds indicate the confidence intervals around this value. 'Protest' denotes that a protest against the executive takes place; the opposition is described as 'Strong' if it has enough congressional votes to remove the president on impeachment charges (or as 'weak' otherwise). In all simulations the opposition's unity and the president's legislative powers are set at the sample's median value, scandals are assumed to be present, and the opposition is assumed to have the votes to initiate accusations against the president and to declare the president incapacitated.

shows that the opposition in Latin America often has the capacity to oversee the executive, although this power is sometimes misused for partisan reasons or invoked in opportunistic manner only when the president is very unpopular.

CONCLUSIONS

Though Latin America's opposition is so little studied that we were forced to begin this review with definitions, our analysis uncovered crucial political roles for the legislative groups not aligned with the president. Not only have they played important policy roles, but they have also not infrequently helped to bring down sitting executives.

In summary, we developed six themes. First, due to the combination of presidentialism and multipartism, defining the opposition in Latin America requires a mixture of US and European-based approaches. In most cases we borrowed the European idea that the opposition are those parties without cabinet membership, but recognise that presidential coalitions are inherently less stable and less supportive of the president than parliamentary coalitions. Second, using this definition, we showed that there is great diversity in the size and cohesion of opposition forces in Latin America. Some presidents have been successful in building over-sized coalitions, some face cohesive opposition majorities, and others face only small and divided groups in the legislature.

A third finding was that there is no necessary relation between the strength of the president and the strength of the opposition. This odd finding is the result of the two distinct sources of a president's strength: constitution (legal powers) and legislative support. Shugart has shown that presidents with weak partisan powers are often endowed with strong constitutional powers.[29] In addition, we have found that many presidents with weak legislative support build coalitions to secure themselves. Further, and perhaps most importantly, the same party fragmentation that prevents a strong presidential majority in Congress often prevents the unity of the opposition, allowing the president to co-opt members of the opposition or to deploy his proactive powers.

Our final three findings relate to the role of the opposition in policy, oversight, and the removal of presidents from office. Our fourth finding was that the opposition does not distinguish itself significantly from other parties in its responses to questions about participation in legislation or the budget, though there was much cross-national differentiation. In several countries, however, the opposition did see oversight as a much more important role for the legislature than did the governing parties. This finding seems to have a direct relation to the survival of the president. Our fifth finding was that while attempts to check executive power historically often led to democratic breakdown, presidents who have been willing to form coalitions have been less exposed to military conspiracies, even if those coalitions have not constituted a legislative majority. Finally, however, while military coups have become much less common in Latin America, the opposition continues to play an important role in removing presidents from office via impeachment and other legal (or quasi-legal) procedures. This role, however, is contingent on the activation of the public as well as the size and strength of the opposition.

NOTES

1. K. Strom, 'Minority Governments in Parliamentary Democracies: The Rationality of Non-Winning Cabinet Solutions', *Comparative Political Studies*, 17 (1984), pp.199–227.
2. O. Amorim Neto, 'Presidential Cabinets, Electoral Cycles, and Coalition Discipline in Brazil', in S. Morgenstern and B. Nacif (eds.), *Legislative Politics in Latin America* (Cambridge: Cambridge University Press, 2002), pp.48–78; G.I. Deheza, 'Gobiernos de coalición en el sistema presidencial: America del Sur' (Doctoral dissertation, European University Institute, 1997); J. Zelaznik, 'The Building of Coalitions in the Presidential Systems of Latin America: An Inquiry into the Political Conditions of Governability' (Doctoral dissertation, University of Essex, 2002).
3. S. Mainwaring, 'Presidentialism, Multipartism, and Democracy: The Difficult Combination', *Comparative Political Studies*, 26/2 (1993), pp.198–228.
4. J. Linz and A. Stepan, *Breakdown of Democratic Regimes* (Baltimore, MD: Johns Hopkins University Press, 1978); J. Linz, 'The Perils of Presidentialism', *Journal of Democracy*, 1 (1990), pp.51–69; A. Stepan and C. Skach, 'Constitutional Frameworks and Democratic Consolidation: Parlamentarism versus Presidentialism', *World Politics*, 46 (1993), pp.1–22; J. Linz and A. Valenzuela, *The Failure of Presidential Democracy* (Baltimore, MD: Johns Hopkins University Press, 1994); J. Linz and A. Stepan, *Problems of Democratic Transitions and Consolidation* (Baltimore, MD: Johns Hopkins University Press, 1996).

5. D. Altman, 'The Politics of Coalition Formation and Survival in Multi-Party Presidential Democracies: The Case of Uruguay, 1989–1999', *Party Politics*, 6 (2000), pp.259–83; Amorim Neto, 'Presidential Cabinets, Electoral Cycles, and Coalition Discipline in Brazil'; Deheza, 'Gobiernos de coalición en el sistema presidencial'; Zelaznik, 'The Building of Coalitions in the Presidential Systems of Latin America'.

6. J. Foewaker, 'Institutional Design, Party System and Governability. Differentiating the Presidential Regimes of Latin America', *British Journal of Political Science*, 28 (1998), p.665.

7. J. Cheibub, A. Przeworski and S. Saiegh, 'Government Coalitions and Legislative Success under Parliamentarism and Presidentialism', *British Journal of Political Science*, 34 (2004), pp.565–87.

8. Altman, 'The Politics of Coalition Formation and Survival in Multi-Party Presidential Democracies'.

9. D. Altman, 'The Politics of Coalition Formation and Survival in Multiparty Presidential Regimes' (Ph.D. Dissertation, University of Notre Dame, 2001); T. Beck, P. Keefer, G. Clarke, P. Walsh and A. Groff, 'Database on Political Institutions (DPI2004)', *The World Bank* (Washington, 2006), available from http://econ.worldbank.org/staff/pkeefer; Deheza, 'Gobiernos de coalición en el sistema presidencial'.

10. Coalition data for presidential regimes is not easily available, and definitions of coalitions often vary from study to study. We compiled information from multiple sources: Deheza, 'Gobiernos de coalición en el sistema presidencial' (Appendix 2) offers information on nine South American countries (Argentina, Bolivia, Brazil, Chile, Colombia, Ecuador, Peru, Uruguay and Venezuela) between 1958 and 1994; Altman, 'The Politics of Coalition Formation and Survival in Multiparty Presidential Regimes', offers information on nine multiparty systems (Argentina, Bolivia, Brazil, Chile, Ecuador, Panama, Peru, Uruguay and Venezuela) between 1979 and the mid or late 1990s (depending on the country); and Beck *et al.*, 'Database on Political Institutions (DPI2004)', *The World Bank*, offers information on the 18 countries between 1975 and 2004, but identifies no more than three coalition members in any given year. We treated a party as a member of the government coalition when at least one of the sources identified it as such.

11. M. Laakso and R. Taagepera, 'Effective Number of Parties: A Measure with Application to Western Europe', *Comparative Political Studies*, 12 (1979), pp.3–27.

12. Deheza, 'Gobiernos de coalición en el sistema presidencial'.

13. A. Mejía Acosta, 'Crafting Legislative Ghost Coalitions in Ecuador: Informal Institutions and Economic Reform in an Unlikely Case', in G. Helmke and S. Levitsky (eds.), *Informal Institutions and Democracy: Lessons from Latin America* (Baltimore, MD: The Johns Hopkins University Press, 2006), pp.69–84.

14. Deheza, 'Gobiernos de coalición en el sistema presidencial'.

15. S. Mainwaring and M.S. Shugart, 'Conclusion: Presidentialism and the Party System', in S. Mainwaring and M.S. Shugart (eds.), *Presidentialism and Democracy in Latin America* (Cambridge: Cambridge University Press, 1997), pp 394–439.

16. M.S. Shugart and J.M. Carey, *Presidents and Assemblies. Constitutional Design and Electoral Dynamics* (Cambridge: Cambridge University Press, 1992).

17. Shugart and Carey, *Presidents and Assemblies*, Chapter 8.

18. J.M. Payne, D. Zovatto, G.F. Carrillo Florez and A. Allamand Zavala, *Democracies in Development – Politics and Reform in Latin America* (New York: Inter-American Development Bank and International Institute for Democracy and Electoral Assistance, 2002), added a seventh criterion – the reversionary point for the budget in the case that the president's proposal is rejected by Congress. We did not include this item for the estimation of the index, but some of our scores are greater than the ones presented by Shugart and Carey in *Presidents and Assemblies* (Table 8.2) because of occasional differences in our interpretation of particular constitutions. For instance, while Shugart and Carey coded the Venezuelan constitution of 1961 as a 0 in terms of legislative powers, we interpreted Article 173 as allowing for partial veto (overridden by simple majority), Article 228 as preventing Congress from

increasing budgetary items, and Articles 190 and 227 as giving the president exclusive rights to initiate budgetary amendments, yielding a total score of five points.

19. Amorim Neto, 'Presidential Cabinets, Electoral Cycles, and Coalition Discipline in Brazil'; G. Negretto, 'Government Capacities and Policy Making by Decree in Latin America: The Cases of Brazil and Argentina', *Comparative Political Studies*, 37 (2006), pp.531–62.

20. Shugart and Carey, *Presidents and Assemblies*, Chapter 9, and M.S. Shugart, 'The Inverse Relationship Between Party Strength and Executive Strength: A Theory of Politicians' Constitutional Choices', *British Journal of Political Science*, 28 (1998), pp.1–29.

21. On a decade of Salamanca's survey of parliamentary elites, see M. Alcántara Sáez (ed.), *Políticos y Política en América Latina* (Madrid: Fundación Carolina – Siglo XXI, 2006).

22. Original wording: 'Pensando en el trabajo que desempeña como Diputado, ¿cuál es el grado de importancia – mucha, bastante, poca o ninguna – que otorga Ud. durante su actividad parlamentaria a los siguientes aspectos? (Elaborar leyes; elaborar el presupuesto; controlar el gobierno).'

23. S. Morgenstern, *Patterns of Legislative Politics: Roll-Call Voting in Latin America and the United States* (Cambridge: Cambridge University Press, 2004).

24. See Linz, 'The Perils of Presidentialism'; Stepan and Skach, 'Constitutional Frameworks and Democratic Consolidation'; Linz and Valenzuela, *The Failure of Presidential Democracy*.

25. Deheza, 'Gobiernos de coalición en el sistema presidencial', see Appendix 2. Data on military coups were collected from P.H. Smith, *Democracy in Latin America: Political Change in Comparative Perspective* (Oxford: Oxford University Press, 2005), Appendix 2.

26. One-tailed Z-test is 1.906 (normal approximation to the binomial).

27. F. Hagopian and S. Mainwaring (eds.), *The Third Wave of Democratization in Latin America: Advances and Setbacks* (Cambridge: Cambridge University Press, 2005).

28. The countries considered in the analysis (and the first year in the sample) are: Argentina (1983), Bolivia (1982), Brazil (1985), Chile (1990), Colombia (1980), Costa Rica (1980), the Dominican Republic (1980), Ecuador (1980), El Salvador (1984), Guatemala (1986), Honduras (1982), Mexico (1982), Nicaragua (1985), Panama (1989), Paraguay (1989), Peru (1980), Uruguay (1985), and Venezuela (1980). Peru in 1992 was eliminated from the sample because Congress was closed by the end of the year, but including this observation in the sample did not alter the results.

29. M. Shugart, 'The Inverse Relation between Party Strength and Executive Strength: A Theory of Politicians' Constitutional Choices', *British Journal of Political Science*, 28 (1998), pp.1–29.

Parliamentary Opposition after Apartheid: South Africa

ROBERT A. SCHRIRE

Most observers regard 1994 as the dramatic beginning of a new democratic South Africa. For the first time in history, all adult South Africans were eligible to vote in a general election and most did so with enthusiasm. For several centuries whites had ruled South Africa, first as a colony where the colonial power ruled in partnership with white settlers, later as a white ruled independent state, the Union of South Africa, from 1910 to 1961 and then as a republic. The transition to a racially inclusive political system was seen as a dramatic break from the past. And of course in many important ways it was.

These changes, however, tended to mask important continuities. For nearly a century South Africa had a fully-fledged parliamentary system. Until the 1960s a small minority of black South Africans even participated in parliamentary elections and through indirect representatives in the legislative process itself. Although this participation ended in the 1960s, the core framework of democratic government for the white community remained in place. Whites have thus experienced a lengthy history of democratic government.

From the 1970s whites responded to growing black political demands by supporting increasingly authoritarian governments. Power was centralised in the office of the prime minister (later state president), and the civil servants involved in security issues became increasingly powerful and autonomous. During the final years of political struggle between 1984 and 1989, parliament became increasingly marginalised as President P.W. Botha created an executive system based upon the power of security officials from the defence and intelligence departments.[1]

However, for white South Africans, democratic institutions remained in place and white leaders were chosen democratically at party conferences. Indeed the apartheid government actually sought to expand the parliamentary system to include the so-called African homelands, several of which were granted 'independence', as well as to coloureds and Asians who were granted their own separate legislative bodies.

Although parliament granted the imperial presidency of P.W. Botha the authority to wage a total strategy against the African nationalist 'onslaught', it never gave up the authority to reclaim its traditional powers and prerogatives. Indeed the resignation of Botha and the election of F.W. de Klerk as the new president in 1989 went some way towards restoring the primacy of traditional civilian institutions and practices.

The transition to democracy, although not without violence, represented a negotiated settlement between black and white interests as represented by the African National Congress (ANC) and the National Party (NP) respectively.[2] Although the ANC was committed to a 'normal' democracy with full citizenship for all black people, it recognised the harm that power centralisation had done to the country's economy and society. During the negotiations the NP, as the previous beneficiary of centralisation, was now determined to create new and effective institutional restraints on the exercise of political power. It therefore became possible to devise a compromise between black power and white interests. Arduous negotiations produced agreement on a new political order based in part on the existing system but which incorporated important modifications to contain and decentralise political power and authority.

Below we will discuss the new institutional framework negotiated between 1990 and 1994 and embodied in the final constitution of 1996. However, it is important to emphasise the continuities. Unlike former colonies such as Nigeria and Kenya where British designed institutions were a foreign import, the 1996 constitution represented modifications to a long-standing system. Although urban Africans were largely excluded from any form of political participation, most rural Africans had legislative systems in the so-called homelands,[3] while from 1984 coloureds and Indians participated in separate ethnic chambers of the South African Parliament. Thus the new constitution emerged from an earlier parliamentary system and in many ways may be seen as more a reflection of organic change than radical transformation. South Africa is thus an old and a new democracy simultaneously!

CONSTITUTIONAL REALITIES

The constitutional negotiations between the government and the ANC which began formally in 1990, culminated in an agreement on an interim constitution in 1994. This was followed by general elections and the new legislature was given two years to draft a final constitution which would come into effect after it had been ratified by the new Constitutional Court. This dramatic event took place on 8 May 1996 and after the minor changes the Court required had been accepted, the final constitution was signed into law by Nelson Mandela on 10 December 1996. A new chapter in the country's history had formally begun.

As noted, the constitution remained rooted within a centralised paradigm. It is neither a genuine presidential system nor a federation although it has aspects of both. The major innovation was provision for a genuine separation of powers and a bill of rights containing a wide range of political and socio-economic rights. A Constitutional Court was established to be the ultimate arbiter of legitimacy. The president remained the key political actor in the polity. Although not a member of the legislature, his cabinet must with two possible exceptions come from members of parliament. The president has both legislative and executive functions and must assent to bills before they become laws and he has the power to send bills to the Constitutional Court for advice if he has doubts about their legality.

Parliament is the legislative organ of government and is elected for a five-year term although provision exists for its early dissolution. Its two major functions are to pass legislation and to hold the executive accountable. In addition it is a forum for national debates and acts as an electoral chamber for the election of the president (a formality given that the ANC president becomes de facto the nation's president). It has two chambers: the 400 member National Assembly (NA), and the 90 member National Council of Provinces (NCOP). The NCOP was established as a compromise measure to placate those who had advocated a federal system. It is supposed to represent the interests of the provinces although many question its relevance. Given that the NA is by far the more important chamber, this article will focus largely on the NA.

The electoral system underpinning the NA is based upon strict pro-portional representation. Each party draws up a list of candidates in order of preference and strict proportionality determines the electoral results. The lists are constituted as follows: 200 members are elected from a national list while the remaining 200 are elected from provincial lists from each of the nine provinces. However, each voter casts only one ballot. There is a very low barrier to entrance to parliament which makes it relatively easy for even minor interests to obtain representation. A party that can win more than 0.25 per cent of the vote can thus win a parliamentary seat.

Until the 2004 elections members of parliament were prohibited from changing parties and should any member lose his/her party membership, their parliamentary seat would also be forfeited. However, a constitutional amendment now makes it possible for legislators to switch parties under specific circumstances: after each election there are two periods where a window of opportunity for floor crossing opens up but only when at least ten per cent of existing party members in parliament wish to defect. Party defectors may not sit as independents but must either join another party or establish their own.

When several opposition parties supported the amendment, they may not have fully understood its consequences. The ten per cent threshold makes it relatively easy for members of small parties to meet this criterion and defect. However, the ten per cent threshold makes it all but impossible for legislators to defect from the ANC because some 28 members would have to agree to defect to make it possible. The legislation caused great unhappiness in both the ANC and opposition parties. The former rewarded defectors with patronage which alienated loyal ANC members who were not so rewarded while opposition parties were frequently decimated. The ANC congress in December 2007 agreed to support opposition requests for its repeal and in early 2008 the relevant parliamentary portfolio committee agreed to its repeal.

The NA controls its own internal arrangements and procedures although the constitution mandates that minority parties are entitled to participate in the work of both the NA and its array of committees. Members of the NA nominally elect their own internal officials including Speaker and Deputy Speaker, although in practice the ANC leadership decides which candidates will fill which position. The ruling party also appoints the Leader of the House to handle government business.

The engine room of parliament is the committee system where the details of proposed legislation may be scrutinised and officials summoned to account for their activities. Committees have considerable authority including the right to hold public hearings and commission reports from public officials. Acting through the NA they may compel any person or institution to comply with a summons for information.

The portfolio committees can exercise considerable influence in fulfilling their mandate of monitoring the performances of each government department. All legislation is first processed there. The major opposition parties would have representation in all of these committees and by tradition the Joint Committee on Public Accounts is chaired by an opposition member.

PARLIAMENTARY PARTIES AND OPPOSITION

South Africa's system of proportional representation makes it possible for even minor interests to gain parliamentary representation. As a result a large number

TABLE 1
ELECTION RESULTS IN THE NATIONAL ASSEMBLY OF SOUTH AFRICA 1994–2004

Party	1994	Seats	1999	Seats	2004	Seats
ANC	62.65	252	66.35	266	69.68	279
DP/DA	1.73	7	9.56	38	12.37	50
IFP	10.54	43	8.58	34	6.97	28
UDM	–	–	3.42	14	2.28	9
ID	–	–	–	–	1.73	7
NP/NNP	20.39	82	6.87	28	1.65	7
ACDP	0.45	2	1.43	6	1.6	6
VF/VF+	2.17	9	0.80	3	0.89	4
UCDP	–	–	0.79	3	0.75	3
PAC	1.25	5	0.71	3	0.73	3
MF	0.07	0	0.30	1	0.35	2
FA	–	–	0.54	2	–	–
AEB	–	–	0.29	1	–	–
Azapo	–	–	0.17	1	0.27	2

Note: ANC African National Congress, DP/DA Democratic Party/Democratic Alliance, IFP Inkatha Freedom Party, UDM United Democratic Movement, ID Independent Democrats, NP/NNP National Party/New National Party, ACDP African Christian Democratic Party, VF/VF+ Freedom Front, UCDP United Christian Democratic Party, PAC Pan Africanist Congress, MF Minority Front, FA Freedom Alliance, AEB Africaner Unity Movement, Azapo Azanian Peoples' Organization.
Source: Figures adapted from A. Venter and C. Landsberg, *Government and Politics in the New South Africa* (Pretoria: Van Schaik, 2006), p.208.

of parties have emerged with some parliamentary representation only to vanish later from the political scene. The most important results from the first elections in 1994 and the most recent in 2004 are summarised in Table 1. In 1994, seven parties, including the ANC won parliamentary representation while in 2004 12 parties achieved this feat. All six opposition parties represented in 1994 survived to win seats in 2004 but of the six, only two managed to increase their parliamentary representation. In 2004, four new parties managed to win seats.

However, the overwhelming characteristic of all three elections since 1994 has been the dominance of the ruling ANC. Indeed this dominance has grown as the ANC has increased its share of the vote while the opposition parties have lost support. The ANC grew from 62.65 per cent of the vote in 1994 to 69.68 per cent in 2004. The strongest opposition party in 1994 obtained 20.39 per cent of the vote compared to 12.7 per cent in 2004. Thus the gap between the ANC and its closest rival grew from 42 per cent in 1994 to a massive 57 per cent in 2004.

We may categorise parliamentary parties as follows.

Liberation Parties

Three parties are represented in parliament as a consequence of their role in the liberation struggle: the ruling ANC, founded in 1912, and the oldest liberation movement in South Africa, the Pan Africanist Congress (PAC) founded in 1959 and the Azanian Peoples Organization (AZAPO).

The ANC was essentially a protest movement until it was banned in 1960 when many of its leaders, including Nelson Mandela, were either incarcerated or went into exile to continue the struggle.[4] Its historic rival, the PAC, broke away from the ANC in 1959 to become a more militant and Africanist oriented movement. However, it too was banned in 1960 thereby preventing it from developing effective organisation and resources. Despite these setbacks, it is surprising given this history that it has not been able to develop a larger support base. It is one of the few parties which attempts to mobilise black voters exclusively and its advocacy of land reform and African nationalism has not won widespread support despite their potential popularity.

The ANC, as the ruling party, has had to move to the centre to govern effectively. It has had to balance its mildly socialist inclinations with the restraints imposed by a uni-polar and globalising world. Its core strategy has been to seek maximum economic growth within the restraints imposed by a powerful union movement. This has entailed meeting the core demands of labour (minimum wages, union recognition, job protection), creating at least a basic welfare system for some of the truly indigent, and following pragmatic economic policies which include conservative budgeting and attempts to create a black capitalist class.[5] Because this is a delicate balancing act, the party is showing signs of growing internal divisions between its centrist and more radical wings.

Historically White Parties

Two such parties contested the 1994 elections: the National Party (NP), which had been the dominant party in South Africa from 1948 until the negotiated settlement, and the Democratic Party, subsequently known as the Democratic Alliance (DA) which traced its origins to 1959 when a liberal group of parliamentarians split from the conservative United Party to form the Progressive Party, for many years represented solely by Helen Suzman in parliament.

Both parties had originally represented whites in the all-white parliament but after 1994 had sought to increase black support. Neither was able to make a decisive breakthrough as the election results confirm. In an attempt to unite the white/coloured vote and use this as a base to attract African voters, the two agreed to unite under the name Democratic Alliance in 2000. However the union brought together two indigestible entities and was aborted in 2001.[6] Following the 2004 elections, which saw the NP now renamed New National Party (NNP) almost obliterated and the DA becoming the largest opposition party, the NNP disbanded and its leader joined the ANC. However most of its former supporters joined the DA.

Both parties sought to redefine themselves as centrist. The NNP tended to stress its Christian roots and sought to emulate the conservative Christian parties in France and Germany. The DA sees itself as a classic liberal party with an emphasis on free markets and individual rights.

Regional/Ethnic Parties

Several such parties exist, the most important being the Zulu-based Inkatha Freedom Party (IFP) whose support is concentrated in the KwaZulu-Natal (KZN) province and has been led since its founding in 1975 by Mangosuthu Buthelezi.[7] Whites have several small parliamentary parties including the Freedom Front Plus while the Indian based Minority Front is also a minor player. These parties have experienced continual decline in support since 1994.

The IFP has historically been an important player because initially it controlled the KZN provincial government and, given its support base amongst Zulu traditionalists there and in hostels in Johannesburg, had a considerable potential for initiating political violence. It was established as a Zulu cultural organisation at a time when non-ethnic African parties were prohibited by the white regime. The IFP sees itself as a conservative party in terms of both economic policies and social issues. Its major demand has been for a greater degree of regional autonomy and securing more entrenched rights for traditional authorities.

Morality Parties

Given the influence of religion in South Africa, it is not surprising that a party representing conservative moral values should have won representation in parliament. The African Christian Democratic Party (ACDP) advocates a policy based upon fundamentalist religious values. Not surprisingly it was one of only two opposition parties to increase its support between 1994 and 2004 from two to six. The party sees itself more as a pressure group than a government-in-waiting and seeks to influence policy in a socially conservative direction. It opposes gay rights and abortion and is a strong advocate of the death penalty.

Parties of the Disaffected

These parties generally emerged from leadership splits within existing parties. The United Democratic Movement (UDM), the first such party, emerged when Bantu Holomisa, a prominent ANC leader in the Eastern Cape, fell out of favour with the ANC hierarchy and left the party to found the UDM with similarly disaffected former leaders from the NP. More recently Patricia de Lille resigned from the PAC to form the Independent Democrats (ID). Both parties have found it difficult to move beyond the politics of personalities and develop both a national support base and a credible set of policies. Nor have they been able to create an attractive ideology or vision.

THE BEHAVIOUR OF THE ELECTORATE

As a functioning democracy, the dominance of the ANC and the weakness of all the opposition parties is a reflection of the opinions of the electorate. A critical factor that will shape the future will be the attitudes and behaviour of the electorate. While some observers believe that many voters make their political choices on the basis of their interests, most analysts maintain that history and race are the critical determinants and that elections take the form of an ethnic census.[8] The country's population of about 44 million is made up of 75 per cent Africans, 13.6 per cent whites, 8.6 per cent coloured people, and 2.6 per cent Indians. Although several parties exist to represent African interests, including AZAPO, and the PAC, more than 80 per cent of African voters support the ruling ANC. Almost all whites vote against the ANC as do a majority of coloured voters. Most of this support goes to the DA.

As a result, the ANC is assured of remaining in power indefinitely unless and until these dynamics change. For the present, neither perceptions of government corruption and incompetence nor opposition alternatives will change the political landscape. The ANC will continue to make history and opposition parties will have to function within that context.

Given that less than 15 per cent of the electorate is white, developments within the black community – primarily the African and to a lesser extent the coloured community – will be decisive. It is also these communities which suffer from extensive poverty, ill-health (including HIV/AIDS) and poor education. It is therefore probable that, in time, policies and parties to the left of the ANC will have greater appeal when the ties of loyalty to the ANC weaken.

The contemporary irony is that the major parliamentary opposition parties – the DA and the IFP – are parties of the centre-right while the pool of potential opposition voters is largely left of centre. Thus opposition philosophies and policies have limited appeal to most black voters. In addition political loyalties are largely path dependent and both parties have found it almost impossible to escape the legacy of the past and reinvent themselves as value driven organisations. The growing support of the DA between 1994 and 2004 was a direct result of the implosion of the NP, which, as we noted earlier, was disbanded after its dismal 2004 election results.[9] Yet the DA has less voter support than that enjoyed by the NP at its zenith in 1994. So growth prospects appear bleak. Voters regard the DA as too white and the IFP as too Zulu. And because neither party has been able to broaden its electoral appeal, their leadership remains predominantly white for the DA and too Zulu for the IFP.

Logically we would expect parties of the left to constitute the official opposition. However the only radical parties in parliament – the PAC and AZAPO – have been able to attract less than ten per cent of the vote won by the centre right. This is not a reflection of their policies, as we noted earlier. The ANC has been remarkably successful in consolidating its position as the heir to the liberation struggle and, despite its pragmatic policies and frequent policy failures, it has been able to hold intact its core support base. Thus far identity politics has consistently trumped class interests. The dynamics behind this success fall outside the scope of this paper but include the enormous advantages derived from control over the patronage machine of the state, clever strategies of co-opting talented ANC opponents, and the powerful symbolism of its role in the liberation struggle.

We may therefore summarise the most important political realities as follows: the electorate at present does not include a significant uncommitted block of voters which could be decisive in an election. No swing vote exists. The results of each election are path dependent which creates a static and highly predictable outcome. The opposition parties accept that for the present they can do little, if anything, to increase their support. Their criticisms of the ANC, even when valid, have almost no impact on the electorate. The success of the centre-right (DA/IFP) in mobilising its largely racial/ethnic constituencies has not been matched by the ability of the left/populists to mobilise their potential supporters. As a result parliament is not an accurate reflection of the national distribution of interests and orientations. The right is over-represented, the left under-represented. A country with a black majority has a largely white opposition! This explains why parliament has not been successful in performing its function as a forum for genuine debate.

The consequences of a racially defined electorate are significant. The ANC is confident that its position is unassailable. The opposition parties are lacking in motivation and find it increasingly difficult to attract competent people into their ranks. Lacking the resources of office, they face what frequently appear to be overwhelming odds in a game where the playing field clearly favours the incumbents. And as recent election results confirm, the opposition parties are losing rather than gaining support.

OPPOSITION STRATEGIES

In general, opposition parties seek one or more of the following: to become the ruling party, to become a partner in a coalition government, to influence policy, to protect and further the interests of their key constituencies, and to represent and give prominence to broader values and ideologies.

As our earlier discussion indicated, the distinctive characteristic of politics is the near hegemony of the ANC in government and the poor short-term prospects of the opposition parties. What strategies have opposition parties adopted in response to this reality?[10] We will focus on two important issues: opposition strategies towards the ruling party, and towards other opposition parties.

The Opposition and the Government

Opposition parties in comparative perspective reveal a wide range of attitudes and strategies towards the government. In some countries, the opposition or parts of it regard the ruling party as illegitimate and use the platform of parliament to continue 'war' in a different context. To some extent this was the approach of the few liberals and communists who were elected to legislative positions in South Africa prior to 1950. Since 1994, none of the parliamentary opposition parties have challenged the legitimacy of the new political order. The debate within the opposition has been over different opposition strategies such as robust, co-optive and cooperative opposition.

Robust opposition is shaped by both the rules of the political game and by deep-seated ideological/policy differences. The Westminster system tends to produce a robust style of political debate between the government and the opposition and South Africa's political engineers tried to avoid this pattern of politics.

However, the DA, which has engaged in robust politics, has been rewarded by the electorate. This tactical decision was not a reflection of major policy differences between the ANC and the DA. The DA has accepted Britain as its appropriate model and attacks most government initiatives with vigour and eloquence irrespective of the merits of the policies themselves. Opposition for the sake of opposition is how many voters view this strategy. And it is clear that the DA's constituency supports this approach as the success of the party's 'Fight Back' campaign in 1999 confirmed. Most whites and many coloured voters want a 'tough' opposition and the DA caters to this demand, at least at the level of rhetoric.[11]

An alternative strategy was followed by the New National Party. Its leaders believed that the fragile post-1994 democracy made robust opposition dangerous because it would increase racial tensions and encourage the authoritarian tendencies lurking within the liberation movement. The fragile process of transforming the ANC from a liberation movement into a normal political party/government had to be encouraged.

The NNP therefore followed a policy of cooperative opposition. It sought to cooperate with the ANC whenever possible and sought policy concessions through quiet negotiations. Its style of political debate was conciliatory rather than robust. The policy failed and was a major factor behind the implosion of the party. The key factor was that the NNP misread the wishes of its largely white and coloured working class supporters who had been led to hate the ANC by the party itself and wanted a strong and robust opposition. The DA read the mood of this segment of the electorate far more accurately and the 2004 elections can be viewed as a referendum within opposition politics between robust and cooperative strategies. The robust approach emerged strongly victorious, constituting the beginning of the end for the once all-powerful NNP.

Other factors contributed to the NNP's demise. The party had experienced more than 40 years of uninterrupted power and had no real conception of how to conduct itself as an opposition party. Its only leader of stature, former president and Nobel laureate F.W. de Klerk, quit active politics leaving behind a divided and demoralised party. And they were also a victim of their own propaganda success – for decades they had convinced most of the white electorate that the ANC was a terrorist and Marxist movement which would destroy the country if it came to power. To see the NNP now cooperating with its erstwhile enemies was a step too far for most of its former supporters who now switched their support to the robust opposition, the DA.

Today at least two parties, the ID and the UDM, attempt to follow a strategy of cooperative opposition. Indeed both parties were created as a protest against the perceived weaknesses of the ANC and what they saw as the sterility of robust opposition. Thus far, neither party has been able to follow the strategy effectively and both have lost considerable support.

The final strategy has been that of co-optive opposition. Electoral rivals have participated in coalition governments dominated by the ANC despite their on-going rivalry. Under the terms of the interim constitution of 1994, all parties which obtained at least five per cent of the vote were entitled to cabinet seats. Nelson Mandela included both the IFP and the NNP in his first cabinet although the NNP later left the national government. Although this provision was not included in the final constitution, Mandela's successor in 1999 offered the IFP cabinet representation which was accepted. However, after the 2004 elections the offer to the IFP was withdrawn.

Both the IFP and the NNP sought to combine participation in government with opposition to the government. Clearly this was a strategy which was beyond the capacity of their leaders, perhaps beyond the realm of the possible, and was strongly condemned by many of their supporters. Today only one cabinet position is filled by a non-ANC member.

Inter-opposition Strategies

All opposition parties face the same challenge of making a political impact in the context of ANC dominance, and thus share a common interest in making the opposition more effective. However, they have been unsuccessful in developing cooperative strategies amongst themselves. Splits within the opposition rather than consolidation have been the trends within parliament.

The decision to merge the Democratic Party with the NNP illustrates this reality. Because of the restraints of the electoral system, which at that time made defections impossible, a merger into a single party was not possible. The two parties decided to cooperate under the rubric of the Democratic Alliance as an interim measure. However, the partnership was short-lived and soon disintegrated with considerable acrimony. Although personalities played an important role, the key problem was the failure to integrate two very different political cultures: the hierarchical and community oriented Afrikaner approach of the NNP with the more individualist English oriented approach of the DP.

Some attempts have been made to create greater cooperation between the two largest surviving opposition parties – the DA and the IFP. Both parties advocate similar conservative economic and social policies. However the attempts have failed because although all opposition parties have common interests, simultaneously they are also rivals. Opposition parties are competing for the same 30 per cent of the electorate opposed to the ANC. At present the ANC's hold over its support base appears to be secure and is reinforced by the trend whereby their disillusioned supporters do not defect to other parties but either withdraw from political activity or engage in direct community action. This creates a zero-sum game for the opposition parties because gains in the support of one party come at the cost of a loss of support for another opposition party. And this clearly limits the willingness of inter-opposition cooperation because the issue of relative gains and losses will dominate all strategic calculations. Given the destructive consequences of this and the reality that even opposition cooperation will not produce major gains, opposition leaders seem more concerned with their relative position than with striving to increase the overall effectiveness of the opposition. This accounts in large part for the absence of concerted efforts to coordinate or unite elements within the opposition. Calls for opposition unity make good rhetoric but seldom produce results.

THE ROLE OF PARLIAMENT

Constitutional Parameters

In order to understand the role played by the opposition, we need to examine more broadly the role that the constitution carves out for the legislature. In the constitution, parliament is mandated with several functions including policy-making and executive accountability.

The formulation of public policy entails both the passage of broad legislation and the subsequent drafting of more detailed administrative regulations. Parliament is the nominal law-maker but it is widely accepted that in most democracies legislatures legitimate policies formulated elsewhere. Policy proposals are usually prepared by the executive, which in practice means senior departmental officials with ministerial guidance. The role of the legislature is largely formalistic in the passage of legislation and few important laws are initiated from within the legislature itself. The engine room of the NA is the committee system, designed to 'monitor, investigate, enquire into and make recommendations relating to any aspect of the legislative programme, budget, rationalization, restructuring, policy formulation or any other matter it may consider relevant, of the government department or departments falling within the category of affairs assigned to the committee'.[12] This grants considerable potential authority to these committees. In addition special committees have been established to deal with broader aspects of government policy, the most important being the Special Committee on Public Accounts (SCOPA). Opposition members are entitled to representation on all these committees on a proportional representation basis and by tradition SCOPA is chaired by an opposition member.

Alongside policy-making, democratic theory tends to consider accountability and oversight to be the most important legislative functions.[13] Under apartheid, the legislature was quite rightly viewed as the rubber stamp of the executive, a characteristic found in most Westminster-type systems. The approach of government members was to provide the executive with unvarying support while the opposition impotently opposed government policies. The 1996 constitution was designed to strengthen the oversight capabilities of parliament and created institutional capacity for this end. The critical element is the committee system described earlier. The degree of oversight that takes place will be shaped by the leadership and party orientations in these committees. The constitution does provide parliament with more powers than its predecessor enjoyed. Some argue that the committees even have the power to vote against or reduce a departmental budgetary request.

Political Dynamics

What is the record of parliament since 1994 in terms of policy-making and effective oversight of the executive?[14] In the early stages of the new parliamentary democracy most of the legislators came from the formerly excluded communities and election to the legislature represented a steep learning curve. Some 13 years later, it is becoming possible to analyse more enduring trends in the exercise of political power.

The key reality shaping legislative–executive relations is the dominant role played by the ANC both within and outside parliament. We traced earlier the growing numerical dominance of the ANC. How, if at all, has this influenced the role of parliament? A key political reality is that most executives prefer autonomy to effective legislative oversight. Members of the executive usually believe that their superior access to information gives them a special wisdom while legislators are seen as careerists who benefit from making dramatic claims despite limited information.

A large number of laws had to be changed in a post-apartheid society, and parliament, especially between 1994 and 2001, had a heavy workload processing dozens of bills. This may have contributed to a trend whereby most laws require very extensive administrative regulations by the minister to become effective. And these regulations are not sent back to parliament for assent. Thus a very important source of law-making takes place outside the legislature, reducing its impact both on law-making and oversight.

Given the ANC's history as a liberation movement and the general tendency in other democracies towards executive dominance,[15] it should come as no surprise that this trend has also emerged in South Africa. The ANC leadership has been determined to dominate the parliamentary process and ensure that no independent institutional powers emerge. And as we shall see they have formidable weapons to achieve this.

The foundation of ANC power lies in its electoral support which gives it a massive parliamentary majority. The electoral system also gives the party leadership a powerful mechanism to control most aspects of legislative behaviour. In the absence of any form of constituency representation, all legislators enter parliament on a PR list. And the party leadership has considerable influence over the formulation of the list of parliamentary candidates. Independent ANC legislators who defied the party line would be in great danger of being excluded from the party list for future elections. They might even lose their seat in parliament by being redeployed, expelled or suspended from the party. Although this power of the party elite over ANC parliamentarians has been used to neutralise outspoken legislators, its very existence is so effective that it is rarely necessary to exercise these powers.

Another important element of power is the authority structure within the legislature and the parliamentary party. Once again the ANC hierarchy makes all of the critical decisions – the choice of Speaker and Deputy Speaker of the NA, the chairs of the various committees, and the ANC chief whip and his/her deputies. These are formidable powers indeed. Thus overall parliament rarely if ever takes a stand opposed to by the executive.

The role of parliament in policy-making is therefore marginal. ANC dominance also makes it difficult for the ANC parliamentary caucus to exercise any real degree of oversight over their party colleagues in the executive. In general the expectation is for the opposition parties to seek to hold government accountable while the task of the ANC backbenchers is to rally round the government.

There have been a few exceptional cases. In 1999, the Mandela government entered into a complex series of arms agreements with European suppliers to purchase billions of dollars of military equipment. Accusations of large scale corruption around the deals soon surfaced and SCOPA, the appropriate parliamentary committee, began an investigation into alleged corruption by members of the executive. In the SCOPA investigation of alleged bribery and corruption in the award of the arms deal the ANC representative joined with the opposition in challenging the government. However, he did not receive support from his colleagues and indeed was criticised by the ANC hierarchy. Shortly afterwards he left parliament a somewhat disillusioned man.

When the ANC executive is united, little space exists for independent action within the NA. However, when the party is divided, some limited space is opened up for parliamentary initiatives. This was experienced during 2007 when the ANC was deeply divided over the leadership issue following President Mbeki's dismissal of Deputy President Jacob Zuma. Several ANC legislators seized the unusual opportunity of executive weakness to assert some parliamentary prerogatives. Ministers have been criticised for delivery failures, bills have been sent back to government for redrafting, and committee hearings have been unusually open in criticising aspects of executive performance. Perhaps the most dramatic example of this took place in March 2007 when a portfolio committee unanimously rejected a government-sponsored report on the escape of an important suspect from prison. Despite clear evidence that prison officials had cooperated in the escape, the government report white-washed its officials, a finding strongly rejected by the parliamentary committee. Later, however, the ANC caucus asserted itself and repudiated the conclusions of the ANC-led committee.

At its national congress in December, 2007, the ANC rejected Thabo Mbeki's bid to continue as ANC president and elected Jacob Zuma as his successor. However Mbeki will continue to be president of South Africa until elections are held in 2009. This dual authority structure has enabled parliament to exercise some independence from the executive. However, when authority has been consolidated and the ANC president is once again president of the country, executive dominance is likely to be restored.

The Role of the Opposition

We have seen the limited role that parliament has played as an institutional actor in both policy-making and executive oversight. This makes the task of creating an effective opposition unusually difficult and many voters express the critical view that the opposition is both ineffective and irrelevant.

It is clear that the political dynamics of South African politics and the institutional characteristics of parliament itself make it very difficult even for the most competent of opposition parties to make an impact. In general, if ruling parties make history, opposition parties have to try to survive within that history. All the cards are stacked against the opposition, at least for the present.

Incumbency creates two paths to resources. The ANC controls the state which gives it enormous powers of patronage. And as a result of ANC dominance, major interest groups, especially business, will provide resources to the ruling party either to avoid possible sanctions or to gain advantages such as lucrative state contracts.

Opposition parties have access to neither. In addition to these resources, the state provides direct funding to political parties for election costs. Once again strength creates more strength. In the 2004 elections, public funding to the parties was allocated on the basis of the proportion of votes they had won in the previous elections. The ANC received R42,573,853, the IFP R5,050,841, and the DA R7,087,153. Because the ANC increased its share of the vote in 2004, it will get an even greater share of the public funding for elections in 2009.

Opposition parties, as we noted earlier, have found it difficult to cooperate with each other because they are competing for the same pool of voters. Party leaders thus have a very limited incentive to cooperate. As one party leader argued, 'I would love to cooperate with other larger parties but they are so much better at public relations than we are that in the end they will claim the lion share of the spoils'.[16] And past history has shown that in the absence of the spoils of office, it is difficult to maintain party unity. The amalgamation of smaller parties into a larger party may actually increase problems of party unity without increasing opposition effectiveness as the abortive DA/ NNP union confirmed. Given that the overall prospects of growth for the opposition are so poor, it becomes difficult to motivate potential voters and even more difficult to attract talent to parliament. Many of the most able opposition parliamentarians have left parliament because of the frustrations of ineffective opposition. Ironically the ANC has faced similar problems: its enormous majority means that an ordinary parliamentarian has a very limited role to play in the NA. This frustrates the able and ambitious who frequently find the rewards of the business sector more attractive. It also acts as a disincentive for talented outsiders who might otherwise have followed a political career.

Opposition members are sometimes spread too thin to make a genuine impact. As we saw earlier, even the larger opposition parties have a limited number of representatives and each member may have to serve on several committees simultaneously, stretching their already limited resources. For smaller parties the situation is worse, with a single member having to serve on up to 14 committees simultaneously.

However, it does not follow that the opposition is irrelevant. Even if we accept that neither parliament as a whole nor the opposition are able to influence policy significantly or hold the executive accountable to any great extent, other critical functions for a viable democracy may nonetheless be performed.

One of the key functions of a legislature is representation. This is particularly important in a multi-ethnic polity where one group is predominant. For white, coloured and Asian voters, opposition parties create the framework for their representation and indeed opposition parties such as the DA and IFP are largely ethnic/racial parties. This is not to claim that these minorities are not represented in the ANC itself. Indeed not only are they well represented in parliament but the cabinet itself has white, coloured and Indian ministers. However, given their minority status, their ANC representatives have a lower profile in the ANC than they have in the opposition parties.

Minorities may feel that they too have a stake in the system because of their highly visible representation in opposition parties. While we may regret the racial composition of South Africa's party system, we must accept that it mirrors many of the divisions within the larger society and may have positive as well as negative effects.

In less divided societies with a floating vote, parliamentary debates and personalities have some impact on party fortunes. A charismatic opposition leader able to take on the government leaders effectively will raise his party's morale and perhaps cause doubts within government ranks. And the powerful media may communicate this to the interested public with implications for voter behaviour. These dynamics are weak in South Africa. Such is the dominance of the ruling party that even the most brilliant of opposition speakers will have at best a marginal impact. A recent example was the exchange on HIV/AIDS between opposition leader Tony Leon and ANC President Mbeki. Although any fair reading of the debate must score Leon the overwhelming victor, it produced barely a ripple in either parliament or society.

However, parliament does serve as an important mechanism for the recruitment of political talent. It is of vital importance for the viability of democracy to have an effective opposition. Changes in government after decades of effective one-party dominance in Mexico, India and Scandinavia show that change can happen suddenly and unexpectedly. It is vital for a potential alternative government, even if constituted from several minor parties, to exist in parliament.

Perhaps another way of looking at the importance of opposition is to turn the question on its head. Instead of asking if the opposition is effective in terms of its ability to influence policy or hold the government accountable, we should perhaps ask what the implications for governance would be if the opposition ceased to exist. The very existence of a vocal opposition may have many subliminal consequences: officials will be less corrupt because of the fear of exposure, policies will be more carefully formulated to minimise criticism, interests that might have been ignored will be placed on the agenda. These are important realities despite the difficulty of documenting them.

Finally we should keep in mind the linkages with the global village. South African politics now takes place before a global audience of investors, consumers, and decision-makers. Much of what they learn about the country comes directly or indirectly from the activities of the opposition. For example, while the government has a clear interest in minimising discussions about the levels of crime, the reverse applies to the opposition. Crime is thus placed on the political agenda for all in the audience, local and foreign, to see, with important implications for the country's economic prospects and political standing.

The opposition may thus be more important and effective than is often appreciated. The overall impact of its activities may be greater than the sum of its parts. And the fact that the ruling party takes many of its criticisms seriously confirms this reality.

It lies beyond the scope of this article to examine the power map of the polity or the structure of power within the presidency and the executive.[17] However, given the dominant role played by the ANC hierarchy in shaping the role of parliament, a brief summary of the key elements may be useful.

In many democracies, parties have increasingly become election machines designed to mobilise the electorate. Although broad policies on key public issues will have been formulated by the party, the government of the day will have considerable autonomy to make policy. Key members of the civil service will play a critical role in this process.

In contemporary South Africa, with high levels of political mobilisation and the memory of the struggle very much alive, the organs of the ANC are influential in shaping the details of public policy. Indeed party and state are thoroughly intertwined. Most members of the cabinet are also ANC leaders and will participate in key ANC organs such as the National Working Committee and the National Executive Committee.

One might have predicted that the cabinet would gradually become more influential over time but this has not happened. Part of the reason may be the multi-party coalitions which have characterised many of the post-apartheid cabinets. Leaders from other parties such as the NNP and IFP served in several cabinets, thus weakening executive cohesion. In addition, the cabinet has been weakened by the increasing power of the presidency. Thabo Mbeki is by nature a centraliser and he has established a large and powerful office to assist him. Indeed one of the criticisms made of his presidential style has been his attempt to centralise power in his office. Recently the party has demanded, with some success, that the leading role of its key organs be re-established.

In many democracies, party caucuses have a special status independent of the party at large. In the UK, for example, the parliamentary caucus of the Conservative Party is recognised as an autonomous body that determines its own leadership and has considerable leeway in deciding its policy priorities. In South Africa the ANC caucus similarly demanded special status separate from the party at large. However, in 1998 the ANC national congress rejected this request, reinforcing the subordinate status of the ANC parliamentary members to the party at large.

The parliamentary caucus of the ANC, aware of the degree to which it has been marginalised, has responded by establishing study groups to specialise in the various policy areas. But given that they are all mere agents of the party on the PR list and given the relative paucity of backbench talent, they have not been able to take many effective policy initiatives.

From the perspective of both the cabinet and the power brokers in the ANC, their view of the role of their parliamentary members is to support the government, pass all government bills, and leave the oversight function to the opposition parties. To a large extent they have been successful.[18]

Perhaps the unusual degree of power exercised by the ANC as an organisation is reflected in the current presidential race to succeed Mbeki. Although it is a tradition for candidates not to campaign openly for high office, not one of those who are seen as the leading candidates comes from either parliament or the national cabinet. All of the major potential candidates are senior party officials ranging from ANC deputy president Jacob Zuma, Motlanthe, the secretary-general, and NEC members Ramaphosa and Sexwale. The only serving cabinet member who is seen as a possible president is defence minister Lekota who is also the ANC national chairman.

WHERE IS THE REAL OPPOSITION?

Under apartheid, with black people excluded from effective political participation, white opposition parties in parliament did not represent the real opposition to the government. Not much has changed since apartheid imploded. Institutionalised politics does not reflect the real configuration of forces in the political economy. A largely non-African opposition, with some Zulu support, confronts a dominant party representing the vast majority of the African population. As long as elections are mere racial censuses, this reality will continue. Clearly government is not all-powerful. Important restraints exist from business, the global community and the courts. But as we have shown above, the parliamentary opposition does not constitute a major source of opposition. Where then does the real opposition lie?

It is perhaps an irony that the 'genuine' opposition is part of the ruling alliance. During the protracted struggle against apartheid, the forces of the left – the ANC, South African Communist Party (SACP) and the trade federation Congress of South African Trade Unions (COSATU) – all cooperated against a common enemy. When victory was finally achieved, neither COSATU nor the SACP was prepared to oppose the ANC behemoth and lose the material benefits flowing to the new regime. They have remained within the ruling alliance where they have sought, with limited success, to influence government policy. Indeed dual ANC/SACP party membership has been permitted and all the SACP members who are in parliament have been elected wearing their ANC hats!

The ANC is thus a 'broad church', and its many divisions are only contained by the power of patronage. Increasingly, members of all three alliance partners are questioning the wisdom of continuing with the alliance. The general pattern in most African states has been for the power of the ruling party, backed by the resources of the state, to increase while the union movements have atrophied. This is a fate COSATU is determined to avoid.

Thus far the symbolic power of the ANC has intimidated its alliance partners, forcing them to try to influence policy from behind the scenes. Despite growing anger over their failures, they remain committed to the alliance in part because the impending retirement of President Mbeki has created an opportunity to influence the choice of his successor. Should they fail to elect a left-wing candidate, they may be forced to re-evaluate their strategic options, including the continuation of the alliance itself.

Given the dominant role of the ANC, groups within civil society have not attempted to challenge the ANC's hegemony. Rather they have mobilised to influence policy in ways which serve their interests. Business has created direct links to the government, thus bypassing the opposition parties. Social movement groups like the Treatment Action Campaign, which seeks to increase the resources devoted to the treatment of HIV/AIDS, has developed a highly effective public campaign to mobilise public opinion to put pressure on the government. Under apartheid, the real opposition was located outside parliament in the trade unions and civic movements. It is perhaps an irony that they continue to constitute the real opposition and operate largely from outside parliament despite the enfranchisement of the black population.

CONCLUSIONS

Politics in South Africa contains a high degree of duality. On the one hand a constitution sets out the rules of the political game and parliament, the executive and the courts function in a relatively orderly and harmonious way. On the other hand electoral politics does not produce an outcome which reflects the underlying interests of the population. The 'first world' of institutional politics bears little relationship to the political attitudes and interests of the rural poor, the unemployed or those living under the sway of traditional authorities. The party systems reflect the past: racial politics, the struggle, the apartheid legacy. A genuine realignment in which interests and genuine identity issues determined the nature and support of parties would probably bear only a passing resemblance to the status quo.

Over time this realignment may come. At some point the ANC may split into its constituent parts. Most analysts predict that the Left will desert the alliance under the leadership of the SACP and COSATU.[19] However, it is also possible that the Right will gain in strength and that a coalition of the moral right-wing, traditional leaders, business and the new middle class could unite to form a new opposition to the right of the ANC. This of course, assumes that democratic politics will survive. Many analysts argue that ANC dominance is so entrenched that it threatens the spirit of democracy itself. They argue that the party would use the full resources of the state, including repression, to ensure that its hold on power is not threatened.

A critical issue will be the political responses of the poor and working poor. It is generally accepted that no government, no matter how uniquely talented, could within a decade produce the desperately needed socio-economic miracles: reduce unemployment from some 40 per cent to a more manageable level, reduce the high levels of inequality, control the spread of HIV, build houses for the poor and meet the many other demands for a better life.

At present the growing disillusionment with delivery failures and high levels of corruption within the ANC has not eroded the loyalty of most of its supporters. Even those who have benefited least from a majority government remain loyal in the expectation that things will improve. Many of those alienated from the party have chosen to exit from politics and withdraw their vote entirely. The critical reality is that disillusionment has not led to an increase in votes for the opposition.

This will have important implications for the future. While most of the disillusioned have exited from politics, many former political activists have become involved in community action and protests. Violence over the slow pace of land reform and the poor quality of urban services has become increasingly prevalent. A key issue will be whether the country will face growing extra-parliamentary political protests as were experienced in the 1980s in response to government failures, or whether those presently alienated will rejoin system politics and support new opposition parties when the present system begins to unravel.

Will growing opposition be institutionalised and brought back into parliamentary politics or will it remain outside the system expressing itself in protests and violence? This may well be the decisive element in determining what sort of South Africa will emerge when ANC support begins to weaken.

NOTES

1. See K. Grundy, *The Militarization of South African Politics* (Bloomington: Indiana University Press, 1986); A. Seegers, 'South Africa's National Security Management System', *Journal of Modern African Studies*, 29 (1991), pp.253–73.
2. P. Waldmeir, *Anatomy of a Miracle* (London: Penguin, 1997) contains a perceptive analysis of the negotiations.
3. J. Butler and R. Rotberg, *The Black Homelands of South Africa* (Berkeley, CA: University of California Press, 1977).
4. See N. Mandela, *Long Walk to Freedom* (Randburg: Macdonald, 1994). An excellent collection of documents is contained in T. Karris, *From Protest to Challenge*, Vol.5 (Bloomington: Indiana University Press, 1997).

5. A. Hirsch, *Season of Hope: Economic Reforms under Mandela and Mbeki Durban* (Scotts-ville: University of KwaZulu-Natal Press, 2005).
6. A perceptive analysis of these dynamics is contained in H. Kotze, 'A Consummation Devoutly Wished?', in R. Southall (ed.), *Opposition and Democracy in South Africa* (London: Frank Cass, 2001).
7. The classic study of the IFP remains G. Mare and G. Hamilton, *An Appetite for Power* (Johannesburg: Ravan Press, 1977). The IFP's performance in the 2004 elections is described by L. Piper, 'The Inkatha Freedom Party: Between the Impossible and the Ineffective', in J. Piombo and L. Nijzink (eds.), *Electoral Politics in South Africa* (New York: Palgrave Macmillan, 2005), pp.148–65.
8. An analysis which concludes that voters are rational actors and not ethnic vehicles is R. Mattes, 'South Africa: Democracy without the People?', *Journal of Democracy*, 13 (2002), pp.22–36. The alternative view is strongly expressed by H. Giliomee, J. Myburgh and L. Schlemmer, 'Dominant Party Rule, Opposition Parties and Minorities in South Africa', in Southall (ed.), *Opposition and Democracy in South Africa*, pp.161–82.
9. For a description of how the NNP fared in its last parliamentary election in 2004, see C. Schulz-Herzenberg, 'The New National Party: The End of the Road', in Piombo and Nijzink, *Electoral Politics in South Africa*, pp.166–86.
10. A summary of opposition strategies is provided in R. Schrire, 'The Reality of Opposition in South Africa', in Southall (ed.), *Opposition and Democracy in South Africa*, pp.135–48.
11. For an in-depth analysis of the DA's campaign strategy in the 2004 election, see S. Booysen, 'The Democratic Alliance: Progress and Pitfalls', in Piombo and Nijzink (eds.), *Electoral Politics in South Africa*, pp.129–47.
12. Quoted by L. Nijzink, 'Opposition in the New South African Parliament', in Southall (ed.), *Opposition and Democracy in South Africa*, p.62.
13. The classic statement remains R. Dahl, *Regimes and Opposition* (New Haven, CT: Yale University Press, 1973).
14. An interesting survey of a decade of South Africa's parliament can be found in Piombo and Nijzink (eds.), *Electoral Politics in South Africa*.
15. See J. Simon, *British Cabinet Government* (London: Routledge, 1999); A. Lijphart, *Parliamentary versus Presidential Government* (Oxford: Oxford University Press, 1992).
16. Interview with opposition leader, Cape Town, 3 Feb. 2007.
17. See R. Calland, *Anatomy of South Africa* (Cape Town: Zebra Press, 2007) for an innovative attempt to provide a political power map.
18. It is telling that in the ANC Policy Discussion Document released in March 2007 in preparation for the National Conference in December the chapter entitled 'Legislature and Governance' merely lists the much debated issues of electoral system reform, floor-crossing, the abolition of some or all provinces, as well as some issues around ethics and post tenure rules for public representatives. Nowhere in the document does the ANC present its vision of the role of the National Assembly in social transformation or discuss its views on the importance of parliament as the country's main body of elected representatives.
19. This is certainly the consensus view of almost all political commentators and President Mbeki himself is on record as predicting such a split at some time in the distant future.

Parliamentary Opposition and its Alternatives in a Transnational Regime: The European Union in Perspective

LUDGER HELMS

The contention that there is no such thing as parliamentary opposition at the supranational European level[1] belongs to the more established hypotheses concerning European governance, which have rarely and only more recently been challenged. Given the wide range of competing interpretations of the EU system as a whole, this widespread negative (and often tacit) scholarly consensus is remarkable. However, as long as there is no agreement on some of the more fundamental issues of European governance, such as whether the European Union has a 'real' parliament, or whether it can be reasonably characterised as a parliamentary system of government, any positive consensus on the more specific issue of parliamentary opposition would be even more remarkable.

This attempt to assess the manifestations of parliamentary opposition, as well as its limits and alternatives, in the European Union is based on a comparative politics approach that challenges the entrenched *sui generis* paradigm in European Union research. The decision in favour of such an approach rests on the proposition that the European Union may be meaningfully described as a political system whose specific properties can be understood better through explicit or implicit comparison with other political systems.[2] While the heuristic benefits of such an approach are obvious, there are potential pitfalls in studying the European Union from a comparative perspective. One of the better known problems relates to the inclination of many scholars to compare, and contrast, empirical aspects of supranational European governance with idealistic assumptions about the democratic process in European (and other) nation-states.[3] Another source of 'miscomparing'[4] emanates from confining comparisons to the level of structural features without duly taking into account their functional dimension. Genuine comparisons have to include the search for functional equivalents[5] – a strategy of comparison that allows comparing different systems without denying their particular structural features.

More specific problems of studying parliamentary opposition in the European Union relate to the EU's character as a multi-level system.[6] Only an analysis that includes at least the two major levels (the supranational and the national level), and the manifold interdependencies between them, may hope to produce realistic insights into the working logics of European governance. The striking neglect of studying the relationships and interdependencies between the European Parliament and the national parliaments of EU Member States, which provide the key arenas of parliamentary opposition at either level, has been highlighted more recently.[7] However, it would be rather unconvincing to attribute the notably limited knowledge of opposition politics in the European Union exclusively to a lack of scholarly interest. As Peter Mair has argued in a recent paper, there are some problems concerning the opposition issue in the European Union that trouble European citizens as much as EU scholars, and many aspects of the larger problem result from the complex and confusing interdependencies that exist between the different levels of political action.[8] Thus, any serious attempt to understand the workings of parliamentary opposition in the EU has to devote particular attention to the specific relations and non-relations between the relevant actors at different levels that have a stake in the systemic function of parliamentary opposition.

A closer look reveals that part of the problem with studying parliamentary opposition in the European Union is even more fundamental. Indeed, there can be no conceptual and empirical clarity about the sources and manifestations of parliamentary opposition in a given polity in the absence of a sufficiently clear understanding as to what or whom the opposition is directed against. Even if the search for a reference point of the parliamentary opposition and its actions is confined to the level of other institutional or institutionalised actors,[9] there is no natural answer to this basic question.

Traditional approaches to studying parliamentary opposition, which have been devised in the context of parliamentary democracies, consider the 'governing majority' (comprising the political executive, that is, the cabinet, and the supporting political parties in parliament) as the natural antagonist and central point of reference of the parliamentary opposition. In the bulk of works on parliamentary opposition in non-parliamentary regimes, which lack the specific fusion-of-powers structures that characterise parliamentary democracies, the executive branch (or simply the president) has been identified as the closest equivalent of the 'executive/parliamentary majority' nexus in parliamentary democracies. While this is of limited help when it comes to defining the parliamentary opposition, it provides a reasonable starting point for devising more specific and sophisticated concepts.[10]

Matters in the European Union are somewhat more complicated. On the one hand, there is a strong inclination among scholars, politicians and citizens to consider the Commission, which displays many features of a cabinet, as the European Union's core executive. From this perspective, both the Parliament and the Council are conceived of as the first and second legislative chambers of a supranational bicameral system. On the other hand, it is possible, and equally convincing, to consider the Commission and the Council as two interdependent components of a 'dual executive'.[11] This view is particularly compelling if the focus is on the structural features of the three major actors to be found at the European level (the Commission, the Council, and the Parliament). There are obvious problems with considering the Council – which is composed of the political 'chief executives' of EU Member States – a genuinely 'legislative' actor.

Adopting this second view, the natural starting point for any analysis of parliamentary opposition in the European Union would be to study the political structures and processes inside the European Parliament and its relations with the Commission and the Council. The complex nature of the EU polity requires us to expand this focus, though. The analysis of manifestations of parliamentary opposition in the European Parliament is to be complemented by an analysis of parliamentary opposition in the EU Member States. Given the multi-level character of the European Union, it is necessary, however, to reach beyond established notions of parliamentary opposition, and develop a conceptual focus that accounts for the opposition functions of both the minority and majority parties in national parliaments.

A more complete picture would emerge if these assessments were complemented by a thorough analysis of possible 'functional equivalents' of parliamentary opposition at the European level. While a more detailed examination of other oppositions, and their relationship with the parliamentary opposition, cannot be provided here for reasons of space alone, it would seem useful to highlight by way of conclusion some of the more prominent 'co-actors' and 'contenders' of the parliamentary opposition at the European level.

Perspectives that conceive of the European Parliament as a unitary actor have by no means been confined to the constitutionalist school of executive–legislative relations research. Indeed, as Simon Hix, Tapio Raunio and Roger Scully have rightly observed,[12] some of the most theoretically advanced work in the field by authors such as George Tsebelis and Geoffrey Garrett draws on this understanding.[13] From here, it is only a small step to considering the European Parliament as the institutional embodiment of parliamentary opposition at the European level.[14]

As to the legislative powers of the European Parliament, the series of reforms carried out since the early 1970s transformed the Parliament 'from a lobbyist to a co-legislator'.[15] Initially, Parliament's power in the legislative arena was effectively limited to a consultative role. According to the rules set by the Treaty of Rome (signed in 1957 and put into force the following year), neither the Commission nor the Council were obliged to accept any of the amendments proposed by the Parliament. Even the very modest consultation powers of the Parliament remained long disputed. It was only in 1980 that a ruling of the Court of Justice confirmed that no legislation could be adopted by the Council unless the Parliament had formally issued its opinion. In constitutional practice, this judgment provided the Parliament with a certain amount of power, as it was now able to delay, or threaten to delay, issuing an opinion on a pending bill.

Apart from more specific changes to the procedure for adopting the annual budget, which slightly increased parliamentary influence, it was the major treaties of 1987, 1993 and 1999 that progressively enhanced the legislative powers of the European Parliament. The Single European Act of 1987 introduced the 'cooperation procedure'. Even though this new procedure applied only to a strictly limited number of articles in the treaty, it marked an important change. There were now two readings of legislation in the European Parliament, and the Council's ability to overturn parliamentary amendments was reduced. Moreover, the Parliament for the first time effectively had some agenda-setting power (through its amendment powers), though its capacity to act remained conditional upon the support of the Commission and the Council.

The Maastricht Treaty of 1993 effectively replaced the cooperation procedure by the 'co-decision procedure', a change that would revolutionise the relations between the Parliament and the Council. The new procedure established a conciliation committee (composed of an equal number of representatives from the European Parliament and the Council) that would be activated if there were no consensus on a given bill after two readings in each institution. However, under the Maastricht version of the co-decision procedure, the Council clearly remained the more powerful part of the European 'two-chamber legislature'. In case the conciliation committee failed to reach an agreement, the formal procedure allowed the Council to re-propose the bill in its original version, leaving the Parliament with a blunt 'take-it-or-leave-it' option. Thwarting the expectations of the governments in the Council which had hoped to be able to use this procedure as a disciplinary measure against the Parliament, the latter rather used its first opportunity to reject a draft bill under consideration (a directive in the field of telecommunications). This occasion, the first ever on which the European Parliament successfully blocked a piece of EU legislation, marked an important precedent that influenced successive revisions of the formal rules of legislative co-decision.

When the Treaty of Amsterdam introduced a revised version of the co-decision procedure in 1999, it hardly broke new ground. Rather, it closed the gap between the now well-established informal practice of legislative co-decision and the effectively suspended formal rules. From now on, no new legislation to which the new procedure applied (mostly regulations concerning the EU single market) could be passed without the explicit consent of a (simple) majority in the European Parliament and a qualified majority in the Council. The Constitutional Treaty that was signed by the political chief executives of all the EU Member States in 2004 but effectively buried after negative referendum results in France and the Netherlands included the proposition to make the co-decision procedure the standard procedure concerning almost all EU legislation. Even without this extension of the co-decision procedure, the current European Parliament's power status in relation to the executive is considerably more impressive than at any previous stage of European integration history.

Whereas the effects of legislative co-decision procedures within the European Parliament (including in particular the structural concentration of workload in a handful of parliamentary committees, and a marked decrease in the overall number of non-legislative resolutions and initiative reports[16]) have been too obvious to be denied, the exact influence of the Parliament in the legislative arena has continued to be a matter of contention. A recent study that draws on a survey among a select group of practitioners of EU affairs found a 'Council-centric view' to mark the most accurate depiction of legislative decision-making at the European level.[17] One author has argued more specifically that the more recent variant of the co-decision procedure may not be judged an unqualified success for the European Parliament.[18] Another found the European Parliament to be 'somewhat tame in its efforts to check the council in the legislative process'[19] – an assessment that is based in particular on the small proportion of co-decisions being lost on account of a parliamentary veto. But the identified 'tameness' of the Parliament in the legislative process is in line with the widespread perception among MEPs that their ability publicly to control the Council is generally fairly limited.[20]

Overall, however, there has been a broad consensus that the developments since 1979 have gradually turned the European Parliament into a rather powerful legislative assembly that can be classified, in Michael Mezey's influential categories, as a legislature with 'strong policy-making power'.[21] Similarly, the European Parliament has been described as what Nelson Polsby called a 'transformative legislature' – a legislature capable (and willing) to leave its powerful mark on the legislative decision-making and policy process.[22]

To the extent then that the European Parliament as a whole is considered an actor that can meaningfully be understood in terms of parliamentary opposition, the structural opportunities for powerful parliamentary opposition at the European level can be said to have gradually, and significantly, increased over recent decades. However, the analysis of the capacities of the European Parliament in the legislative process has to be complemented by an assessment of the Parliament's ability to hold the Commission accountable.

Spectacular manifestations of increased parliamentary control, such as in 1999 (see below), do not change the fact that the formal powers of the parliament to control the commission have remained more limited than its legislative powers. Individual responsibility of Commissioners to the Parliament has remained an unfulfilled ambition that would not even have been satisfied by the implementation of the ill-fated Constitutional Treaty. More importantly, there has been no institutionalised opportunity for the Parliament to force the Commission to resign on the basis of a simple no-confidence vote. The closest equivalent of an 'unqualified' vote of no-confidence to be found at the European level is the right of Parliament to censure the Commission on the basis of a two-thirds majority in the vote which has to be produced by an absolute majority of MEPs – a device that bears closer similarity to the rules for impeachment in the United States than to even the most restrictive variants of the no-confidence vote in parliamentary democracies.[23]

No balanced assessment can deny the fact that there has been quite a remarkable expansion of the Parliament's power in the investiture procedure of the Commission since 1993.[24] The Maastricht Treaty ruled that the Council must consult the Parliament regarding its nominee for the post of Commission President, whereas the Amsterdam Treaty granted the

Parliament a vote on the Council's nominee for President of the Commission and the Commission as a whole. However, the increased control powers of the Parliament in the Commission-building process cannot meaningfully be considered a compensation for its specific limitations in voting the Commission out of office. Therefore, occasional assessments that consider the European Union a 'parliamentarised regime', if not a full-blown parliamentary system, are clearly premature. David Judge and David Earnshaw are right to maintain that 'even after Nice the "parliamentarization" of the Commission remains an aspiration'.[25]

This said, more recent political dynamics have moved the European Union closer to a type of regime following the logics of parliamentary democracies than the formal rules concerning executive–legislative relations in Strasburg and Brussels would have us guess. The key event, which served as a powerful trigger for all successive developments regarding the relationship between the European Parliament and the Commission, was the resignation of the Santer Commission early in 1999.

A brief account of the events may not go amiss. The crisis developed out of allegations over irregularities and mismanagement within the Commission, revolving in particular around the actions of two Commissioners, Edith Cresson and Manuel Marín. Having examined these allegations, the Budgetary Control Committee of the European Parliament voted (with a narrow margin of 14 to 13 votes) in favour of granting the Commission budgetary discharge for the 1996 EU annual budget on 11 December 1998, thereby officially advising the plenary of the European Parliament to grant discharge. However, even though the President of the Commission, Jacques Santer, declared that he would treat the matter of discharge as one of general confidence in the Commission, the Parliament in its vote on 17 December 1998 denied discharge.

Adopting Santer's line of argument, the leader of the Socialist group in the European Parliament announced that she would file a motion of censure against the Commission, but added that her group would vote against its own motion, thereby effectively converting a vote of no-confidence into a vote of confidence in the Commission. This motion was later on accompanied by a 'real' motion of censure that was supported by a coalition of MEPs from all party groups. Both motions were withdrawn on 14 January 1999, though, after the Socialists tabled another motion that demanded the creation of an independent committee of experts to investigate the series of allegations. However, a smaller group of MEPs led by the Greens tabled a new motion of no-confidence and insisted on a vote. While this motion failed to win a majority, no fewer than 232 MEPs voted in favour of it (against 293 no votes and 27 abstentions), which marked the largest number of MEPs ever to support a Commission censure motion.

Two months later, the Committee of Independent Experts completed its first report, in which it cleared most Commissioners of the charges brought against them but harshly criticised the Commission as a whole for lacking an appropriate sense of responsibility. The Commission learned of these criticisms through a leak, and resigned in the early hours of 15 March 1999 even before the official release of the report. However, this critical report alone can hardly explain the course of events. A crucial factor driving the decision-making processes within the Commission was the announcement by the leadership of the Socialist group in the European Parliament on 14 March that it had changed its position and would now support a vote of no-confidence, thereby making a two-thirds majority for a censure of the commission highly likely. Thus, it can be argued that, while formally no final censure vote was held, the Commission was effectively censured by the Parliament.[26]

Even more remarkable than this incident were the fundamental changes at the level of political coalitions that came to the fore during the crisis. 'For the first time', as Simon Hix and his co-authors note, 'a coalition of "governing" political groups, which were represented in the Commission, supported the Commission against a smaller group of "opposition" parties, mainly to the left of the socialists'.[27] This marked a spectacular departure from the familiar pattern of informal 'grand coalition politics', the close cooperation between the two major parties – the conservative European People's Party (EPP) and the Socialists (PES) – that had characterised the political process in the European Parliament for many years up until the late 1990s.[28] A more immediate cause for the gradual demise of the informal grand coalition, however, was the breakdown of the long-standing agreement between the two largest parties to 'share' the presidency of the European Parliament (that is, to alternate office every two-and-a-half years) in the aftermath of the 1999 European elections. Needless to say, this episode, as well, has to be viewed in a broader context: After the 1999 European elections had produced a historically low turnout, there was a significantly increased common interest and desire amongst the major political groups in the European Parliament to compete more vigorously on legislative and internal issues, not least in order 'to signal to the outside world that the EP was a "real" parliament'.[29]

In retrospect, the resignation of the Santer Commission in 1999 marked the beginning rather than the end of a new chapter in executive–legislative relations at the European level. Both the Prodi and the Barroso Commissions (in office from 1999 to 2004, and since 2004 respectively) faced a considerably more self-confident Parliament, willing to use its formal and informal powers to control the Commission. Prodi in particular found it hard to dispel the widespread 'impression of weak leadership',[30] which also reflected the fact that he and his team of Commissioners had to govern under the conditions of 'divided government' (a left-wing-dominated Commission facing a conservative majority in the European Parliament). The somewhat difficult formation of the Barroso Commission marked the return to 'unified government', based on narrow conservative majorities in both the Commission and the Parliament. Unlike his Christian Democrat predecessor Santer, Barroso and his team came to experience a remarkably strong opposition from a majority of members of the PES.

As argued above, 'government–opposition patterns' in the European Parliament constitute a rather recent phenomenon. The very emergence of these new patterns, however, would not have been possible – in fact not even conceivable in theory – without a reasonable amount of internal cohesion of the parties involved. While this marks a considerably older dimension of politics in the European Parliament, it took some time to develop.

In the early stages of European integration, during the first post-war decade, deliberate attempts were made to establish a mode of representation that would avoid party cleavages as much as territorial/national cleavages. During the first months of the Common Assembly – the predecessor of the European Parliament in existence from 1951 to 1957 – members sat in alphabetical order. This particular sitting order survived for only half a year, though. It was replaced by a new order that was organised on the basis of ideological affinity. The European Parliament inherited these ideology-based structures of internal organisation. That said, the position of individual members continued to be relatively strong, especially in comparison with most parliamentary regimes. In the Rules of Procedure of the European Parliament, individual MEPs rather than groups remained the primary actors up until the late 1970s (though political groups have been officially recognised since 1957). It was the introduction of direct elections to the European Parliament (applied for the first time in 1979) that marked the beginning of a fundamental change in the internal organisation of the Parliament with party groups gaining ever more ground, largely at the expense of individual members.[31]

However, it is easy to overestimate the direct impact of the change in electoral rules on structural developments within the European Parliament. Elections to the European Parliament have remained strikingly different from parliamentary elections in both parliamentary and presidential regimes. In the minds of EU citizens, European elections have largely continued to be 'second-order elections',[32] defined by a limited relevance in terms of both politics and policies. However, this is by no means the only aspect that has made elections to the European Parliament distinctive. Even more important to our context is the fact that European elections have mainly been fought by national parties over national issues with the parties' positions regarding European integration remaining marginal; moreover, incumbent parties that have lost EP elections have often managed to win subsequent national elections.[33]

Taking these different aspects into account, Simon Hix and his collaborators notice a striking 'electoral disconnection' between EU citizens and their representatives in the European Parliament that has important implications:

> The absence of a clear electoral connection means that political developments inside the European Parliament, such as the evolution of the transnational political groups, cannot be explained by external collective interests of the MEPs. Because European Parliament elections are fought by national parties rather than the transnational political parties in the European Parliament, the MEPs in a particular European political group are unlikely to be rewarded by voters in the next election if they acted collectively to secure their previous manifesto promises. Equally, the MEPs or transnational parties are unlikely to be punished for failing to act on previous electoral promises.[34]

The same authors demonstrate at a later stage of their analysis that it is the gradual increase in the power of the Parliament that marks the single most important factor explaining the notable increase in cohesion of the European political groups.[35] This driving force has been powerful enough to counteract other factors, such as the growing internal national fractionalisation of the parties, in particular, which has had a significant negative impact on cohesion. The analysis of roll call voting dating from 1979 to June 2004, presented by Hix *et al.*, suggests that transnational political parties in the European Parliament are more cohesive than national groups of MEPs, and are increasingly so.[36] While there has been no strictly linear increase in party cohesion within any party group from the first directly elected European Parliament (1979–84) through to the fifth (1999–2004), all six major party groups being represented in the fifth parliament had higher cohesion scores than in any previous parliament. In the fifth parliament, the Greens, the Socialists and the Liberals achieved the highest scores of party cohesion.

The degree of party cohesion, that has been considered to be 'almost as high as in some European national parliaments and certainly higher than in the US Congress',[37] is all the more remarkable as the resources of the political groups for disciplining their members are comparatively limited. Despite a developed system of party whips and party coordinators, and the institutionalised opportunity to expel a member from the group, direct control of the European political groups over their members is weak in comparison with the far-reaching powers of the parliamentary party groups in most parliamentary democracies. In particular, the European parties do not decide whether or not an MEP will get a chance to stand for re-election. Moreover, some of the intra-parliamentary business, such as the assignment of positions to individual MEPs, is handled at the level of European party leaderships and the national party delegations. In the absence of many of the usual devices designed to secure a reasonable voting discipline of members belonging to a particular group, 'cohesion [in the European Parliament] is facilitated by intra-group committee-based division of labour, willingness to build compromises, inter-institutional requirements, and by ideological affinity inside the groups'.[38]

Even so, what about the ideological dimensions of party politics in the European Parliament? As Hix, Noury and Roland demonstrate, there have been major alterations in the ideological structure of the party system over time. Whereas in the first three directly elected parliaments (1979–94), the party system was basically split into two blocs – a left bloc (consisting of the Socialists, the Radical Left and the Greens), and a right bloc (composed of the European People's Party, the Liberals, the British Conservatives and their allies, as well as the French Gaullists and their allies), later parliaments have been marked by a different party system, in which the Liberals occupied a position between the two major parties of the left (the Socialists) and of the right (the European People's Party).[39] A recent expert survey seeking to determine the policy positions of the major political groups in the European Parliament shortly before the 2004 elections arrived at broadly compatible findings. On what appeared as the two most salient dimensions (taxes versus spending and EU federalism), it found there to be three major party blocs: a redistributive left and pro-integrationist bloc (the PES, the Greens, and GUE/NGL); a second block (the EPP and ELDR) located centre-right of the redistributive spectrum but broadly pro-integrationist, and a third bloc (UEN and EDD) located on the economic right while being distinctly Eurosceptic.[40] Also, the results of the expert survey provided strong support for the two-dimensional model of policy competition put forward by Hix, Noury and Roland, which is based on two orthogonal dimensions consisting of classic issues of left–right socioeconomic policy on the one hand and support for European integration on the other.[41]

Will the dynamics that have driven and shaped the evolution of party politics in the European Parliament over recent decades persist in a significantly enlarged Union? As Hix and his co-authors emphasise for the period 1979 to 2004, the various enlargements of the EU have not had a significant effect on party cohesion in the European Parliament.[42] At first sight, this appears to have remained true beyond the 2004 European elections. An empirical study by Hermann Schmitt and Jacques Thomassen focusing on the immediate effects of the 2004 European elections suggests that the recent Eastern enlargement has had a surprisingly limited impact on the distinctiveness and internal cohesion of political groups in the European Parliament.

With or without the new members – the EP groups look very much the same, both with regard to their left–right and their pro–anti-EU position. The new Eastern parties – that is to say: those who have joined one of the traditional groups – fit in very well. Neither the positions of those groups relative to one another have changed much, nor have they lost their cohesiveness.[43]

However, it remains to be seen what mid- and long-term effects the recent Eastern enlargement of the Union 2004/7 will have. The incomplete consolidation of parties and party systems in Central Eastern Europe,[44] and the largely persisting differences between East and West,[45] make it difficult even to formulate a medium-term prognosis.

THE ROLE OF NATION-STATE-BASED PARLIAMENTARY OPPOSITION IN EUROPEAN GOVERNANCE

Again, any assessment of the role of the nation-state-based parliamentary opposition in the European multi-level system has to begin with determining who is the opposition's reference actor. If this actor is deemed to be the national government, it makes sense to consider the non-governing parties in the national parliaments as the parliamentary opposition. Historically, the independent role of the opposition parties in European policy was rather limited in most countries, which had more to do with political preferences than with limited institutional opportunities. There was a notable inclination amongst the political elite of many countries to develop 'bipartisan policies' in the field of European integration policy. However, over the years, the domestic patterns underlying the European policies of national governments have become more diversified. As Ronald Holzhacker notes, 'the process of parliamentary scrutiny over EU matters in the member states is no longer exclusively about finding a national consensus, but increasingly mirrors the rough and tumble of real politics'.[46] Reflecting this development, more recent research has started paying closer attention to the institutional opportunity structure of opposition parties in scrutinising governments in EU affairs.[47] Needless to say, the impact of institutions varies; it tends to be strongest when generous institutional resources meet with favourable political conditions. In parliamentary democracies, opposition parties can usually make the most of the available institutional devices if they face a minority government. It does not come as a surprise, therefore, that in a comparative case study (including Germany, the Netherlands, Denmark and the UK) the opposition parties in the Danish *Folketing* were found to be the most powerful parliamentary opposition actors.[48]

However, the political influence of national opposition parties and, more specifically, their possible contribution to the systemic function of democratic opposition in European governance is not necessarily confined to checking their national governments. As multi-level co-operation between national parliaments and the European Parliament has increased – there are now many forms of collaboration and exchange involving national MPs and MEPs[49] – even parties that are largely excluded from decision-making at home can have some impact through the transnational political group in the European Parliament with which they are affiliated. Obviously, a more specific contribution to the systemic function of democratic opposition at the European level only comes to bear if, or when, a particular political group in the European Parliament happens to pursue policies that challenge the political course of the Commission.

The power to control governments in the national parliamentary arena is largely concentrated in the hands of the majority parliamentary party groups. Having long been identified as the main losers of European integration, most parliaments, and the governing parties in parliament more specifically, gained some new powers to scrutinise and check their governments in the field of EU politics and policy more recently.[50] This notwithstanding, there can be no doubt that European integration, and its domestic repercussions, has tipped the balance of power between national parliaments and executives toward the latter,[51] and that recent parliamentary reforms have been unable to reverse this trend. Other comparative studies suggest that the 'Europeanisation' of European parliaments has by no means erased the more fundamental institutional differences between different models of parliamentary government.[52] Co-governing devices have remained a feature far more typical of, for example, the German system than of the British Westminster system.[53] However, the changing political environment of national parliaments as players in a multi-level process has led to remarkable conceptual re-assessments of the systemic use of different devices of control with many observers now considering public scrutiny as being possibly more valuable than co-governing behind closed doors.[54] This line of argument is compatible with the findings of fuzzy-set analyses which underscore the importance of the public, and which have led to the more specific contention that 'a Eurosceptical public opinion increases the probability of the legislature subjecting the government to tighter scrutiny in EU affairs'.[55]

The crucial problem in our context relates to the fact that many of those activities cannot convincingly be described as parliamentary opposition. They are clearly better characterised in terms of what Anthony King has labelled the 'intra-party mode', the decision-making process within the 'governing majority', that is, the executive and its supporting parties in parliament.[56] Even if we take into account the wide range of possible activities of parliamentary oppositions in democratic politics and policy-making, which may include a fair amount of co-governing behind closed doors, it seems appropriate to draw a terminological and theoretical line between 'opposition' on the one hand and the broader category of 'control' on the other. Otherwise, we risk losing much of the conceptual orientation for a deeper understanding of the democratic process in parliamentary democracies (and beyond) that is provided by the fundamental distinction between government and opposition.

That said, there are scenarios in which the activities of the majority parliamentary parties in national legislatures can be meaningfully understood in terms of 'opposition politics'. In legislative decision-making at the European level, national governments, or individual ministers for that matter, may veto a policy proposal that has climbed the legislative agenda. In doing so, they assume the role of an opposition actor. From a perspective that conceives the European Union as a 'bicameral system', these activities could be classified better as manifestations of legislative opposition. Yet this particular kind of legislative opposition of individual governments at the European level normally draws on parliamentary support at home. This amounts to a scenario in which the governing parliamentary party groups at the national level effectively perform the role of parliamentary opposition at the supranational level, though they act exclusively through their respective governments.[57]

CONCLUSIONS: PARLIAMENTARY OPPOSITION AND ITS ALTERNATIVES IN THE EUROPEAN UNION

The European Union has been described as a 'compound international polity in which governing activity is highly diffused through multiple authorities'.[58] Developing a broader international perspective, the same author found the EU's governance system to be 'more highly compound than those of even the most compound national polities, such as the United States'.[59] Such assessments can be carried over to the specific field of political opposition. As much as, or perhaps even more than, the United States, the European Union is a political system in which political opposition in its various forms is virtually 'ubiquitous', as Nelson Polsby has stated in the American context.[60] This is even true for institutionalised forms of oppositions or 'checks and balances', which are, in any polity, complemented by a host of only partly institutionalised or non-institutionalised forms of opposition.

There are two actors or institutions which are particularly well positioned to check the activities and policies of the Commission as the European Union's core executive and the nearest equivalent to the government in parliamentary regimes: the European Court of Justice and the comitology system. What has become known as 'comitology' is a system of committees composed of national government officials who scrutinise the Commission's implementing measures of EU legislation (though in practice the borders between scrutiny and co-determination of implementation policy tend to be somewhat blurred).[61] The creation of the comitology committees, whose beginnings date back to the early 1960s, reflected the attempt 'to prevent the emergence of a centralized executive power in Europe'.[62] Over the past decades, the comitology system has developed into a highly complex transnational bureaucratic network that many observers find is itself in need of better control.

Unlike the comitology system, the European Court of Justice cannot be characterised as the Commission's direct 'opponent' whose frame of reference is confined to monitoring the work of the Commission.[63] A large proportion of the Court's activities relate to ensuring that national governments comply with their obligations under the EU treaties and EU legislation; giving preliminary rulings on references by national courts marks another important component of the Court's activities. However, this notwithstanding, the Court may no doubt be meaningfully described as a powerful check on the EU executive.

In the more recent literature, a less obvious form of opposition directed against the policies of the Commission (and the other supranational decision-makers) has been identified. Referring to the non-compliance of national governments with EU directives, Gerda Falkner and her collaborators speak of 'opposition through the backdoor'.[64]

Whereas there can be no doubt that these (and other) manifestations of opposition are politically important, and would deserve closer analysis in their own right, the key question in our context is how significant all this is in terms of parliamentary opposition. As to the non-compliance of national administrations with EU directives, it is difficult to identify any involvement of or even a more direct relationship with parliamentary opposition, except of course in the sense that governments failing to comply ultimately draw on a parliamentary power base that can be expected to support this sort of opposition more or less explicitly. Major reservations apply even with regard to policy-making and policy implementation in federal states, which usually have more powerful parliamentary oppositions, because the implementation of decisions made at the federal level can hardly be considered to be among the core tasks of the parliamentary opposition. That said, the party factor underlying the government/opposition divide does matter. Especially in federations, such as in Germany, where the implementation of federal laws are more or less completely left to the administrations at the sub-federal level, state administrations controlled by the party that represents the parliamentary opposition at the federal level are more likely than others to develop activities that may meaningfully be described in terms of political opposition.

What structural or functional equivalents, and relations, to parliamentary opposition can be identified when looking at the two other major institutionalised opposition actors at the supranational level? While national government officials remain the dominant players in the comitology system, there is no denying that the system has been gradually 'parliamentarised'. The most recent comitology reform of June 2006, which introduced a new procedure (the so-called 'regulatory procedure with scrutiny'), has been rightly hailed as a 'major breakthrough for the European Parliament',[65] putting the Parliament and the Council in some, if not in all, categories of delegated legislation on more or less equal footing. In terms of political (if not precisely parliamentary) opposition, the effects of this latest reform on the opportunity structure of other players may be more important. As Schusterschitz and Kotz have noted, 'it might be more interesting for lobbyists to approach members of Parliament with the aim of getting them to vote against a measure the lobby opposes'.[66]

While historically the relationship between parliaments and courts has been extremely close (and continues to be so in some countries, such as Britain), even the most generous interpretation of veto player regimes in contemporary democracies could not convincingly treat courts as *parliamentary* veto or opposition actors.[67] That said, in some countries, such as Germany or France, constitutional courts, and the existence of abstract norm review more particularly, belong to the most powerful components of the institutional opportunity structure of the parliamentary opposition. Some observers have gone as far as to characterise the opportunity of a qualified parliamentary minority in the French National Assembly or the Senate to invoke the Constitutional Council as the only serious institutional weapon of the otherwise poorly equipped parliamentary opposition in the Fifth French Republic.[68] However, this precise option does not exist at the European level. While Article 230 of the EU Treaty confers upon the European Court of Justice the right to review the legality of EU legislative and executive acts adopted by the Commission, the Council, the Parliament and the European Central Bank (as well as acts intended to produce legal effects on third parties) only some but not all actors involved or affected can bring an action to the Court. This opportunity exists for the Council and the Commission as well as for any EU Member State[69] (and for private citizens who feel directly affected by a decision), but not for the European Parliament. The Parliament, as the European Central Bank, can only bring actions to the Court when it comes to protecting its own prerogatives. Therefore, parliamentary opposition through the European Court of Justice is only possible to the extent that parliamentary groups at the national level opposing a political decision at the European level are sufficiently powerful to ensure that their country invokes the Court on the basis of Article 230.

Alongside these institutionalised devices and channels for voicing opposition and dissent, there are many non-institutionalised forms of opposition in the European Union, as in any liberal democratic polity, that should not be left completely outside our focus. There is now a highly developed transnational system of interest group representation at the European level. Whereas the Commission has a vested interest in pursuing an integrative policy towards interest groups in order to strengthen its own legitimacy,[70] it is possible to discern winners and losers of European integration amongst different interest groups.

> Generally speaking, multinational companies and large firms have adapted well to the EU policy-making environment. Some voluntary associations and advocacy groups, used to cooperating on an international scale (e.g. Greenpeace, World Wildlife Fund, Amnesty International) have also developed effective cross-national lobbying strategies ... However, many smaller firms and national groups still find dealing with the European Commission a rather daunting prospect.[71]

Particularly at the level of restricted 'thick' institutions, which may be distinguished from more open and 'thin' institutions, such as very large conferences and seminars, the major key players dominate the scene.[72]

Compared to the degree of transnationalisation of professional lobbying in the European Union, transnational activism by EU citizens is still in its infant stages. The majority of actions are carried out by domestic actors and are aimed at domestic public or private targets. A study edited by Dough Imig and Sidney Tarrow focusing on the period 1983 to 1997 found evidence of a moderate increase in transnational activism within the European Union, though.[73] 'Europeans were moderately more likely to take to the streets in protest against the European Union, its agents, and its policies after 1992 – although still much less often than they protested against domestic grievances.'[74] However, the involvement of different groups tends to be strikingly different. Generally, occupational groups, especially workers, fishermen and farmers (who experience the often painful realities of economic integration in its most direct forms) are significantly more likely to protest against the European Union than the 'new social movements', such as environmentalists.

Another important dimension of the larger picture of European governance in the early twenty-first century concerns the transformation of the public sphere within the European Union. The available research on this particular aspect of European integration leaves no doubt that recent dynamics at this level have weakened rather than strengthened parliamentary oppositions and other social actors at both the national and the supranational level. As Ruud Koopmans concludes in his major research paper:

core state actors such as heads of state and government, cabinet ministers and central banks are by far the most important beneficiaries of the Europeanisation of public debates, in whichever form it occurs. Legislative and party actors – those actors from the core of the political system who are directly accountable to the electorate – are much less well represented in Europeanised public debates, both in an absolute sense and even more so relative to government and executive actors.[75]

As the same study reveals, there is an interesting correlation between the discursive influence of individual actors and their amount of support for and opposition to European institutions and integration. With few exceptions, such as the underrepresented but generally pro-European group of researchers and scientists, 'actors who are less influential in Europeanised public debates tend also to be more critical of European institutions and less supportive of the integration process than actors whose voices are more prominent in Europeanised public debates'.[76]

At least two major conclusions emanate from the analysis above. First, it is obvious that there *are* specific manifestations of legislative politics at the European level that can be meaningfully described in terms of parliamentary opposition. While in many, or even most, cases and situations the European Parliament as a whole performs the role of a parliamentary opposition actor within the European decision-making system, its activities have come to be complemented by more traditional manifestations of parliamentary opposition that draw on the political support of a reasonably coherent group of MEPs. Those structures and activities are supplemented by different manifestations of parliamentary opposition which are based at the national level of EU Member States, but which nevertheless affect the political process at the supranational level. That said, even when taken together these different manifestations of parliamentary opposition in the European multi-level system do not fully satisfy the normative and empirical expectations characterising most established notions of parliamentary opposition in parliamentary democracies. In particular, there have been no devices specifically designed to enable parliamentary opposition actors to play a decisive role in producing alternations in governmental office at the European level. This striking inability of the parliamentary opposition at the European level to serve as an 'alternative government' has been accompanied, and compounded, by a more latent structural weakness of parliament-based oppositions at both the national and the supranational level in shaping the European public agenda.

Secondly, it is important to note that the somewhat debilitated parliamentary opposition in the European Union is part of a highly complex multi-level system of checks and balances, which includes a host of different actors and institutions. As impressive as this group of potential veto players the EU executive faces may be, the present system fails to generate a satisfactory degree of democratic accountability. There is an overwhelming consensus among scholars of European governance that the characteristic absence of democratic accountability (of which direct accountability of executives to parliaments marks only one, if particularly crucial, component) is not being compensated by the multiplication of control mechanisms and the emergence of new control and accountability regimes.[77] The introduction of direct democratic devices at the European level (and their inception or expansion at the national level) may be considered a valuable, if not unproblematic, contribution to the task of strengthening responsive and responsible government in the European Union. Their impact is, however, bound to be limited to special occasions. The most promising route towards further democratising the European Union would appear to be the introduction of specific institutional devices that bind the EU executive and its most senior representatives more closely to the political will of European citizens and their agents in the European Parliament.[78] That said, institutional reforms alone will not be able to solve the European Union's much-debated 'democratic deficit'. Parliamentary government, while being in some ways an elite-centred form of democracy, can only flourish with a reasonable amount of support from those being represented by governments and oppositions.

NOTES

1. In this article, the terms 'supranational level' and 'European level' are used as interchangeable synonyms to refer to the level above the European nation states and within the territory and functional boundaries of the European Union.
2. Notions of the European Union (or the European Community) as a political system have been around since the early 1970s. See L.N. Lindberg and S.A. Scheingold, *Europe's Would-Be Polity* (Englewood Cliffs, NJ: Prentice-Hall, 1970). The core text in contemporary European Union studies is S. Hix, *The Political System of the European Union* (London: Palgrave Macmillan, 2nd edn., 2005).
3. This point has been raised, among others, by A. Moravcsik, 'In Defence of the "Democratic Deficit": Reassessing Legitimacy in the European Union', *Journal of Common Market Studies*, 40 (2002), p.605.
4. G. Sartori, 'Comparing and Miscomparing', *Journal of Theoretical Politics*, 3 (1991), pp.243–57.
5. J. van Deth 'Equivalence in Comparative Political Research', in J. van Deth (ed.), *Equivalence in Comparative Politics* (London and New York: Routledge, 1998), pp.1–19.
6. See, for example, J. DeBardeleben and A. Hurrelmann (eds.), *Democratic Dilemmas of Multilevel Governance: Legitimacy, Representation and Accountability in the European Union* (Basingstoke: Palgrave Macmillan, 2007); M. Egeberg, *Multilevel Union Administration: The Transformation of Executive Politics in Europe* (Basingstoke: Palgrave Macmillan, 2006); I. Bache and M. Flinders (eds.), *Multi-Level Governance* (Oxford: Oxford University Press, 2004).
7. K. Neunreither, 'The European Parliament and National Parliaments: Conflict or Cooperation?', in K. Auel and A. Benz (eds.), *The Europeanisation of Parliamentary Democracy* (New York: Routledge, 2006). Originally special issue of the *Journal of Legislative Studies*, 11/3–4 (2005), pp.466–89.

8. P. Mair, 'Political Opposition in the European Union', *Government and Opposition*, 42 (2007), pp.1–17. Note that Mair's focus is on the broader subject of political opposition rather than parliamentary opposition.

9. There is no obligation to make such a confinement, though. Building on the seminal work of Kirchheimer, Shapiro and Dahl, Mair has recently distinguished between 'classical opposition' which is directed at the policies of the government, 'opposition of principle' directed at the polity, and the 'elimination of opposition' which is directed only against the personnel of government. See Mair, 'Political Opposition in the European Union', p.5.

10. As to the United States as the world's best studied non-parliamentary democracy, there is a strong tendency to consider one of the two major parties in Congress as the key opposition actor at the level of governmental institutions. During periods of 'unified government' the minority party in Congress can be easily identified as the nearest equivalent of the parliamentary opposition in parliamentary democracies. The situation becomes more complex and complicated during periods of 'divided government'. Then, the majority party in Congress can be considered the key legislative opposition actor, though it may be argued that in this case the 'legislative opposition' mode is partially replaced, or complemented, by 'presidential opposition' exerted by minority presidents. See L. Helms, 'Five Ways of Institutionalizing Political Opposition: Lessons from the Advanced Democracies', *Government and Opposition*, 39 (2004), pp.40–45.

11. Hix, *The Political System of the European Union*, pp.41–46, 72 passim.

12. S. Hix, T. Raunio and R. Scully, 'Fifty Years On: Research on the European Parliament', *Journal of Common Market Studies*, 41 (2003), see pp.195–6.

13. See for example G. Tsebelis, 'The Power of the European Parliament as a Conditional Agenda-Setter', *American Political Science Review*, 88 (1994), pp.128–42; G. Garrett, 'From the Luxembourg Compromise to Co-Decision: Decision Making in the European Union', *Electoral Studies*, 14 (1995), pp.289–308.

14. While, obviously, only part of the actions of the European Parliament can be reasonably described in terms of opposition and dissent, this (alone) does not render the institution-based opposition focus useless. Consensus-seeking and consensus-building mark central components of the political activities of parliamentary oppositions in most democratic regimes outside the Westminster tradition, and even in the bulk of Westminster democracies oppositions tend to be less invariably scathing and destructive than many textbook accounts suggest. See the contribution by André Kaiser to this volume.

15. S. Hix, A.G. Noury and G. Roland, *Democratic Politics in the European Parliament* (Cambridge: Cambridge University Press, 2007), p.18.

16. A. Maurer, 'The Legislative Powers and Impact of the European Parliament', *Journal of Common Market Studies*, 41 (2003), pp.236–8.

17. T. Thomson and M. Hosli, 'Who Has Power in the EU? The Commission, Council and Parliament in Legislative Decision-making', *Journal of Common Market Studies*, 44 (2006), pp.391–417.

18. According to Charlotte Burns, 'the EP has not necessarily been made better off by the reforms of co-decision ... Under co-decision II, because the loophole that allowed the EP the opportunity to delay legislation has been closed, the parliament can find itself under pressure to reach agreement with the council in conciliation or face the prospect of failed legislation'. C. Burns, 'Co-Decision and Inter-Committee Conflict in the European Parliament Post-Amsterdam', *Government and Opposition*, 41 (2006), p.246.

19. C. Lord, 'Democratic Control of the Council of Ministers', *Österreichische Zeitschrift für Politikwissenschaft*, 36 (2007), p.132.

20. Lord, 'Democratic Control of the Council of Ministers', p.131.

21. D. Judge and D. Earnshaw, *The European Parliament* (London: Palgrave Macmillan, 2003), p.25. For the concept by Mezey referred to above see M. Mezey, *Comparative Legislatures* (Durham, NC: Duke University Press, 1979).

22. A. Kreppel, *The European Parliament and Supranational Party System: A Study in Institutional Development* (Cambridge: Cambridge University Press, 2002), p.1; see N.W. Polsby, 'Legislatures', in F.I. Greenstein and N.W. Polsby (eds.), *Handbook of Political*

Science, Vol. 5: Governmental Institutions and Processes (Reading, MA: Addison-Wesley, 1975), pp.257–319.

23. Unlike the no-confidence device in parliamentary democracies, impeachment as constitutionalised in the United States is strictly speaking a device of judicial rather than political control. That said, the element of politics involved in constitutional practice can be very strong, as the impeachment procedure against President Clinton in 1998/99 demonstrated. Indeed, a survey published early in 1999 found more than three-quarters of Americans convinced that this impeachment was more about politics than about the investigation of possible crimes. See *National Journal*, 20 Feb. 1999, p.501. For a broadly focused analysis of impeachment in the United States, see M.J. Gerhardt, *The Federal Impeachment Process: A Constitutional and Historical Analysis* (Chicago, IL: University of Chicago Press, 2000).

24. For a detailed analysis of the factors driving this complex process, see C. Moury, 'Explaining the European Parliament's Right to Appoint and Invest the Commission', *West European Politics*, 30 (2007), pp.367–91.

25. Judge and Earnshaw, *The European Parliament*, p.244.

26. For a more detailed empirical analysis of this episode see A. Topan, 'The Resignation of the Santer-Commission: The Impact of "Trust" and "Reputation"', *European Integration Online Papers*, 6 (2002), http://eiop.or.at/eiop/eiop/texte/2002-014a.htm, and N. Ringe, 'Government–Opposition Dynamics in the European Union: The Santer Commission Resignation Crisis', *European Journal of Political Research*, 44 (2005), pp.671–96.

27. Hix *et al.*, *Democratic Politics in the European Parliament*, p.199.

28. The long-standing existence of informal grand coalitions in the European Parliament was structurally favoured by the rules of the EU legislative process. See A. Kreppel, 'Rules, Ideology and Coalition Formation in the European Parliament: Past, Present and Future', *European Union Politics*, 1 (2000), pp.340–62. It is important to note, however, that even at the height of informal grand coalition politics the European Parliament remained, very much like the US Congress and in contrast to parliaments in parliamentary democracies, a legislature in which legislative coalitions tended to be formed for each vote. No less importantly, 'grand coalition politics' has been continued to some considerable extent. Other things being equal, voting together is most likely where the two parties have similar policies, such as on issues of EU integration and external trade. See S. Hix, A. Kreppel and A. Noury, 'The Party System in the European Parliament: Collusive or Competitive', *Journal of Common Market Studies*, 41 (2003), p.327.

29. A. Kreppel and S. Hix, 'From "Grand Coalition" to Left–Right Confrontation. Explaining the Shifting Structure of Party Competition in the European Parliament', *Comparative Political Studies*, 36 (2003), p.75.

30. Topan, 'The Resignation of the Santer-Commission', p.11.

31. Kreppel, *The European Parliament and Supranational Party System*, p.215. Today, as Gail McElroy notes, 'the EP's limits on individual rights are among the most restrictive in Europe. Individual legislators do not possess significant speaking rights or adjournment rights in the EP, and what rights they did have, have been severely circumscribed over the course of the past 25 years'. G. McElroy, 'Legislative Politics as Normal? Voting Behaviour and Beyond in the European Parliament', *European Union Politics*, 8 (2007), p.444.

32. K.H. Reif and H. Schmitt, 'Nine Second-Order National Elections: A Conceptual Framework for the Analysis of European Election Results', *European Journal of Political Research*, 8 (1980), pp.3–45; H. Schmitt, 'The European Parliament Elections of June 2004: Still Second-order?', *West European Politics*, 28 (2005), pp.650–79.

33. C. van der Eijk and M.N. Franklin. 'Potential for Contestation on European Matters at National Elections in Europe', in G. Marks and M.R. Steenbergen (eds.), *European Integration and Political Conflict* (Cambridge: Cambridge University Press, 2004), pp.32–50; S. Hix and M. Marsh, 'Punishment or Protest? Understanding European Parliament Elections', *The Journal of Politics*, 69 (2007), pp.495–510.

34. Hix *et al.*, *Democratic Politics in the European Parliament*, p.28.

35. Hix *et al.*, *Democratic Politics in the European Parliament*, Chapter 5.
36. It is important to note that, in contrast to the legislative procedure in the US Congress, not all votes are roll call. Currently, roll call votes account for about one-third of all votes in the European Parliament. Methodological problems with long-term roll call vote analysis are compounded by the fact that the overall number of roll call votes has experienced a 500 per cent or so increase between the 1979–84 Parliament and the 1999–2004 Parliament. See McElroy, 'Legislative Politics as Normal?', pp.435–6.
37. Hix, *The Political System of the European Union*, p.93.
38. T. Raunio, 'Second-rate Parties? Towards a Better Understanding of the European Parliament's Party Groups', in K. Heidar and R. Koole (eds.), *Parliamentary Party Groups in European Democracies: Political Parties behind Closed Doors* (London and New York: Routledge, 2000), p.246.
39. S. Hix, A. Noury and G. Roland, 'Dimensions of Politics in the European Parliament', *American Journal of Political Science*, 50 (2006), pp.494–511.
40. G. McElroy and K. Benoit, 'Party Groups and Policy Positions in the European Parliament', *Party Politics*, 13 (2007), pp.5–28; The acronyms shown in the text refer to the following parties: EPP – European People's Party, Party of European Socialists – Socialists, GUE/NGL – Confederal Group of the European United Left/Nordic Green Left, ELDR – European Liberal Democrat and Reform Party, UEN – Union for a Europe of Nations, EDD – Europe of Democracies and Diversities.
41. McElroy and Benoit, 'Party Groups and Policy Positions in the European Parliament', p.18.
42. Hix *et al.*, *Democratic Politics in the European Parliament*, p.102.
43. H. Schmitt and J. Thomassen, *The EU Party System after Eastern Enlargement* (Vienna: Institute for Advanced Studies, Political Science Working Paper 105, September 2005), p.15.
44. See, for example, P.G. Lewis, 'Party Systems in Post-communist Central Europe: Patterns of Stability and Consolidation', *Democratization*, 13 (2006), pp.562–83; B. Wessels and H.-D. Klingemann, 'Parties and Voters – Representative Consolidation in Central and Eastern Europe?', *International Journal of Sociology*, 36/2 (2006), pp.11–44.
45. See, among others, J.-E. Lane and S. Ersson, 'Party System Instability in Europe: Persistent Differences in Volatility between West and East?', *Democratization*, 14 (2007), pp.92–110; L. Helms, 'Konvergenz- und Divergenzaspekte der Parteiensystementwicklung in der Ära der Europäisierung: Ost- und Westeuropa im Vergleich', *Österreichische Zeitschrift für Politikwissenschaft*, 34 (2008), forthcoming.
46. R. Holzhacker, 'National Parliamentary Scrutiny over EU Issues: Comparing the Goals and Methods of Governing and Opposition Parties', *European Union Politics*, 3 (2002), p.477.
47. R. Holzhacker, 'The Power of Opposition Parliamentary Party Groups in European Scrutiny', in Auel and Benz (eds.), *The Europeanisation of Parliamentary Democracy*, pp.428–45.
48. Holzhacker, 'The Power of Opposition Parliamentary Party Groups in European Scrutiny', p.443.
49. There has been a standing invitation to members of national parliaments to participate in committee meetings of the European Parliament, in addition to other multilateral and bilateral meetings, such as meetings between the EP national sub-groups and national MPs. Also, parliaments of many Member States are represented in Brussels and have been provided with official office space. MEPs, for their part, are normally allowed to attend meetings of their national parliament's European Affairs Committee, and sometimes even have the opportunity to participate in the preparation of bills by submitting comments and questions. K. Neunreither, 'The European Parliament and National Parliaments', pp.466–89.
50. T. Raunio and S. Hix, 'Backbenchers Learn to Fight Back: European Integration and Parliamentary Government', *West European Politics*, 23/4 (2000), pp.142–68. The involvement of specialised committees, access to information, and the constitutional right or political power to 'mandate' ministers through issuing voting instructions are widely believed to mark the three most important indicators of the level of control. T. Raunio, 'Holding Governments Accountable in European Affairs: Explaining Cross-National Variation', in Auel and Benz (eds.), *The Europeanisation of Parliamentary Democracy*, pp.321–3.

51. H. Kassim, 'The Europeanization of Member State Institutions', in S. Bulmer and C. Lequesne (eds.), *The Member States of the European Union* (Oxford: Oxford University Press, 2005), pp.285–316; T.A. Börzel and C. Sprungk, 'Undermining Democratic Governance in the Member States? The Europeanisation of National Decision-Making', in R. Holzhacker and E. Albaek (eds.), *Democratic Governance and European Integration* (Aldershot: Ashgate, 2007), pp.113–36.

52. A. Benz, 'Path-dependent Institutions and Strategic Veto-Players – National Parliaments in the European Union', *West European Politics*, 29 (2004), pp.875–900.

53. This can be seen to represent a more general pattern. As Vivian Schmidt has highlighted, parliaments in federal systems, such as Germany, Austria or Belgium, were in general more successful in their attempts to secure new powers in relation to the central executive than their counterparts in unitary states (such as Britain or France). V. Schmidt, 'Democracy in Europe: The Impact of European Integration', *Perspectives on Politics*, 3 (2005), pp.764–5.

54. See, for example, Benz, 'Path-dependent Institutions and Strategic Veto-Players', p.897.

55. Raunio, 'Holding Governments Accountable in European Affairs', p.336.

56. A. King, 'Modes of Executive–Legislative Relations: Great Britain, France, and West Germany', *Legislative Studies Quarterly*, 1 (1976), pp.11–36.

57. The conceptual perspective put forward here is to be distinguished from apparently similar, but different perspectives, such as that put forward by Katrin Auel and Arthur Benz. The authors differentiate between 'internal' and 'external' veto players: Whereas governments or individual ministers may assume the role of 'internal veto players when challenging the policies of a supranational agenda-setter, governments may face the opposition of 'external veto players', including in particular the national parliaments, at home. K. Auel and A. Benz, 'The Politics of Adaptation: The Europeanisation of National Parliamentary Systems', in Auel and Benz (eds.), *The Europeanisation of Parliamentary Democracy*, p.378.

58. Schmidt, 'Democracy in Europe', p.761.

59. Schmidt, 'Democracy in Europe', p.762.

60. N. Polsby, 'Political Opposition in the United States', *Government and Opposition*, 32 (1997), p.511.

61. M.A. Pollack, 'Control Mechanisms or Deliberative Democracy? Two Images of Comitology', *Comparative Political Studies*, 36 (2003), pp.125–55.

62. R. Dehousse, 'Comitology: Who Watches the Watchmen?', *Journal of European Public Policy*, 10 (2003), p.809. As to the functional dimension of the comitology system, the same author has rightly pointed out that 'although comitology is at times depicted as a kind of institutional hydra, it is to a large extent a natural development. Any system of two-tiered government, particularly when it opts for decentralized implementation of rules adopted at central level, as has been the case in the EC, will be inclined to develop structures of this kind, as can be seen in the emergence of 'executive federalism' in Canada ... or of *Politikverflechtung* in Germany', p.800.

63. K. Arter, 'The European Court's Political Power', *West European Politics*, 19 (1996), pp.458–87; W. Mattli and A.-M. Slaughter, 'Revisiting the European Court of Justice', *International Organization*, 52 (1998), pp.177–209; C.J. Carrubba, 'The European Court of Justice, Democracy, and Enlargement', *European Union Politics*, 4 (2003), pp.75–100.

64. G. Falkner, M. Hartlapp, S. Leiber and O. Treib, 'Non-Compliance with EU Directives in the Member States: Opposition through the Backdoor?', *West European Politics*, 27 (2004), pp.452–73.

65. G. Schusterschitz and S. Kotz, 'The Comitology Reform of 2006: Increasing the Powers of the European Parliament without Changing the Treaties', *European Constitutional Law Review*, 3 (2006), p.74.

66. Schusterschitz and Kotz, 'The Comitology Reform of 2006', p.89.

67. The perception of constitutional courts as veto players has however become firmly established in recent research on liberal democracies. See N. Alivizatos, 'Judges as Veto Players', in H. Döring (ed.), *Parliaments and Majority Rule in Western Europe* (Frankfurt and New York: Campus, 1995), pp.566–89.

68. X. Vandendriessche, 'Le parlement entre déclin et modernité?', *Pouvoirs*, 99 (2001), p.66.

69. The grounds on which these actors may invoke the Court include doubts about the European Union's competence, possible infringements of the EU Treaty and more specific procedural requirements.
70. J. Greenwood, 'The Future of Consultation with, and Participation by, Interest Groups in the European Union', *Transnational Associations*, 4 (2005), pp.219–30.
71. S. Mazey and J. Richardson, 'Interest Groups and the Brussels Bureaucracy', in J. Hayward and A. Menon (eds.), *Governing Europe* (Oxford: Oxford University Press, 2003), p.219.
72. Mazey and Richardson, 'Interest Groups and the Brussels Bureaucracy', p.223. This notwithstanding, even the direct impact of the major and more powerful interest groups on European decision-making seems to be rather limited. This is at least what case studies from various policy fields suggest. According to Irina Michalowitz, 'the weak directional power of lobbyists at the European level even in cases in which they are well equipped may result from the character of the European political system as a system with very weak electoral and indirect control. Lobbyists are not able to threaten effectively'. I. Michalowitz, *Assessing Conditions of Influence of Interest Groups in the EU* (Institute for Advanced Studies, Vienna, Political Science, Working Paper 106, November 2005), p.23.
73. D. Imig and S. Tarrow (eds.), *Contentious Europeans: Protest and Politics in a Europeanizing Polity* (Lanham, MD: Rowman & Littlefield, 2001).
74. S. Tarrow, *The New Transnational Activism* (Cambridge: Cambridge University Press, 2005), p.87.
75. R. Koopmans, 'Who Inhabits the European Public Sphere? Winners and Losers, Supporters and Opponents in Europeanised Political Debates', *European Journal of Political Science*, 46 (2007), pp.183–210, see p.205. Koopmans' study covers three different dimensions of Europeanisation: 'supranational Europeanisation which refers to the role of actors and institutions from the European level in public debates in national news media', 'vertical Europeanisation' which occurs when national actors address or refer to European institutions, issues, legal frameworks, norms or identities, and 'horizontal Europeanisation' which is meant to include increased attention for actors and institutions from other European countries in national news media.
76. Koopmans, 'Who Inhabits the European Public Sphere?', p.206.
77. See, for example, M. Bovens, 'New Forms of Accountability and EU-Governance', *Comparative European Politics*, 5 (2007), pp.104–20; S. Puntscher-Riekmann, 'In Search of Lost Norms: Is Accountability the Solution to the Legitimacy Problems of the European Union?', *Comparative European Politics*, 5 (2007), pp.121–37; Y. Papadopoulos, 'Problems of Democratic Accountability in Network and Multilevel Governance', *European Law Journal*, 13 (2007), pp.469–86.
78. See, also in this vein, A. Follesdal and S. Hix, 'Why There is a Democratic Deficit in the EU: A Response to Majone and Moravcsik', *Journal of Common Market Studies*, 44 (2006), pp.533–62.

Making Sense of Opposition

PHILIP NORTON

Opposition, as this volume has shown, is a complex phenomenon. It is taken as intrinsic to a democratic society, yet it is a nebulous concept. It permits of several definitions. It stipulates a relationship – standing in some form of disagreement to another body – but that, as Rodney Barker has noted, can encompass very different phenomena.[1] Che Guevara led an opposition movement. David Cameron is Leader of the Opposition in the UK Parliament. There is very little relationship between the opposition activities of the two. Clearly, we need to refine the term.

Barker identified six meanings of the term,[2] but his list is not exhaustive. In essence, though, the definitions he offered can be subsumed within two broad categories. The first is where a body opposes the existence of the state. These bodies may be peaceful or they may wage war, but whatever form they take they do not accept the legitimacy of the state. The second is what Sartori has described as 'constitutional opposition'[3] and it is this that forms the basis of our concerns in this study. Here, the term comprises bodies that accept the legitimacy of the state and as such are prepared to work within the structures and processes stipulated by the constitution.

They may disagree with the regime in power but they seek to affect its activities, even its existence in office, by working within the extant constitutional framework. The margins may be somewhat blurred. As Sartori noted, one may have a responsible and constitutional opposition, one may have a constitutional and non-responsible opposition, and one may have an opposition that is neither responsible nor constitutional. This last category, notes Sartori, may come to constitute a form of contestation rather than opposition; as such, it blurs the distinction between the two categories.

In this volume, the concern has been a specific type of opposition falling under the second category: that is, parliamentary opposition. The reach encompasses opposition that is constitutional, but it does not rule out opposition that is non-responsible. Indeed, as is clear from the foregoing pages, parliamentary opposition can take different forms. Even within the rubric of parliamentary opposition, the term still permits of different definitions. Let us begin by teasing out those definitions before advancing a number of theoretical propositions.

TYPES OF OPPOSITION

The use of the term 'opposition' occurs in different ways even within the rubric of parliamentary opposition. It is used in the context of *the Opposition*, *opposition parties*, *opposition*, and *extra-parliamentary opposition*. These different usages are apparent from the contributions to this volume, as is the importance of their meanings for theorising about parliamentary opposition.

The Opposition constitutes the principal, usually the largest, non-government party. The use of both the definite article *and* a capital O distinguish it from the combination of parties, and other bodies, which exist outside the governing party. As André Kaiser has shown, the concept of an official Opposition is especially well understood within Westminster parliaments. In the UK, the second largest party is designated as the official opposition and its leader becomes Leader of the Opposition (a term first coined in Canada), a position recognised and defined in statute for the purposes of according a salary to the office-holder. Recognising that it is a constitutional and responsible opposition, it is styled Her Majesty's Loyal Opposition.[4]

Opposition parties comprise all those parties that do not form the government. The category thus extends beyond (but also includes) the second-largest party, though its confines are not as clear as the term may suggest. It is usually taken to refer to parties that have achieved seats in the legislature, though it may also encompass all recognised parties outside government, whether or not they have seats in the legislature. Even within the legislature, the term is not as watertight as it may appear. A party in government may at times adopt an oppositional position. This has been seen in the case of South Africa and, as experience in Austria, Belgium and the Netherlands reveals, a coalition party may oppose a proposal from another coalition party. As we have seen in the case of Austria, it is not unknown for this to happen even after the proposal has gone through Cabinet. In Scandinavia, opposition parties may at times constitute support parties for the government. However, the essential point for our purposes is that the term refers to particular actors in the parliamentary system.

The term *opposition* encompasses not only opposition parties but also different forms of relationship. It covers relationships between parties (opposition parties in relation to government) but also relationships that may exist within parties as well as outside the context of party. We refer to opposition rather than to *the* opposition (definite article, small 'o') because – as Morgenstern, Negri and Pérez-Liñán record – it is possible, especially in a presidential system, for an executive to face multiple oppositions. Indeed, there is a range of possible relationships. Here, the work of Anthony King is especially relevant. The significance of his work is apparent from several of the contributions to this volume. In his seminal article in 1976, King identified five modes of executive–legislative relations: the opposition, inter-party, intra-party, non-party and cross-party modes.[5] As Kopecký and Spirova note, these have been refined into three modes by Andeweg and Nijzink, though we retain the original as having utility for our purposes in discussing the multi-faceted nature of opposition.

The *opposition mode* is that which is taken as the usual and most visible aspect of the relationship between executive and legislature, that is, where there is conflict between the party in government and the party, or parties, in opposition. This mode, as King notes, is defined by conflict. The politicians in the different parties fight for the spoils of victory. They have no incentive to agree: 'their aim is not accommodation but conquest'.[6] This, especially in Westminster systems, is seen as being at the heart of parliamentary opposition. The 14th Earl of Derby in 1841, quoting another politician, declared 'The duty of an Opposition [is] very simple ... to oppose everything, and propose nothing'.[7] Even Dahl's definition of opposition ('*B* is opposed to the conduct of government by *A*') inclines in this direction.[8] It is also the most visible aspect of parliamentary opposition in other systems as well. It is the means by which opposition parties distinguish themselves from the party in government and hence the basis on which they seek to form the government in future. However, it is not the only mode that helps us to understand the potential for opposition within a parliamentary context.

The opposition mode is premised on the existence of coherent and essentially unified parties. The battle is between political armies, with each party's parliamentarians serving as disciplined soldiers. This, as we have seen, usually constitutes the reality of parliamentary behaviour. Cohesion is a feature of parliamentary parties. This is clear from the contributions to this volume, as well from other studies of discipline and cohesion.[9] The internal cohesion of parties is demonstrated most notably in hard data deriving from roll call votes, as in the case of Hungary and the Czech Republic. 'Party votes' – votes in which 90 per cent or more of one party vote on one side and 90 per cent or more of another party on the other – are a feature of western democracies. However, disagreement between parties is not the only form of opposition, and though it may be the most important in symbolic terms and in highlighting the limitations of government, it is not the most important in terms of affecting policy outcomes.

The *inter-party mode* is the first of two modes that helps us identify opposition from within. In this case, it is opposition from a party within a coalition. Coalitions have been a feature not least of pillarised societies, such as those of the Nertherlands, Belgium and Austria. Though, as Andeweg, de Winter and Müller show, there has been de-pillarisation in these countries, coalitions remain a feature of each one. Even during pillarisation, the existence of grand coalitions, encompassing all pillar parties, was not as frequent as may be thought; even some pillar parties variously existed outside the government. There was thus scope for the opposition mode to exist. However, what is important for our purposes is the scope for disagreement among the parties to the coalition. The parties have to be held together. Though coalitions may face the legislature as a body united on measures laid for approval, the period leading up to presentation may be marked by conflict between the coalition partners. This is well documented by Andeweg, de Winter and Müller in their study of post-consociational democracies. As they record, a variety of mechanisms are employed in Belgium to ensure the cohesion of the parties to coalition. Sometimes the mechanisms work and sometimes they do not. As they record, there 'is a demanding code of conduct enforcing the collective and collegiate behaviour of ministers, but in case of very heterogeneous cabinets it is nevertheless often violated'.

The *intra-party mode* encompasses opposition within a party. Parties may have organised or temporary groupings operating within their ranks and these groupings may not always approve of the line taken by the party leadership. Richard Rose identified factions and tendencies within parties.[10] Factions comprise those within a party 'who seek to further a broad range of policies through consciously organised political activity'. Tendencies are those with shared views on a particular issue rather than a range of issues and come together only on that issue. Either can be dangerous to a party, especially when in government: a faction may be a constant thorn in the side, but at least may be a known entity. A tendency may suddenly emerge to oppose a policy and, if drawing on a large number of the party's parliamentarians, may be a threat to the government's capacity to get the measure through.[11] Factions or tendencies within the governing party (or parties), once they reach a number sufficient to deny the government a majority, become (assuming opposition parties are united in voting against the government) veto players.

Those within a party who disagree with the policy or policies of the party leadership may express their disagreement through voice and vote, but for some – notably in new democracies – the option of exit is also employed. As we have seen in the case of Bulgaria, Hungary and the Czech Republic, defections from parties (in some cases, defections by parties) have been a feature of parliamentary politics. However, as a parliament becomes more established, defection rates appear to decrease; this has been the case in Hungary and the Czech Republic, but is less apparent in the less developed Bulgarian parliament. Defections have also been a marked, and continuing, feature of the Polish *Sejm*.[12] Defections, though, are not exclusive to new democracies, and take place in long-established legislatures, including those with high levels of party discipline, such as the UK Parliament, and those with weak party discipline, notably the US Congress. Such defections are not necessarily confined to occasional individual 'floor crossers'.[13]

The *non-party mode* and the *cross-party mode* differ from the other modes. The others derive from seeing opposition as conflict. Opposition, however, may be negative or constructive. The former is how the term tends to be regarded, not least in Westminster systems, and forms the basis of the opposition mode. In practice, this does not characterise accurately opposition in the UK, or – as we have seen – in many other legislatures. Being in 'opposition' does not necessarily entail a negative stance in relation to all parties advanced by government; it merely stipulates that one is not in government. Achieving election to government may be achieved through a constructive approach to the determination of public policy. The non-party mode can encompass a negative or constructive approach, while the cross-party mode encompasses a constructive, or at least consensual, approach.

The *non-party mode* is distinctive, then, for being able to encompass a negative or constructive approach and, as the name implies, for operating outside the context of party. It covers members coming together on a basis of shared interests or backgrounds, independent of party. The groupings may be informal or may achieve some organisational identity. Such a grouping may exist to pursue interests that conflict on occasion with the policies of the government. They may also achieve a reputation for specialised knowledge or expertise that entices the government to elicit their views or co-operation in developing a particular policy.

A good example of the development of a non-party mode is to be found in the UK, where all-party groups have burgeoned in recent years. These are groups which do not form part of the official parliamentary structure, but nonetheless enjoy some institutional recognition – they register their exist- ence and can utilise committee rooms – and draw members from across the political parties.[14] There are country groups and subject groups. The latter are the groups most relevant for our purposes. Some cover shared non-political interests (such as scouting and table-tennis) but others relate to areas of public policy. They cover subjects as diverse as AIDS, child and youth crime, com- passion in dying, environment, equalities, genocide prevention, obesity, prison health, solvent abuse, tourism, and war crime. They constitute one of the most significant growth areas in the UK Parliament. By 1988, there were 103 all-party subject groups. By 2004, there were 303.[15] Some groups may argue against a particular policy, while government may consult others or prove sympathetic to representations made by them.[16] The fact that the groups operate in a non-party mode means that government does not usually see them in the context of opposition, though it may regard some as outlets for the views of particular vested interests.

The non-party mode also encompasses procedures that may be employed by individual members, acting as such and independent of party, including private members' legislation. It also covers – especially important in the context of determining public policy – those occasions when a government may hand an issue over to the legislature to determine the outcome, free of party direction (free votes). A government may be internally divided or may not wish to attract popular opprobrium for taking a stance on a particular social issue. On such occasions, the legislature may fulfil an important role of conflict resolution.[17] However, as there is no formal government position, there is no opposition to government; instead, members form their own supporting or opposing positions on the specific issue. On rare occasions where there is a notable impasse in the system, the legislature may even fulfil an exit function, though that may occur in conditions of partisanship.[18]

The *cross-party mode* is distinctive for emphasising the fact that opposi- tion does not necessarily entail engaging in conflict. Here opposition refers to bodies (parties not in government) rather than to behaviour. For opposition parties to work with government in agreeing public policy is a feature of several of the legislatures examined in this volume. It is a mode characteristic of Germany[19] as well as of Scandinavian countries, but is far from uncommon elsewhere. As we have seen, opposition parties in Latin America variously vote with the majority on contentious issues. Even in the United Kingdom, a paragon of the opposition mode, most government bills are approved on Second Reading (the vote on principle) without opposition.[20] Parties may be in opposition, in the sense of being out of government, but not necessarily in disagreement on a continuing basis with government. Committees may also operate in a cross-party mode. King, in discussing the British House of Commons, regarded select committees – formal parliamentary committees established to investigate particular topics – as examples of the non-party mode. However, we treat them as examples of the cross-party mode, given that members are appointed on a party basis, though once appointed tend to operate (usually but not always successfully) in a bipartisan spirit. King also treated them as having little influence, though he was writing three years before the creation of a series of departmental select committees, possibly the most important reform in the British House of Commons for half a century.[21]

These modes fall under the generic term of opposition. However, there is one other use of the term and that is *extra-parliamentary opposition*. This volume addresses parliamentary opposition, but – as a number of contributions have shown – this cannot be viewed in isolation of external actors. In pillarised societies, parliamentary and extra-parliamentary bodies have united in a particular pillar. With de-pillarisation, the external bodies have become more important as independent actors (and give government greater choice in selecting between options advanced by such bodies). External bodies are also important in other contexts. As Kopecký and Spirova record, parliamentary oppositions in post-communist Europe can refer laws and decisions to the constitutional courts. There is a relatively high use of the 'court option' in Bulgaria, Hungary and (notably) the Czech Republic. Parties in the legislature may also seek to mobilise the extra-parliamentary party organisation, the public or the media in opposition to government or even trigger a referendum as a means of constraining the executive. As we have seen in the context of Latin America, public unrest is a critical variable; when combined with parliamentary opposition, it can result in the downfall of a president. The parties cannot necessarily be seen to be operating within the exclusive confines of an autonomous institution.

These different uses of the term opposition, and the different modes of executive–legislative relations, help explicate the nature of opposition and demonstrate that it constitutes something more than a largely ineffectual body established to engage in conflict with the executive. Indeed, what the contributions to this volume draw out is the rich and multi-faceted aspects of opposition and the consequences that they may have for the political system. These are not confined to what Blondel characterised as legislative viscosity (that is, the capacity to resist a change in the arrangement of molecules – or, in this case, to resist the flow of legislation)[22] but extend also to other functions. However, what is apparent from this volume is that opposition in its different forms has a greater capacity than critics of legislatures concede to affect the outcomes of public policy.

CONSEQUENCES OF OPPOSITION

The contributions to this volume enable us, then, to look at legislatures from the perspective of consequences and to develop a number of theoretical propositions.

A focus on observable decision-making has led critics to contend that legislatures have little or no power. They operate at the margins of the policy process and, as such, hardly merit a great deal of scholarly examination. This perception is longstanding,[23] indeed about as longstanding as the existence of organised, and recognised, parliamentary opposition. The relationship is not necessarily coincidental. Lord Bryce identified the growth of party as a key variable in undermining the power of legislatures,[24] and party forms the basis of structured parliamentary opposition. Because parliaments are seen as marginal, then – as Ludger Helms observes in his opening chapter – there has not been seen to be much point in examining parliamentary opposition.

This perception is flawed at several levels. First, legislatures are not necessarily marginal in the law-making process. Minority governments – whether single party or coalition – may be blocked by a combination of opposition parties. This is illustrated by Morgenstern, Negri and Pérez-Liñán in their study of Latin American countries. Policy outcomes may be affected by actions other than simply voting against government. Opposition parties may exploit institutional opportunities to affect outcomes, such as – as in Japan and the United Kingdom – the requirement for a bill to be passed within a specified time, otherwise it falls. A government may not need the votes of opposition parties to ensure a majority for its measures, but it is likely to need their co-operation to ensure adherence to the rules of the legislative process. Withdrawal of co-operation may make it difficult to overcome certain procedural hurdles (such as where a super-majority is required) or to continue with parliamentary business. There thus tends to exist what has been termed the equilibrium of legitimacy, which neither side (government or opposition) can upset without creating a threat to its own position.[25] If there is a threat it is most likely to come from parties that entertain no hope of being in government and may therefore operate as a constitutional but non-responsible opposition or, most destabilising, those that are not responsible and operate on the borders of what is constitutionally permissible.

In some countries, as this volume has demonstrated, opposition or even a coalition party (disagreeing with another coalition party) may achieve desired outcomes, either by the need for cohesion (inter-party mode) or by a cultural desire for consensus (cross-party mode). Also, as this volume has shown, there is more to opposition than having an impact, or seeking to have an impact, on legislative outcomes. Opposition fulfils a number of functions other than that identified by Packenham as the decisional and these functions can be, and are, significant in democratic polities.[26]

Parliaments, and parliamentary opposition, are not as insignificant, then, as the thesis of parliamentary decline proposes. Indeed, the emphasis on strong government may in itself miss an important point. As Morgenstern, Negri and Pérez-Liñán record, the existence of a strong government does not necessarily denote a weak opposition. It is possible to have a strong executive and a strong opposition. In short, opposition cannot be ignored in a study of political systems. That in itself is an important conclusion to be drawn from the contributions to this volume. However, we can go further in identifying the impact of parliamentary opposition. Different facets of opposition have been identified and analysed in the foregoing pages. Drawing on the work of the contributors, we can draw out the consequences of parliamentary opposition in a number of straightforward theoretical propositions.

First, the Opposition and individual opposition parties are significant actors in exposing Government to public challenge and oversight, but least effective in affecting outcomes of public policy. The Opposition is most likely to form responsible opposition, but smaller opposition parties, especially policy outliers not expecting to be in a future government, are more likely to adopt a critical role and may engage in non-responsible opposition.

The importance of legislatures for fulfilling functions (defined as consequences) other than that of law-making was highlighted by Packenham's seminal work. Opposition parties are central to the fulfilment of many of these functions. That is demonstrated by the contributions to this volume. A great deal of parliamentary time is given over to fulfilling functions other than law-making. Question time is a feature common to many legislatures, but exists independent of the legislative process. Opposition parties may have some input into the timetabling of parliamentary business, if not its outcome.

As Morgenstern, Negri and Pérez-Liñán find in Latin American countries, 'to the extent that opposition legislators identify a distinctive role for themselves, they claim the right to oversee the executive branch'. Legislatures provide an institutional framework for opposition parties to challenge government, to force government to justify itself and to offer alternative policies. They therefore tend to be significant users of parliamentary opportunities and resources. As Andeweg, de Winter and Müller show, there has been greater parliamentary activity in Austria and the Netherlands, and to a lesser extent Belgium, as de-pillarisation has taken place; more questions are asked, more amendments put forward, and more committees of inquiry established. As they point out, most empirical evidence 'shows that in the three countries the parliamentary opposition makes disproportionate use of the parliamentary opportunities open to them'. Question time is a central feature of many legislatures, not least Westminster-style legislatures. Where televised, it can be employed by opposition parties to challenge government and to raise their public profile. It is part of the party battle, which may help opposition parties politically, though the partisan activity may be at the expense of how electors view the legislature.[27]

Opposition parties may on occasion achieve some change to public policy, especially where there may be a culture favourable to the cross-party mode of executive–legislative relations (as in the Netherlands), but that is not the principal consequence. In the UK Parliament, the position of government and opposition – in essence, the approach underpinning the legitimacy of proceedings – is expressed in the observation 'the government is entitled to get its business, but the opposition is entitled to be heard'. There are various procedures available to opposition parties, not least the Opposition, to be heard and they variously utilise these procedures to ensure that their voice is heard and, by being heard, force government to respond. The legislative chamber provides the institutionalised means for such an exchange, one that is in the public domain. For opposition parties unable to mobilise a parliamentary majority, the most important weapon they have is the oxygen of publicity.

The Opposition and individual opposition parties are here treated as single actors. Individually, they do not constitute veto players. In a majoritarian system, with a single-party government enjoying a parliamentary majority, that remains the case whether or not they act as individual actors or in co-operation with one another. However, in a situation of minority government, they may, in combination, constitute a veto player. The number of opposition parties is an important variable. As Morgenstern, Negri and Pérez-Liñán show, a fragmented party system – characterised by a large number of parties – militates against partisan votes by opposition parties. The ideological position of parties is also important, even in situations with relatively few opposition parties. As André Kaiser explains, much depends on their relationship to one another in terms of their location on the ideological spectrum. Where opposition parties share similar positions, they are more likely to combine than in situations where opposition parties may be arrayed well to the left and to the right of the point occupied by the governing party.

Second, opposition is most effective as a veto player in the intra-party and inter-party modes of executive–legislative relationships. For a majority governing party, maintaining the support of its own members is a necessary and sufficient condition for achieving desired policy outcomes. For a minimum winning coalition, ensuring the cohesive support of the parties to the coalition is a necessary and sufficient condition. To lose the support of one's own members can be a public embarrassment but may also be a threat to a desired outcome if the number is such as to deny one a majority. A governing party with an overall majority of, say, 19 seats is thus vulnerable if ten of its own members decide to vote against it (assuming a united front of opposition parties) or if 20 decide to abstain from voting. Unless an opposition party can be persuaded to support the government, the dissident members can block the measure from getting through. The stance of opposition parties, as we have seen, is likely to be affected by their ideological distance from the governing party, though the prospect of defeating the government may serve as an inducement to put aside ideological differences with other opposition parties (and closeness to the governing party). In a minimum winning coalition, the defection of a party jeopardises the capacity to achieve passage of a measure and the same considerations apply. In policy-making terms, the most potent 'opposition' threat to a government thus comes not from the opposition but from within government. Indeed, in a dominant-party system such as that of South Africa, it constitutes the only potential source of significant opposition.

There is the important rider, already emphasised, that the capacity of government members and a coalition party to serve as veto players is dependent on all or most opposition parties voting against the government. As we have noted, opposition parties may not necessarily co-operate with one another, especially if there is a large number of them, and some may be ideologically closer to the government than other opposition parties and, indeed, closer to government than some of the government's own ideological outliers. In the British Parliament, for example, left-wing Labour MPs may vote against a Labour Government only to find the Conservative Opposition voting with the Government or abstaining from voting. In the vote on war with Iraq in 2003, for example, a large body of Labour MPs voted against the government, but the government achieved a large majority with Conservative support.

Third, opposition is most effective in contributing to policy formation in the cross-party mode of executive–legislative relations. Here, opposition parties serve not as veto players but as persuasive actors in a consensual process. Opposition parties oppose the continuation in office of the governing party – seeking to replace it at the next election – but are not necessarily opposed to particular measures and may seek, or be invited, to play a role in the development of those measures.

The cross-party mode is intrinsic to the culture of systems that are essentially consensual. We distinguish these from those, such as the pillared systems of countries like Belgium and the Netherlands, where the culture is more one of accommodation, with coalitions being constructed on the basis of political necessity and with the partners to that coalition not always willing to go along with a proposal emanating from within the coalition. Parties need to agree to get a measure through, hence the capacity to be a veto player, but in a consensual system the government may already have its majority but nonetheless seek the involvement of other parties in order to maximise support and, presumably, improve the quality of the policy.

The non-party mode may also make a contribution to policy formation, but our assumption is that such a relationship is not likely to operate on as regular a basis as the cross-party mode, where organised parties exist on a continuous basis and may have an institutionalised role in the process of policy delibera-tion. Our theoretical supposition is that non-party formations are more likely to be temporary and to have a sporadic input in policy deliberations.

The five modes of executive–legislative relationships identified by King thus enable us to tease out the complexities of parliamentary opposition. It is worth stressing that a legislature is not confined to a particular mode. As King demonstrated, more than one mode operated in each of the parliaments he analysed. There may be a predominant mode (opposition in the UK, cross-party in Sweden), but other modes may, and do, operate and the emphasis may change over time. Indeed, as we have seen, political circumstances create new conditions and the forms of opposition change. This has been well illustrated in the case of the post-communist countries as well as in those countries of western Europe characterised by de-pillarisation. As the study by Kopecký and Spirova demonstrates, the different modes provide us with a useful con-ceptual tool.

What the research of this volume shows is that the potential for opposition to affect policy outcomes is much more varied than the traditional view of par-liamentary opposition, deriving largely from perceptions of the Opposition and opposition as conflict, allows.

FUTURE RESEARCH: DIFFERENT DIMENSIONS OF OPPOSITION

This volume has furthered our understanding of the nature of opposition. It has drawn out the different facets of parliamentary opposition, but it has done so largely in the context of a single body, that is, *a* legislature. The focus has not been exclusive; as we have seen, the position is complicated where second chambers exist, as in the case of Australia, Canada, Japan and the United Kingdom. However, our theoretical focus largely derives from this one-dimensional perspective.

The picture becomes more complex, because there is the potential for a greater number of relationships to exist, where there is more than one legisla-tive chamber. We thus treat as two-dimensional a system that has a bicameral national legislature and as three- or multi-dimensional those systems that have more than two legislative chambers: that is, federal nations. As André Kaiser shows, the position is especially complex in those systems that are bicameral *and* federal. Small parties, with concentrated strength, may exert greater influ-ence – through being in government in a state legislature – than a large party (the Opposition) with greater, more broadly based support at the national level. A party may operate as government at one level and as an opposition party at another. A national government may thus have to face several ways in dealing with 'opposition'. In a federal system, where powers may be concurrent, a state legislature may serve as a veto player.

There is another dimension to be factored into the equation. The relevance of this dimension is demonstrated by Morgenstern, Negri and Pérez-Liñán, and that is a presidential system of government. There is the potential for opposition *within* the executive branch, though that is not exclusive to presidential systems. (The bureaucracy may be a force in its own right, but our primary concern here is with parties.) Here, the relevant division for our purposes is between the executive and legislative branches. Morgenstern, Negri and Pérez-Liñán draw out the various relationships that exist under a separation of powers. They factor in bicameralism. The potential for multiple opposition relationships is enhanced when federalism comes into play. The USA is the best-known but not the only example of a presidential, bicameral *and* federal system. Brazil is another good example. The position in the USA is less complex than it might otherwise be by virtue of being a two-party system. The parties are sufficiently ideologically indistinct and porous to encompass any nascent third party. In a nation that is socially as well as institutionally fragmented (with multiple parties – as tends to be the case in Latin America – and multiple legislative chambers), the potential for different forms of opposition to exist is at its maximum.

Nor is this the only multi-dimensional arrangement (presidential, bicameral, federal) now in existence. The European Union offers a similar multi-dimensional system, but with the added dimension that, as Ludger Helms vividly demonstrates, it is not always clear what constitutes the executive that is the focus of parliamentary opposition. The EU has what may be deemed a dual executive – the Commission and the Council of Ministers. (There is the further complication that broad directions may be decided by the European Council.) The Council of Ministers also has a dual personality. It exists to fulfil executive functions but it also serves to fulfil legislative functions. It is thus deemed by some analysts, as well as by the European Parliament, to constitute the second chamber of a bicameral system.[28] The position is further complicated by the position of national parliaments, which may stand in opposition to the position taken by their respective governments,[29] but which may also play a greater collective role as a result of greater collaboration[30] and may be accorded a more formal role in future treaties. The proposed European Reform Treaty empowers national parliaments to refer proposals back to the Council of Ministers. There thus exist different levels at which opposition may be expressed and the potential for multiple oppositions, with opposition at times coming from executive bodies.

The one-dimensional analysis is thus most pertinent in nations such as New Zealand and Sweden (unicameral and unitary) – and approximately two-thirds of nations have unicameral legislatures[31] – but needs building on in cases of bicameral federal nations, such as Australia, Canada, and Germany, and most especially in nations that are bicameral federal and presidential, and in the *sui generis* case of the European Union. Here, we see the scope for opposition to exist in several guises, including in the form of a legislature or government. For the governing party at national level, a state legislature may constitute opposition, but conversely for the state government, the national legislature or executive may equally constitute a crucial veto player.

Our conclusion is not dissimilar to that of Dahl's in looking at the wider context of opposition in western democracies: 'there exist a great variety of different patterns of opposition in democratic systems'.[32] These patterns, Dahl noted, differed according to a range of characteristics, some of which could be explained and others not. He sought to give some shape to the nature of oppositions. This volume has done the same in the context of parliamentary opposition, but with the same recognition of what further work needs to be undertaken. There is considerable scope for developing the study of parliamentary opposition. The contributions to this volume have enriched our knowledge and theoretical grasp of such opposition – of its complexity and its importance – and the value of parliamentary opposition as a subject for further study and theorising. This volume constitutes not so much a conclusion to a study of opposition as a powerful platform for further research.

NOTES

1. R. Barker, 'Introduction', in R. Barker (ed.), *Studies in Opposition* (London: Macmillan, 1971), p.4.
2. Barker, 'Introduction', p.5.
3. G. Sartori, 'Opposition and Control: Problems and Prospects', *Government and Opposition*, 1/2 (1966).
4. See R.M. Punnett, *Front-Bench Opposition* (London: Heinemann Educational Books, 1973).
5. A. King, 'Modes of Executive–Legislative Relations: Great Britain, France and West Germany', *Legislative Studies Quarterly*, 1/1 (1976), pp.11–34.
6. King, 'Modes of Executive–Legislative Relations', p.18.
7. A. Jay (ed.), *The Oxford Dictionary of Political Quotations* (Oxford: Oxford University Press, 1996), p.114.
8. R. Dahl, 'Preface', in R. Dahl (ed.), *Political Oppositions in Western Democracies* (New Haven, CT: Yale University Press, 1966), p.xviii.
9. See, for example, R.Y. Hazan (ed.), *Cohesion and Discipline in Legislatures* (London: Routledge, 2006).
10. R. Rose, 'Parties, Factions and Tendencies in Britain', *Political Studies*, 21 (1964), pp.34–46.
11. See, e.g., P. Norton, 'Parliament', in A. Seldon and K. Hickson (eds.), *New Labour, Old Labour* (London: Routledge, 2004), pp.190–206, for the vulnerability of the 1974–79 Labour Government in the UK to factions and tendencies as well as opposition parties.

12. E. Nalewajko and W. Wesołowski, 'Five Terms of the Polish Parliament, 1989–2005', special issue of *The Journal of Legislative Studies*, edited by P. Norton and D.M. Olson, 13/1 (2007), pp.74–6.
13. In the UK, a body of predominantly Labour MPs defected in 1981 to form a new party, the Social Democratic Party (which later merged with the Liberal Party).
14. See *Guide to the Rules on All-Party Groups* (London: House of Commons, 2005), accessible at www.parliament.uk/documents/upload/PCFSGroupsRules.pdf.
15. P. Norton, *Parliament in British Politics* (London: Palgrave Macmillan, 2005), p.127.
16. See Norton, *Parliament in British Politics*, pp.127–8.
17. R. Packenham, 'Legislatures and Political Development', in A. Kornberg and L.D. Musolf (eds.), *Legislatures in Developmental Perspective* (Durham, NC: Duke University Press, 1970), pp.521–37.
18. See Packenham, 'Legislatures and Political Development'.
19. See King, 'Modes of Executive–Legislative Relations'; and L. Helms, 'Perspectives on Government and Opposition in Unified Germany', *Politics*, 18/3 (1998), pp.151–8.
20. R. Rose, *Do Parties Make a Difference?* (London: Macmillan, 2nd edn., 1984), pp.79–83.
21. See, e.g., G. Drewry (ed.), *The New Select Committees* (Oxford: Clarendon Press, rev. edn., 1989).
22. J. Blondel *et al.*, 'Legislative Behaviour: Some Steps towards a Cross-National Measurement', *Government and Opposition*, 5/1 (1970), pp.67–85.
23. P. Norton, 'General Introduction', in P. Norton (ed.), *Legislatures* (Oxford: Oxford University Press, 1990), pp.4–5.
24. Lord Bryce, *Modern Democracies* (London: Macmillan, 1921), pp.390–91.
25. P. Norton, 'Playing By the Rules: The Constraining Hand of Parliamentary Procedure', *The Journal of Legislative Studies*, 7/3 (2001), p.28.
26. Packenham, 'Legislatures and Political Development'.
27. See K. von Beyme, *Parliamentary Democracy: Democratisation, Destabilization, Reconsolidation* (London: Palgrave, 2000), p.81. On Question Time in the UK House of Commons, see M. Franklin and P. Norton (eds.), *Parliamentary Questions* (Oxford: Clarendon Press, 1993).
28. See P. Norton, 'How Many Parliamentary Legislatures Are There?', *The Journal of Legislative Studies*, 10/4 (2004), pp.6–7; and D. Judge and D. Earnshaw, *The European Parliament* (London: Palgrave Macmillan, 2003), pp.307–8.
29. See R. Holzhacker, 'The Power of Opposition Parliamentary Party Groups in European Scrutiny', in K. Auel and A. Benz (eds.), *The Europeanisation of Parliamentary Democracy* (New York: Routledge, 2006). Originally special issue of the *Journal of Legislative Studies*, 11/3–4 (2005), pp.428–45.
30. Lord Norton of Louth, 'National Parliaments in Europe: Recent Developments', in J.Th.J. van den Berg, L.F.M. Verhey and J.L.W. Broeksteeg, *Het Parlement* (Nijmegen: WLP, 2007), pp.209–18.
31. See L. Massicotte, 'Legislative Unicameralism: A Global Survey and a Few Case Studies', *The Journal of Legislative Studies*, 7/1 (2001), pp.151–70.
32. R. Dahl, 'Patterns of Opposition', in Dahl (ed.), *Political Oppositions in Western Democracies*, p.347.

Index